S e x ,

L o v e ,

a n d   F a s h i o n

HARMONY BOOKS / NEW YORK

Bruce Hulse

Sex,

Love,

and

Fashion

A

Memoir

of a

Male

Model

All rights reserved.
Published in the United States by Harmony Books,
an imprint of the Crown Publishing Group,
a division of Random House, Inc., New York.
www.crownpublishing.com

Harmony Books is a registered trademark and the Harmony Books
colophon is a trademark of Random House, Inc.

Library of Congress Cataloging-in-Publication Data
Hulse, Bruce.
    Sex, love, and fashion: a memoir of a male model / by Bruce Hulse.
    1. Hulse, Bruce. 2. Male models—United States—Biography.
  3. Love—Psychological aspects. 4. Self-actualization (Psychology)
  I. Title. II. Title: A memoir of a male model.
    HD8039.M772U55   2008
    746.9'2092—dc22
    [B]   2007043361

ISBN 978-0-307-38168-2

Printed in the United States of America

DESIGN BY BARBARA STURMAN

10 9 8 7 6 5 4 3 2 1

First Edition

This book is dedicated to:

my wife, Katrina, who taught me true love

my mom and dad, who loved me unconditionally and showed me it's what's inside that counts

my lifeguard buddy Pat Scullin, who taught me the art of storytelling

my model buddies—Todd Irvin, Tommy Preston, Russell James, and Nick Constantino—tried and true friends

Doc X, who showed me how to face death with an open heart

Bruce Weber, my mentor and guide, who showed me the joy and adventure in photography and modeling

my "superagents," Martha North, Chris Forberg of Public Image, and David Todd and April Anyse of Nous Models

Contents

Author's Note

Some of the dialogue in the book has been recon-
structed from memories that are not always exact or
complete; therefore it may not reflect precisely what
was said at the time. My intent is to allow the reader
to fully understand and experience the events and
conversations described in this book. I have done my
best to portray my life accurately. I have also changed
the names of some of the people in this book to honor
their desire for privacy.

Let go of your worries
and be completely clear-hearted,
like the face of a mirror
that contains no images.
If you want a clear mirror,
behold yourself
and see the shameless truth,
which the mirror reflects.
If metal can be polished
to a mirror-like finish,
what polishing might the mirror
of the heart require?
Between the mirror and the heart
is this single difference:
the heart conceals secrets,
while the mirror does not.

—RUMI

Foreword

by Russell James

It was 1989. As I sat in my seat waiting for the flight from Lisbon to Hamburg to board, I had my fingers crossed that the much-coveted "open seat" next to me would remain just that—open. But just as the door was about to close, a blue-eyed, black-haired giant of a man cast a formidable shadow over me. He stowed his bag overhead and sat down in the seat that now looked more like a stool under him. I felt like the entire scene should have been in slow motion while a Levi's soundtrack should have been playing, for this man (and I say this as a heterosexual male) was one good-looking rooster. I mean . . . really good-looking.

I braced myself. Anyone this good-looking was going to be, well, intellectually challenged. Just as I was thinking Please don't speak, *he began to speak. By the time we got to Hamburg I had silently*

condemned myself as obnoxious, uneducated, and worthy only of living in a lonely tower somewhere. His name was Bruce Hulse. He was charming, sincere, humble, well-educated, a philosopher, smart as hell, and really, really funny. I admit it—I had a crush. We became firm friends and over the following six years I came to know Bruce as not only a dependable friend, but as a spiritual and compassionate icon in my life. Perhaps most of all, and to really drive the nail through my heart, I was in awe of his profound effect on the opposite sex. Bruce was not a man of boastful conquests, but when it came to him and women all I can say is, "Shit just happened." He had that certain winning combination of DNA that is impossible to explain. Think you have an impenetrable ego? Well, take a stroll through a European city, Manhattan, or Miami Beach with your mate Bruce Hulse by your side. It's as if one vanishes beside him. Women wobble and men seem to hunch a little as his massive frame and calm disposition cast a spell

admirers worldwide, who simply could not envisage the world's hottest bachelor off the market. Surely this was a marketing gimmick? To my delight B Hulse has proved to be the most loyal and devoted husband anyone could aspire to be. And fatherhood? What a dad! He can now be found on any given Sunday coaching a baseball game for his son's team or at the beach with his daughter in tow.

Bruce's only fault? Over all these years it's been his infuriating gentlemanlike quality "not to tell." So now I have to buy the bloody book! I can only hope and pray that he will—at long last—reveal the secrets of all those days (and nights) before Katrina. I have oh so many questions about those times back in Miami Beach, Paris, Milan, and New York City. Come on, you hot rooster! I've waited fifteen years for this!

over the walkway. Inevitably it is only minutes before someone under the hex engages him in conversation under the pretext of "Are you . . . ?" or, "Didn't we meet at . . . ?" I saw some of the world's greatest beauties throw themselves in his path, all measure of self-restraint and public appearance cast aside. To add to the mystery, the calmer, wiser, and more centered Bruce became, the more his female fan club grew.

Then in 1993, Bruce (or "B Hulse" as he was affectionately known) surprised us yet again when he announced his pending marriage to the beautiful Katrina. I could almost hear a collective gasp from his

---

RUSSELL JAMES is a former model and one of the world's leading photographers, with twenty years' experience of celebrity, fashion, and exotic location shoots. His work has appeared in fine art galleries, most every major magazine, and many coffee-table books. He is also a celebrated director.

Sex, Love, and Fashion

1

Ebb and Flow

The ocean glittered like a million diamonds in the Mexican sun. The beach was gold, the sky sapphire blue. I stood barefoot in the hot sand, my head thrown back in the light breeze as I responded to the direction of the photographer for *GQ* magazine. I felt relaxed and confident as she asked me to turn this way and that—to bend, to smile, to hold the pose. An experienced professional at the top of my game, I was doing a job I loved in an impossibly spectacular setting: a secluded, palm-fringed cove on the edge of the Pacific Ocean.

"Now I'd like some shots of you bodysurfing, Bruce," the photographer told me. I smiled. I was looking forward to washing off the gritty mix of sand and suntan lotion, and I couldn't imagine a better way. I'd loved to surf ever since I was a teenage lifeguard in New Jersey; it came as naturally to me as breathing.

I ran into the water in my swim shorts and began riding the waves as the photographer's SLR clicked and whirred. For a moment I completely forgot that this was how I earned my living. I felt like a carefree kid again, a basketball star and straight-A student surfing on Avalon Beach with my buddies, living in a ramshackle house in the dunes, drinking beer and hooking up.

"Okay, Bruce, now I'd like you to ride this horse along the shore," the photographer said. Her name was Pamela Hanson, and I loved working with her. She was so in touch with nature that the images she created were breathtaking. "I want to try to capture the connection between man and animal. Do you think you can help me do that?" Once Pamela had all the images she wanted, I spontaneously stripped off my shorts and climbed back onto the stallion to gallop through the surf, my naked body pressed low against the flanks of this incredible beast. Out of the corner of my eye, I saw that Pamela was still snapping away.

The three other models and the rest of the crew seemed to pick up on my mood, and they all stripped down to enjoy the sun, sea, and sand. When it was time for lunch to be brought down to us from our casita, I was still too stoked to eat. I looked along the coastline to the point where the beach seemed to disappear into the horizon, and I was filled with a sudden urge to run. While everyone else settled in to eat, I took off along the shore alone. It didn't occur to me to put on any clothes.

As I fell into an easy rhythm in the soft sand, I thought about

my dad, something I often did when I ran. I could almost feel him next to me, matching me stride for stride, the way he had when I was small. "Come on, Bruce the Moose," he'd say, "pick it up a little."

Running was a huge part of Dad's life. At six feet two inches tall and 175 pounds, he'd once held the U.S. record in the mile. After he finished college, he became a navy lieutenant on a destroyer in the South Pacific, searching for Japanese submarines. He missed out on the 1948 Olympics in London only because he was too busy to put in the training.

I remember Dad coming home after working all day as a chemist, changing into his New York Athletic Club sweatsuit and taking me to the local track for a run. Sometimes on Saturdays we'd go to the park or do some cross-country running in the woods, jumping creeks and running backward up hills.

When I was eleven years old, Dad gave me a book by the visionary Australian coach Percy Cerutty, one that would change my life. Cerutty wrote about the importance of meditation and yoga, of

My dad in his NYU track-and-field letter sweater outside his home in Stanhope, New Jersey.

focusing on the breath. Like the devoted son I was, I read every word of the book Dad had given me, then put those lessons into practice.

It was my father who had bought me my first surfboard. I remember paddling out on the water at Cape May on the New Jersey shore, about an hour and a half from our home in Havertown, Pennsylvania, and catching my first wave. Fearless, I stood right up and rode it all the way in to the sand. The feeling was exhilarating, like nothing I had ever experienced. It was even better than running. I felt as if I were flying, as if my freedom was a natural extension of the waves. I was hooked.

My father, mother, and three sisters—April, Carol, and Diane—preferred to dig for clams with our dog Inky or hang out on the old boat Dad had bought from an army-surplus store. It was a World

War II landing craft that he'd spent five years restoring. He named it *The Gibbut*, putting together the words *big* and *tub* spelled backward. It was the only boat of its kind in the marina, and its noisy diesel made it stand out even more from the sleek yachts that surrounded it.

I loved that old boat, but I loved surfing more. Dad would drop me off at the beach early each morning with my board tucked under my arm, and I'd spend the rest of the day in the water. I'd grab a quick hot dog for lunch, but then it was right back in; there was no other place I'd rather be. Only at night would I return to *The Gibbut* for supper and a game of hearts with my family.

When my dad was skippering *The Gibbut*, he often wore a dark blue ribbed sweater from his navy days, so that's what I chose to wear for my first-ever photo shoot when I was ten years old. I had a brand-new Instamatic camera, and I'd persuaded my younger sister Carol to take some photos of me in our backyard. We began with some shots of me fooling around and standing on my head. Then I got the idea to dress up for some pictures, and at one point I grabbed Dad's sweater and a black beret I found in my mom's closet. I thought the beret made me look really cool, like a movie star.

I remember that moment—looking in the mirror, combing my hair and styling it for a photo—as the first time I became self-aware. Carol snapped away as I posed for the camera. When the photos came back from the lab, I especially loved the one of me in the beret and sweater. I thought it made me look like a military hero. I thought it made me look like my dad.

That memory came back to me now in Mexico and mingled with my euphoria. I was floating on a runner's high, the feeling that I could effortlessly go on forever. Looking around, I realized that there was no sign of civilization anywhere. No buildings, no people, no roads or cars. I felt like the last man on earth. Out here, all artifice was stripped away. I was man in harmony with nature—running, sweating, listening to my breath. Mind, body, and spirit were perfectly aligned. I was at peace.

Then the thought came into my mind that the crew's lunch break would soon be over and that Pamela would want to start shooting again. Going back would mean working some more—having my hair styled, my skin oiled, and my every feature checked before I could pose with the eyes of the camera and the world upon me. To go back would be to admit that I wasn't the last man on earth after all, just one of billions of people struggling through life, often not very happily, looking for that special connection that could make it all okay.

When I was in my late teens, I had aspired to live a life filled with meaning. I told myself those ideals were still important to me, but somehow I'd gotten got caught up in an industry that sold products by creating the illusion of desire and sex.

Suddenly intensely sad at the thought, I veered right into the ocean, swimming out into the huge waves breaking on the shore. When I could no longer stand, I let the sea wash over me like a baptism. Floating on the waves, drifting with the currents, I wished I could stay in that moment forever. But the spell had been broken.

On shore again I picked up my stride, heading back to the crew and the cameras, the big paychecks and the free designer clothes, and the women—most of all the women. Despite having slept with so many of the world's most desirable women, I was still an incurable romantic. I still believed that one day I would find the life partner who would help me find the truth I sought.

People came into view up ahead. They were all just as I had left them—eating, setting up cameras, putting on makeup and adjusting clothing—going about the business of a fashion shoot in an exotic location. Slowing my stride, I felt as if I had just returned from some sort of parallel universe.

"Hey, where were you?" one of the models asked, shielding her eyes from the sun as she peered up at my six-foot-three-inch silhouette.

"Nowhere special," I said, reaching for a bottle of water from a cooler and drinking it down.

"All right, everybody, let's get back to work!" one of the art directors cried, rising to his feet and clapping his hands together to dust off the sand and to get our attention.

"Okay." I nodded, preparing to set aside my inner life and face the cameras as "The Incredible Hulse," the male supermodel whose life might be envied by one and all—except for someone who actually lived it.

Standing on my head in the backyard for my sister Carol.

2

Early Days

I can't remember exactly when it was that I realized that my mom was an alcoholic, or that she suffered from the clinical depression that would plague me my whole life. I do know that as a little boy I thought it was perfectly natural to get yourself up, wash, dress, make your own breakfast, and pack your lunch, while your mother lay in bed all morning.

"She stays up too late reading," my father would tell my sisters and me, an excuse that seemed plausible when I looked at the piles of books balanced precariously on every surface in the house. "Your mom's always been a night owl. She needs her sleep in the mornings. Let her be."

On weekends we'd hear her voice imperiously calling, "Bill! Bill!" and my dad would hurry to her room with cups of tea until we'd finally hear her shuffle into the bathroom. Once she was up and dressed, she'd act as if nothing were amiss. She'd do the laundry, humming to herself as she folded clothes. She cooked meals, although in a rigid set pattern: hamburgers on Mondays, chicken on Tuesdays, meat loaf on Wednesdays, and so on. She'd bake devil's food cake for my birthdays and angel food cake for the girls, and she wouldn't hesitate to take the paddle to my backside if I wandered off to the creek by myself to search for frogs and snakes for my growing reptile collection.

It was only later in the day, when the drudgery of being a housewife and mother of four had worn her down, that the drinking would begin. Whiskey sours washed down the antidepressants that kept my mother sane, along with the sleeping pills and amphetamines. Herself one of four children from a devout Catholic family, she had eloped with my Presbyterian father after falling in love with him on a blind date. Far too young, pregnant, and disowned by her Czech family for the first few years of her marriage, my mother quickly found that life with the dashing naval lieutenant who had stolen her heart wasn't quite as she'd imagined it.

"*You* kids have been named in alphabetical order," she'd tell me when I was a young boy, when April was at school and Carol and Diane were still quite small. "That way I'll always remember what order you came in."

Stifled by her responsibilities, she escaped into other people's imaginations, devouring book after book. Drinking, chain-smoking, and popping pills also helped, but when I was fifteen years old, her doctor suddenly stopped prescribing her any more of the drugs she'd been taking for years. Not surprisingly, the sudden shock to her system triggered a complete mental and physical breakdown.

One day Mom was home as usual, and the next day she wasn't. Dad told us that she'd been admitted to the Haverford State Hospital, an old-fashioned redbrick mental institution in suburban Philadelphia, where we later learned she was locked in a padded cell while she went "cold turkey."

As a family we tried to pretend that nothing had happened. We were already self-sufficient, so we still got up each morning and made our own breakfasts and took ourselves off to school. Dad did the laundry and grilled steaks for us on the outdoor grill. We did our usual chores, but none of us dared tell any of our friends—we were too ashamed. My sisters and I weren't allowed to visit Mom, but I can remember Dad coming home from those visits looking as wretched as I'd ever seen him. My younger sisters would cry themselves to sleep, sure that they'd never see our mother again.

I would lie in bed thinking of all the bad things I'd done to my mother over the years, like the time I'd caught a garter snake at school and put it in my lunch pail but forgot to tell her. Was I to blame for her illness? I tried not to think of how undiplomatically I'd behaved after I'd seen a friend's parents openly hugging and kissing. I couldn't stop staring. When I returned home that night, I asked my mom, "Why don't you and Dad ever kiss?" She looked up from her book with a sad smile. I realized then that their relationship wasn't like that, and for the first time I began to question everything I'd previously considered normal in my home.

"When's Mom coming home, Dad?" I asked quietly each night when he came in from work.

"Soon, son, soon," Dad would reply, his eyes far away. I tried to

Mom and Dad on vacation in Florida post-retirement.

focus on my happiest memories of Mom, like the times she'd cut my peanut butter and jelly sandwiches into the shapes of little sailboats at lunchtime while I sat watching *Chief Halftown* on TV. Or the time she took me out in the middle of the night on a bullfrog hunt with some professional hunters in waders. Poor Mom—she was terrified of reptiles and she couldn't swim, but she still drove me out to that mosquito-infested creek and waited patiently until I caught myself a big fat frog.

When Mom was eventually released from the mental hospital, she walked back into our lives silent and pale. It was a long time before she told us that she'd had such terrible hallucinations of our being taken from her that she'd finally forced herself to snap out of it. With the help of Dad and her parents (who were by now reconciled to her elopement with a Presbyterian), she was eventually able to overcome her substance and alcohol dependency, although her depression would never leave her for long.

The year after Mom returned to us, I started experimenting with some emotional and physical connections of my own. Ginger was a year older than me, a senior in high school, and she was the prettiest girl I'd ever seen. Blond and outgoing, she came from a wealthy family. Her father was president of the local country club.

"You're cute," she announced to me at a friend's birthday party.

"Oh, thanks."

"You're not like the other boys. You don't chase girls, do you?"

Sixteen and only really interested in sports, I could feel my face reddening. The more we talked, the closer Ginger sat. Before I knew it, we were making out on the sofa. The next day she told everyone we were boyfriend and girlfriend. That summer, after Ginger graduated from high school, we traveled to Ocean City, New Jersey, for senior week. We spent our nights walking from party to party and our days sleeping it off on the beach. It was a special time for us both, and when that summer was over, we were both in the throes of first love.

When I wasn't making out with Ginger that summer, I was hanging out with my buddies Charlie McMurray and Kevin "Doc" Dougherty, working on a garbage truck. Charlie lived in my neighborhood, and I'd known him all my life. Like me, Doc loved playing basketball, so when he moved to our suburb from the city, he and I became instant pals.

The main garbage operator in Newtown Square, Pennsylvania, was "Crazy Bob." His latest recruits, the three of us had a running joke that ours was a great way to make money, because business was "always picking up." We were earning around a hundred dollars a week, which was pretty good money back in 1968. The first day I

Two years old, with my "monk-monk" and bottle, 1954.

showed up for work, I had to wear a surgical mask, because I couldn't bear the stench. But as time wore on, I got used to the odor.

I have fond memories of those hot summers spent hanging off the back of the garbage truck. At lunch we'd pass around a quart of beer. We were constantly goofing off, singing at the top of our lungs and cracking jokes as we made our stops. Of course we always had something to say to the pretty girls we saw on our rounds. By the end of each day, we were soaked in sweat and reeking of rotten vegetables, but we didn't care a bit.

Heaving trash into the back of the truck helped build tremendous body strength, and we regarded our job as a free workout. I was soon in peak physical condition. After our shift was over, we'd head down to an abandoned quarry filled with springwater and jump in to cool off. The water was so clear you could see the old cranes rusting on the bottom. Our courage was measured by how far we'd climb up the rock ledge to dive off the cliffs. The highest drop was nearly fifty feet. I never made it to that ledge, but my buddies did.

There was no limit to my energy and stamina during those summers of '68 and '69. After working on the truck during the day, I played basketball five nights a week in the Narberth Basketball League. It was an outdoor showcase for local high-school players, and the stands were often crowded with college scouts searching for new talent.

On the weekends I'd drive my mom's blue 1952 Mercury out to Avalon Beach to hang out with my buddies Jim Shoemaker and

Billy Glenn, whom I dubbed "Shoe" and "The Glenn." They'd both recently become lifeguards, and they shared a dilapidated shack that looked like a hurricane had recently come through it. Beer cans littered every room, and lifeguards slept three to a bed or on the floor. I took one look around and thought, *This is paradise.* Shoe and The Glenn partied every night, had access to beautiful bikini-clad girls, and got paid to spend all day on the beach. I decided there and then that I would become a lifeguard the following summer.

Ginger got a swimming scholarship to a college in Ohio and dumped me for some guy on the swim team. The rejection stung, but I was single again, and I decided to make the most of it. My grades were good, so my parents didn't mind it when I went out on weekends. That usually meant drinking beer with my jock buddies or smoking a little pot with my hippie friends.

One weekend in January 1970, I went to a party at the house of a friend whose parents never seemed to be around. Some clown thought it would be funny to slip some LSD into my drink, so the next thing I knew, I was tripping my brains out. I lay in one of the bedrooms, unable to move. I'm not sure how long I was tripping, but I remember seeing the destruction of the world that night. I had visions of my friends sharpening knives to stab me with, and I sank into a Dantean hell where people were being tortured and murdered and there was no God. It was as if the scales had

125-pound Haverford Junior High "starting fullback," Havertown, Pennsylvania, 1966.

been ripped from my eyes, and suddenly I saw everything that was wrong with society, culture, and humankind. Everything I had ever believed in was a lie.

There was no denying that there were many bad things happening in the world at the time, most of which I had ignored until that night. My country was at war in Vietnam, where American troops had recently slaughtered innocent villagers at My Lai; Charles Manson and his Family cult had just been arrested for the brutal murders of Sharon Tate and six others; the Black Panther movement was fomenting racial tension; there was terrorism from the Red Brigade in Europe; and the Catholics and Protestants were at war in Northern Ireland. Yet until this moment, my high school's upcoming run for the state basketball championship was the biggest challenge I faced. My eighteen years of life seemed meaningless.

My friends did all they could to snap me out of my LSD-inspired despair, but they couldn't. I remember one of them leaning over me and peering into my eyes.

"Man, Hulse," he said, "you're so messed up you're going to end up at the Haverford State Hospital and you're never going to come out of it!" That didn't do much for my frame of mind, either.

A friend eventually drove me home, where even after the acid wore off, the feelings of terror and confusion continued. I couldn't sleep. I couldn't eat. I tried to go to school and talk to my friends about what I was feeling, but they just didn't understand. Emotionally and physically drained, I finally sat down with my parents and told them what was happening.

"Mom, Dad, someone slipped me some acid at a party, and now I'm all messed up inside," I said, tears streaming down my face. "I'm so confused. I don't understand what's going on in my head. It feels like my brain is going to burst."

My parents were shocked and worried. My mom had been down the rabbit hole of depression, and she didn't want me to go there, too. She held my hand and dried my tears and told me that everything would be all right. My father was a very pragmatic, "let's get it done" type of guy. To his way of thinking, Haverford State Hospital had helped my mother, so now it could help me.

I remembered what my friend at the party had said about Haverford, and I began to shake. I really thought I'd blown it. The star athlete with top grades was going to be locked up in a mental institution for the rest of his life. As a boy I used to walk with my buddies along the railway tracks behind the imposing brick building on the edge of Havertown, and we would dare each other to go near the "crazy people" inside. Now, three years after my mom's hospitalization, I was one of those crazies, sitting in a stark, brightly lit room, afraid that I, too, was having a complete breakdown.

The doctor who admitted me was not particularly reassuring. His eyes showed no compassion, no concern. When he asked me what I was feeling, I asked him, "What's the meaning of life? Why are we here? What's our purpose?"

I could tell by the way he summarily dismissed my questions that he saw me as just another lost and confused hippie, an adolescent punk having a drug-induced breakdown. His response was to offer me more drugs—a dizzying cocktail of antidepressants and tranquilizers that only made me feel worse.

Sitting in that godforsaken place where so many had already lost hope and realizing that I was still a voluntary patient who could leave anytime, I stood up and shook my finger in his face. "You know, I may be messed up, but you're more screwed up than I am." I walked out and went home.

But my troubles weren't so easily left behind. I returned to school at the end of the basketball season, just as the state playoffs were about to start. Our team, the Haverford High School Fords, hadn't made it to the finals for a decade. But we had a lot of good players that year, including me, and hopes ran high.

A few days after I walked out of the mental hospital, I found myself having to play at least two games a week, plus practices, under intense physical and mental pressure, as our team steadily advanced through the playoffs. It started to look as if we had a chance. I would sit on the bus to each game, feeling sick to my stomach and wondering if I could keep it together long enough to even walk onto the court. My biggest fear was that when the game began, I'd just sprint off the court and run away from the crowds and the noise as fast as I could, letting down my family, my team, and virtually everyone I knew.

One of the toughest games I had to get through was at the Palestra gymnasium on the University of Pennsylvania campus, in front of a crowd of ten thousand. Our fans were going crazy. Mom and Dad and my sisters were out there somewhere in the surging sea of faces, cheering us on. I walked into that arena feeling as if my limbs had turned to liquefied lead. I didn't care about the adulation. In fact, I wanted to die. My breathing began to feel ragged and painful in my chest. My head spun. I was sweating. I could hardly think, hardly see. I tasted the fear in my mouth, the bile in the back of my throat. I bit my cheek until I tasted blood.

It was the hardest thing I'd ever done up to that point in my life, but I threw myself into the game. I played like a man possessed, as if my life depended on it. I was on fire. But whenever there was a break for any reason, such as a foul or a time-out, I started panicking again. Anytime I wasn't actually playing gave me a few minutes to remember where I was and why, and it was disastrous for my psyche. I could hear a voice in my head repeating, *I am fucked up! I am fucked*

University of Pennsylvania Palestra, 1970. Pennsylvania High School District I basketball playoffs.

up! I am fucked up! I want to kill myself! I envisioned myself with a gun in my mouth. As soon as the whistle blew again, I shook off my demons and gave the crowd what they wanted.

Halfway through the game, the coach put me defensively on the other team's High School All-American star scorer with instructions to "shut him down." I focused on that guy like he was the devil himself, using every inch of my height to block him. We won the game, and the following day the headlines read HULSE PUTS GLOVE ON WILLIAMS.

The whole team continued to play really well, and the Haverford Fords somehow made it all the way to the finals, in a televised game in front of fifteen thousand fans. The team we were playing was heavily favored to win. Once again I played as if my life depended on it, but this time it wasn't enough: We lost. I looked around the arena at my teammates, my family, and my coach, all sobbing because we didn't win, and I thought, *It was only a basketball game, not the end of the world.* I walked out of that arena dry-eyed and completely numb.

I should have sought more counseling after that, but I didn't know where to look besides Haverford State Hospital. My parents were concerned for my well-being, but they didn't know what to do with me, either. They were children of the Depression, survivors of World War II who didn't understand the confusion raging through me. I talked to my friends about how I felt, but they all thought I was nuts.

"Have another beer, Hulse, and forget about it," they'd say. Beer was their answer to most of life's problems. Their carefree attitude may have served them better than my existential gloom served me, but I couldn't relinquish my need for answers. I sought out anyone who would listen. I talked to the jocks, the hippies, and even the Young Life Christians—who directed me to the Bible, but that didn't resonate with me. The Young Lifers struck me as a bunch of uptight kids just regurgitating what their parents had shoved down their throats.

Having inherited my mother's appetite for reading, I devoured every book I could on spirituality, enlightenment, and the search for happiness. I also began reading *Psychology Today* to try to figure out what was wrong with me, but that didn't help, either. I began writing lists of the things that made me happy, trying to identify the sturdy parts of my fragile world: surfing, being near the ocean, being surrounded by nature. Unfortunately, living in suburban Philadelphia, I was severely limited in my exposure to those things.

Around this time Ginger and I got back together. She'd returned from Ohio and had started training as a nurse. She tried to help me as best she could, although I don't think she ever really understood what I was going through; but it was nice to have someone to hold. One day I was at her parents' enormous mock-Tudor house reading a copy of *Philadelphia* magazine, when I came across an article about a yoga teacher named Guru Amrit Desai. Yoga had interested me ever since I'd read Percy Cerutty's book, but I hadn't read or heard that much about it since then. Desai explained yoga in a way that I really understood. He also talked about the important role of meditation in achieving inner peace and compared the sensation of meditation to listening to God. He was teaching classes in Germantown, the article said; maybe he could help me find my way.

I started taking Guru Desai's classes and found that he was teaching the fundamental principles of yoga as a way to boost physical rejuvenation through movement and meditation. He promised that meditation through yoga would improve my health and give me greater spiritual awareness. The forms and postures were important, but meditation was the key. With the guru's guidance, I was able to detach myself from my surroundings and strip away my negativity. I was left with a sense of calm and tranquillity I had never known.

Shortly after I'd met Guru Desai and started my yoga classes with him, my depression began to lift. It was as if I had found my true purpose: to seek an inner sanctuary. I returned home a different person, but my newfound way of life was hard for my friends to accept. No one at school was practicing yoga. They'd never seen anyone doing the stretches and movements I was now doing before every basketball practice. Some were curious, but most dismissed my regimen as eccentricity. "It's just Hulse," they'd say. "He's a little out there."

At the time I was among the best half-mile runners in the state of Pennsylvania, but I decided to begin running the 120-yard high hurdles instead. Hurdling required me to stretch out more than running, drawing on the flexibility I was developing through my yoga practice. Giving up the half mile was a tough decision to make because of my connection with running and my father, but I had to do what I believed was right for me. I also stopped drinking and focused all my energies on searching for inner peace. I spent the rest of my senior year in high school trying to find a balance between my new world and my old one.

By the time I arrived at Cornell University to study medicine, my depression was gone. I was recruited to play on Cornell's basketball team, which meant I had less time for yoga. The combination of having to keep up with the intense sports regimen, my schoolwork, and my meditation was suddenly overwhelming, especially in a premed program. After much soul-searching and some long discussions with my parents, I changed my major to English. Like my mother, I'd always loved to read, and I thought that maybe I could become a teacher.

Ginger and I were still dating, but she was back at college in Ohio, so we now had a long-distance relationship. Apart from a drunken one-night stand, I was loyal to her, which was easy at Cornell, where the ratio of guys to girls was at least five to one. While my friends complained about the lack of women, I stayed true to Ginger and spent every lunch hour at the swimming pool. I was determined to become a lifeguard in New Jersey with my buddies the following summer, so I swam almost every day. I couldn't wait to get back to the beach.

At the end of May, I traveled to Avalon on a bitterly cold day to take my lifeguard test. Seventy-five lifeguards were needed each summer to watch the six-mile stretch of beach, invaded by some thirty thousand vacationers. Most of the positions were taken by lifeguards who had already passed the test and had been coming back each summer for years. When I arrived at the beach, there were about a hundred other young men warming up. We were all good athletes, mostly college swimmers, football players, and rowers. The test was a half-mile swim in freezing water. The first twenty men to make it around the buoy and back up to the beach would be selected. I was very, very nervous. I knew I was fit, but I also knew that a lot of the competitive swimmers could make it through the water faster than I could.

When the whistle blew, we all sprinted to the water's edge and threw ourselves in. The cold was brutal. A thought flashed through my mind: *Maybe I'll just be a trash man again this summer.* The ocean around me churned with flailing arms and legs. I didn't put my face under the freezing water for fear of getting "ice head," so I only swam backstroke or freestyle. When I finally reached the midway buoy, I realized I was only in the middle of the pack. I'd have to pick up speed coming back toward shore or I wouldn't make the cut, so I powered through every stroke. I had worked too hard to let my chance slip away. There was no way I was going to wait another year.

I exploded out of the water and dashed across the finish line with the very last ounce of strength left in my body. One of the supervisors walked up to where I stood doubled over, dripping and gasping for breath. "Seventeenth," he told me, patting my back. I was too exhausted to respond.

That summer of 1975, my friends and I lived a fantasy. For the princely sum of six hundred dollars, Shoe, The Glenn, and I rented a run-down two-bedroom house on the beach with three other guys for the whole summer. Saigon had fallen, the Khmer Rouge overran Cambodia, and the Middle East was in chaos, yet there we were, oblivious to all that. In 1972, I'd initially missed the Vietnam draft because I was a college student. Then, when the government removed that exemption and gave us all a number, mine was 193. At that time, I would sit with my buddies and watch the televised Selective Service Lottery each week as they drew the numbers that meant young men like me would be yanked out of school and sent to the other side of the earth. It was so surreal. There we were, drinking beer, living in a dream world, and yet, with the shake of that government-owned glass tumbler, any one of us could be on our way to war. Fortunately for me, the draft only went as high as number 171 before hostilities ceased, and here I was now, living on the beach and working as a lifeguard.

One of the kids I came to know on the beach that summer went by the nickname of "Doc X." His real name was Terry Hughes, and he was a fifteen-year-old rebel with attitude, raised by his wealthy grandmother after his parents broke up. He was the only white runner on an otherwise all-black track club in Philadelphia. Most of the other runners in the club had nicknames, and as he was highly political and seriously into Malcolm X, he came up with the moniker that would stick with him for the rest of his life.

Doc X had shoulder-length dark brown hair and the most piercing blue eyes I'd ever seen. He was a terrific surfer, a kneeboarder, which was really adventurous back then. He had a huge problem with authority figures, and he considered lifeguards "beach pigs," as he called them. But when he saw me meditating or doing my yoga each morning on the stand, he realized I wasn't the typical beer-swilling oaf he imagined all lifeguards to be. Doc X was a strict vegetarian, a nondrinking, nonsmoking, anti-drugs fitness freak, so he liked my philosophy on life. As soon as we started talking, we formed an instant connection. In a very short time, Doc X felt like the brother I'd never had.

Then there was "Big Pete" Soderman. Six feet four inches tall,

Left to right: Jim Bonner, me, and Jim Shoemaker, summer of 1971, 78th Street, Avalon, New Jersey.

super-intelligent, and fascinated by my interest in Eastern philosophy, Pete looked like Marlon Brando and drank like a fish. Rob Graham, who was from Canada, was a karate expert who helped hone my own martial-arts skills by turning into "Cato" around our beach house, just like in the *Pink Panther* films—jumping out at me at any moment with a flying kick.

Stuart Hoover, or "Stoover," as we called him, was someone I'd met on my first year at the beach and who kept coming back. He was the cousin of our lifeguard captain, Murray Wolf, known to everyone as "Scarhead." Stoover had to work hard to prove to the rest of us that he could really lifeguard and didn't get his job just because of The Cap. Stoover and I did a lot of running together. We also worked the same construction site in Narberth during a couple of icy-cold winters.

Being at Avalon was great for meeting people and making life-long friendships. I worked from ten in the morning to six in the evening every day, and I spent each night relaxing with my friends. Even though it was against NCAA rules, I found a local summer basketball league to play in so I could practice in the off-season. I planted a garden in the backyard of our house where I grew tomatoes, squash, salad greens, zucchini, and fruit, just as I had watched Mom do back home. At the end of the summer, we dug the garden out, filled the hole with water, and had what we called a "gator party." Everyone took turns running and jumping into the giant mud puddle. It was a true rite of passage and a perfect way to end the season.

At the start of my sophomore year, Ginger transferred from her college in Ohio to attend nursing school in upstate New York, not far from Cornell. We decided to live together, but the only way her parents would allow it was if we got engaged. We'd been together, on and off, for over three years. Although she'd dumped me once before,

I'd learned to trust her again, and I really felt as if I could spend the rest of my life with her, so it seemed like a logical next step. As always, my parents were supportive of my choice. My mother even gave me her mother's engagement ring.

But things didn't work out quite as we planned. Unexpectedly, Ginger didn't take to her nursing classes, and not long after she moved in, she suddenly declared that she was homesick. A few weeks later, she returned to Philadelphia to live with her parents. I was disappointed, but I hoped the move was just temporary. We kept in constant contact, but then one day I received a letter from her. When I opened the envelope, my grandmother's engagement ring fell out onto the floor. I was stunned. I had really thought that things were okay between us. I jumped into my car and drove four hours back to Philadelphia to confront her. Ginger told me quite coldly that she'd fallen back in love with her childhood sweetheart and that they were going to get married. There was nothing I could say to change her mind.

This felt to me like yet another abandonment by a woman. My mother had been absent, mentally if not physically, for much of my teenage years and then had left us altogether for a while. And Ginger was my first love. She had helped me through my breakdown after my acid trip and my mother's hospitalization. For a time she had restored my faith in women. I had loved and trusted her. And now she'd dumped me not once but twice. When she closed the door in my face and ended a pivotal chapter in my life, I walked away from her house heartbroken. I decided that I was never going to put myself in that sort of vulnerable situation with any woman again. Her betrayal cut so deep that it felt almost as damaging to my psyche and my self-esteem as the acid trip. I never wanted to feel such pain again.

3

Finding My Path

When the girlfriend of a basketball buddy at Cornell asked me if I would consider posing for her art class, I didn't understand what was involved at first.

"You've got a great body, Bruce," she told me with a seductive smile. "We always get fat slobs signing up as models, and it would be so much better to have a good physique to draw."

"What does it pay?" I asked.

"Five bucks an hour."

"Sounds good. What do I have to do?"

"Oh, it's easy. You just get undressed and stand in front of the class."

"What? No way!" I didn't realize she meant *nude* modeling. Nudity had never been a source of embarrassment in my family. My father would often walk around naked at home, as would my sisters and I, although my mother never did. But this was different.

She wasn't going to let me off the hook. "What about all your talk of being a free spirit, Hulse?" she asked, frowning. "I had no idea that was all bullshit. You're just a big phony."

Hulse? A phony? That was all the challenge I needed. After mulling it over, I figured I'd give it a try. If it didn't work out, at least I'd have a good story to tell someday.

I showed up to the first art class wearing what had by then become my trademark look—an old, worn army raincoat and combat boots. Class had already started, so I entered the room quietly and stood against a back wall listening to the professor, trying to remain anonymous for as long as I could. There were about thirty students seated at their desks, sketchbooks in hand, presumably waiting for me. Finally the professor looked at me and asked, "Are you ready?" As she did so, every head in the room turned around to look in my direction. That's when I noticed they were all girls!

Nobody had told me that life-class models were supposed to show up wearing a robe, so everyone had to wait while I undressed before I could assume my position on the riser at the front of the classroom. It was a bizarre feeling to be completely nude in a room full of clothed people. I never felt so tall or so naked in my entire life.

"Excuse me, but this is my first time," I mumbled, as if it weren't already obvious. The teacher was understanding and directed me through a series of three-minute poses that weren't too difficult. As time passed, I began feeling more comfortable, but one terrifying thought kept racing through my mind: *Whatever you do, don't get an erection.*

Dreading the embarrassment of having a hard-on in front of a roomful of women staring right at me, I focused on certain spots on the wall and tried to make my mind go blank. I meditated, concentrating on breathing evenly and tuning everything out, which seemed to do the trick. By the end of the two hours, I felt surprisingly at ease. In fact, I found art modeling to be liberating. After class I got dressed and walked around the room to look at the finished drawings. I was curious to see what the artists saw when they looked at me. Some had focused on specific body parts, while others went for the full-body sketch. Thankfully, a few of the drawings were vaguely flattering.

It wasn't long before I became popular around the Cornell art department. Every class I modeled for seemed to be more crowded than the last, I guess because I was in great physical condition from playing basketball night after night. With practice I found I could hold a twenty-minute pose without breaking it. I began to regard the whole experience as a discipline. My arm or leg might fall asleep, but I refused to move, because if I did, I knew that the students' drawings could be ruined.

I also began to get more appreciative looks from girls around campus. I asked a few of them if they ever got turned on while painting or drawing me in class. "Oh, no," they'd insist, "it's strictly art." That didn't always ring true, and one later confided to me how erotic it was for her to draw me.

One morning during an 8:00 A.M. class, I was posing in a chair, leaning back against the wall. I guess a combination of the early hour and the reclined position caused me to doze off. A sense of panic swept over me when I awoke. I knew that when a man goes into full

Summer surf trip, 1971. Getting ready to go to the Outer Banks, North Carolina, in search of waves. From left to right: me, my sister Carol, and Bill "The Glenn" Glenn.

REM sleep, he automatically gets an erection. I didn't know how long I'd been out, but when I glanced down, I saw that my hand was touching my penis, and I wasn't sure if it had been before I went to sleep.

Springing up from my chair, I told the class, "Um, excuse me, I've got a bad leg cramp." Embarrassed, I gathered my things and scurried out of the room without another word. It was the first time I'd broken a pose and the last time I ever modeled nude in an art class.

In the middle of my sophomore year, *Sports Illustrated* published an article about the Cornell basketball team saying that a number of black players had resigned because they felt they were being discriminated against. Our coach was subsequently fired, and the school brought in a new coach from an all-black college in suburban Philadelphia. With the change in leadership, I found myself suddenly cut from the team, which was very traumatic for me. I had identified myself as a ballplayer my whole life. I wasn't the star of the team, but I started almost every game. Being banned from playing basketball caused a sudden and catastrophic identity crisis. I had already decided not to be a doctor. Lately I wasn't even sure about my English studies. And if I wasn't even a basketball player anymore, then who was I?

That summer I was in a thoughtful mood when I returned to Avalon to be a lifeguard. This time I was stationed on the Thirtieth Street beach with a fellow lifeguard named Chris Gilday. Our stand had the distinction of having the best wave breaks in the area because of a nearby pier. Since there were two of us, we were able to alternate shifts in the water, which meant I could surf and watch the beach at the same time. I'd go out with my board for an hour or so, teaching little kids how to surf. I'd sit them on my board and yell, "Okay, stand up now!" whenever a small wave came through. When my time was up, I'd go back so Chris could take his turn.

I couldn't think of a better way to spend my summers than being paid to do some of my favorite things: surfing and patrolling the beach, connecting to nature, enjoying the sun and sea. A summer highlight was the South Jersey Lifeguard Championships, with relay races in swimming, running, and rowing, and I'm proud to say the Avalon Beach Patrol was the reigning South Jersey champion.

I also spent time with Doc X again, who was, as usual, holding court in his grandmother's four-bedroom split-level beach shack.

"Doc X stays in the X Mansion," he used to say. "People come to see Doc X. . . . Doc X doesn't go to see people. That's the Doc X way." His door was open twenty-four hours, and people would drop in day and night to talk to him. He had amazing self-discipline, and his clean living set a great example for the younger kids. It felt good to have my "kid brother" around again. His one weakness was cream-filled doughnuts, which he absolutely loved, but even then he used to limit himself to one or two per summer. When it was time for him to have one, he would bring it home in a box as if it were the Holy Grail, and then he'd stare at it reverentially for several minutes before finally allowing himself to indulge.

He and I used to laugh at the stressed-out businessmen arriving with their families on the weekends, thanking God we weren't one of them. We never wanted anything to do with that lifestyle. Doc was a secret millionaire thanks to his grandmother's oil wells in Texas, but he lived in that old shack and drove around in battered two-hundred-dollar bangers with the words THE DOC X MOBILE spray-painted on the side and an old rack for his surfboards bolted to the roof.

"Surf's up," he'd say suddenly, looking out the window at the Atlantic. "Who's comin'?" I could have been quite content spending the rest of my life catching waves with Doc X.

I learned more about women at Avalon than I ever did at Cornell. The older lifeguards taught me their "Twenty Questions Technique" for picking up girls, and I practiced the technique every chance I got. It started with calling a girl over and then asking several rapid-fire questions, such as "Where are you from?" "What are you up to at the beach today?" and "Are you here with friends?" The more questions I asked, the more confident I got. All the questions would lead up to the most important one of all: "What are you doing tonight?"

The summer eventually ended and, with it, my happiness. Back at Cornell, I realized that without the team spirit provided by basketball, my life had little purpose. I signed up for some acting classes and learned how to fence for theatrical swordfights, but my depression descended on me once again. Unable to pull myself out of it,

Ready for action! Avalon Beach Patrol, 76th Street, 1971. From left to right: me, Jim Bonner, and Jim "Seal Boy" Shoemaker.

I found myself having suicidal thoughts again. My parents, sensing that something was wrong from my telephone calls and letters, drove down to visit and found me sobbing in my room. In between ranting about being kicked off the basketball team and missing Avalon, I told them I wanted to drop out of college altogether.

"I have no idea who I am except when I'm with the other life-guards," I told Mom and Dad. "I think I need to be with people who share my values and goals. Maybe I should move to a commune or something." My father asked me what I wanted to do. "That's just it—I don't know," I said. "I just know I need to find myself and figure out what I really want from life. All I'm sure about is that I don't want to become a white-collar nine-to-five working stiff." Neither of them knew what to suggest.

Even though I'd always hated being alone, I began avoiding my friends, who had already noticed a change in me. I read avidly, losing myself in the words of others, just as my mother always had, looking for escape. I was still crazy about sports, and I became deeply engrossed in shorinji kempo, a martial art that incorporated Japanese Zen Buddhism into its fighting style. Through my interest in shorinji kempo's Eastern philosophy, I came across a book called *What the Buddha Taught*, by Dr. Walpola Rahula, which dispelled misconceptions about Buddhism and made it relevant to contemporary life. Everything Dr. Rahula wrote seemed to be speaking directly to me. He said that if I confronted the truth about myself, I could achieve a state of inner peace. Immediately I changed my major from English to comparative religion and began to study Buddhism.

The word *Buddha* itself means "awakened intelligence," so a Buddhist is literally "one who is awakened." The path of Buddha is the path of intelligence. It is not emotional; it is the pure path of knowing. What most drew me to Buddhism, however, were the Buddha's teachings about how to alleviate suffering and obtain enlightenment. Buddhists believe that we are already everything we hope to someday become. The goal you seek is not something you can achieve; it is not in the future or in some other place. It is in you, yourself, right now. I remember reading that and feeling inexplicably connected with the message. I thought, *This feels good.*

Around the same time, a representative of Guru Maharaj Ji, the acclaimed teenage "Avatar of the Age," and his Divine Light Mission came to our campus to speak. Everything the missionary said about this incredible boy prodigy who had already touched so many around the world seemed to reach my soul. Even though Maharaj Ji's path to enlightenment was more Hindu than Buddhist, he was a living master in the here and now who could show me how to find the inner peace I so desperately sought. My confusion lifted, and my path suddenly became crystal clear. I knew what I had to do. I dropped out of school that afternoon and decided to move to one of the Maharaj Ji's ashrams in Ithaca.

A sudden decision like that might sound odd today, but in the early seventies it wasn't all that unusual for a kid to drop out of school and seek enlightenment. More than forty thousand Americans joined the Maharaj Ji's community across the United States, and many more went to India. I became a vegetarian and decided to dedicate my life to helping others.

The ashram was an old Victorian house not far from the Cornell campus. The house rules came directly from the Maharaj Ji in India, but they were diluted as they came west. One of the chief rules, for example, was that we were supposed to be celibate. That meant no sex and no masturbation; we weren't even supposed to entertain sexual thoughts. Maintaining abstinence was of vital importance to achieving a heightened state of enlightenment. Second sight and supernatural vision were said to be attainable only to those practicing celibacy.

When I first moved into the house, there were two hippie girls in charge who blatantly flouted the celibacy rule by inviting men back to the house for sex. It seemed ludicrous to me that they weren't following the very rules they were in the house to enforce. When they moved out soon after I joined, I was relieved.

In the beginning I liked the way I was living, and for the most part I liked most of the people I shared the house with. I got a job as a carpenter on a construction site, banging nails all day and taking a lot of grief from the foreman and the other workers, who knew I went home to an ashram and handed my paycheck over to the commune.

"You're a frickin' dumb-ass!" they'd yell across the construction site if ever I did anything wrong. If I asked a question, they'd say, "Figure it out for yourself, stupid!" Or, "Surely a spiritual guy like you must know all the answers?" I rolled with the punches, remembering the words of the Tibetan Buddhists: *Build a house for your enemies next door, for they are your greatest teachers, from whom you will learn patience and endurance.* Eventually these hard-ass construction workers were won over by my relentless cheerfulness, and some of them even began coming to me with their problems.

When I got home to the ashram each night, we'd eat together and have meetings and meditations. On weekends we canvassed students at the Cornell campus to try to promote our way of life. The celibacy rule wasn't hard for me at first, because I was able to channel that energy into my spiritual aspirations. I still had strong desires, but I learned how to focus them into my higher being.

But then a senior member of Maharaj Ji's organization came to the house for several weeks. During the day he gave inspiring speeches and lectures, but at night he worked on seducing the women. This was a man who was supposed to be living his life as an example to others. One girl he was chasing came to me because she was so upset by his advances. I did what I could to protect her. Eventually the mahatma left the ashram, but for me the damage had been done. His actions called into question everything I'd been learning. If the leaders weren't following their own teachings, then how valuable could those teachings be? I became restless, and my determination to achieve elevated states of mind began to weaken.

I already knew that several of the women in the house were attracted to me. They would follow me around, showering me with affection that was becoming hard to ignore. After months of celibacy, one night I gave in to temptation. I crept down to one of the girls' room and woke her. Without uttering a word, she led me to the meditation room, where we made love. After such a long stretch of abstinence, we had mind-blowing sex that definitely seemed to take me to a higher plane.

In the days that followed, I became even more confused about my beliefs. I still trusted in the teachings of the Maharaj Ji but realized it was time to move out. When the Maharaj Ji got married at sixteen, breaking his own spiritual discipline of celibacy, a lot of people thought he was a fraud, but I was relieved. I still thought him enlightening and liberating, in a symbolic way. He had shown me that I could have my core beliefs without sacrificing love, sex, marriage, or children. Now all I needed to do was find the right woman.

I went back to Avalon Beach the following summer with an entirely different mind-set. I knew I needed to make some changes to my lifestyle. I traded partying and drinking for meditation and clean living on the beach. A few buddies and I rented a house together and practiced yoga every day. We hosted meditation groups nearly every night and cooked incredible organic dinners with the fresh vegetables I grew in our garden.

Doc X came around a lot and we had long conversations about spirituality and meditation. "Doc X likes what B has to say," he'd tell me. "This could become the Doc X way." He'd set up his bongo drums next to the lifeguard stand and play all day, which drove Scarhead crazy. Doc X and The Cap had an ongoing battle of wills that lasted for years.

I taught many of my lifeguard buddies about my new way of life, and they, too, became followers of the Maharaj Ji. Girls came over to chant and meditate with us, but we never had sex—at least not in the house. That was the one rule we had: If you were following the Maharaj Ji, you had to take sex outside to the sand dunes, our second home under the stars. Girls on vacation dreamed of seducing lifeguards, it seemed. I found it virtually impossible to turn them down, especially after such a long period of celibacy. Like Maharaj Ji, I was only human after all.

Being a lifeguard wasn't only about chicks, though. In fact if we were on duty and caught talking to girls after noon, when the beach became really crowded, we could be suspended without pay. Our job was about looking out for families and children and making sure that people enjoyed themselves safely on vacation. We learned all about northeasters and riptides; we practiced first aid, CPR, and lifeboat training every day. "Nobody drowns on my watch," Scarhead used to growl. And in the thirteen years that I returned each summer to lifeguard on the South Jersey shore, nobody ever did.

Avalon was such a calming, peaceful retreat for me. No matter what was happening to me during the rest of the year, I always made it back to the beach every summer, to take part in the races, to look out for the swimmers and surfers, and to teach the kids, or "surf grommets," how to have a healthy respect for the water. Also the name of a mythical island of Arthurian legend, Avalon was my true ashram.

I took the fall semester off to go on a road trip with my buddy Rob "Cato" Graham in his Volkswagen bus. Rob was also taking a break from school at McGill University in Canada. Our plan was to drive the VW bus to San Diego, where we'd sell it before flying to Hawaii to surf. We worked our way slowly down the East Coast, camping by the side of the road. From September through November, we surfed North Carolina and Florida. We made it as far as San Antonio, Texas, but had to stop to earn money chopping firewood when our funds ran out. Wearying of life on the road, we eventually drove back to New Jersey, and Rob returned to college, promising to make it to Hawaii another time.

I decided to follow his lead and returned to Cornell the next semester to take a degree in Buddhist and Hindu studies. I'm sure I was a royal pain in the ass to my professor, because I was much more interested in the practical side of Buddhism than the academic. "Does enlightenment really exist?" I would ask. "Can I truly experience the state of meditation and freedom from desire that the classic texts describe?"

"I can neither confirm nor deny your question," he'd answer. I desperately wanted to experience the inner peace Buddhism promised me, but it still proved tantalizingly elusive.

I played basketball that summer in a league on the South Jersey shore with many skilled and talented ex–college players. The level of competition was extremely high. One of my teammates was a guy named Joe Cafferky. I'd known Joe since we were kids competing against each other on the playgrounds of Philly. There was no end to Joe's talent. An inch shorter than me, he was a point guard who could jump like no one else I'd ever seen. He'd been captain of the North Carolina State men's basketball team and was now playing professionally for a team in Sweden.

"Hey, Bruce, you know my team's looking for another American," Joe told me one day. One of the managers from Joe's Swedish team came to visit and watched me playing in a summer-league game. When he asked if I'd be interested in playing for his team, I agreed without a moment's hesitation. It would be a tremendous opportunity to see Scandinavia and enjoy a sport I loved. The club would pay me three thousand dollars a month and set me up in a small apartment.

At the end of August 1976, I flew to Stockholm and then on to the team's hometown of Borås. Word of my arrival preceded me. As soon as I landed, I was whisked off to a press conference and interviewed as "the new American." We trained out at the team's facility in Hästhagen, where I couldn't get over the crisp freshness of the air. After practice we'd swim in the lake or sit in the sauna or *bastu,* drinking beer. I remember thinking, *If this is their idea of training camp, I can't wait to see what the off season's like!*

Our team was called Borås Basket, and the symbol on the front of our jerseys was a pair of scissors, a reference to the city's textile-manufacturing base. The Borås Hall arena seated around four thousand people. I knew that everyone was curious to see what I'd be able to bring to the team, and I didn't want to disappoint. My first game was in front of a capacity crowd. I didn't realize until that game how much I missed the sound of fans cheering, and it really got me pumped up. At the opening tip-off, the other team got the ball and lobbed it down the floor to one of their forwards. He was going up for what he thought was a routine layup when I swooped in from behind him and literally pinned the ball against the backboard. I must have been three feet above the rim.

Borås Hall erupted as the fans went crazy. I can still see the look of utter shock on the guy's face when he realized I'd just stuffed him. It was one of the few times in my life I'd made that type of play, but that night at Borås Hall my timing was perfect.

We practiced every day and played a couple games a week, so I soon settled into a steady routine. My friend Joe averaged around thirty points per game and I managed around twenty, so we were a force to be reckoned with. We often traveled to Stockholm and Malmö for games where we'd get together with other Americans playing abroad. After the game we'd go out for dinner and drinks and catch up on news from back home. As the only two Americans

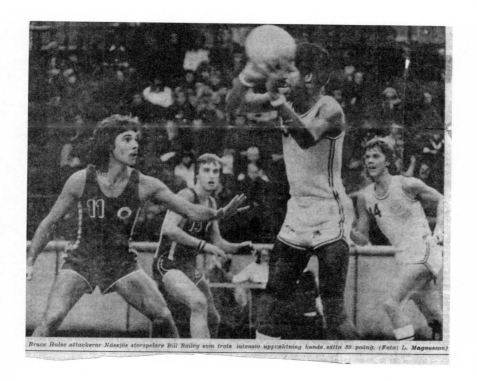

Bruce Hulse attackerar Nässjös storspelare Bill Bailey som trots intensiv uppvaktning kunde sätta 30 poäng. (Foto: L. Magnusson)

on our squad, Joe and I became good teammates and even better friends. We'd meet every morning at the library to read the American newspapers and have coffee, and then we'd go to the local recreation center and play Ping-Pong.

After basketball practice, we often played one-on-one. I have to confess, I can't remember ever beating Joe. He was an absolute monster on the court and would always find a way to win. If he wasn't driving by me down the lane, he was killing me with his outside jump shot. It was small consolation that I was usually able to beat him at Ping-Pong.

Life was simple in Sweden. The winter was long and dark. The sun rose at 10:00 A.M. and set at around 2:30 P.M. There were only two television stations, so if you didn't like what was showing on

Channel 1, you'd better like what was on Channel 2. Every Thursday evening, *Star Trek* aired. It was the only familiar show in a foreign country, so I always looked forward to watching it.

I began dating a beautiful Swedish girl named Annika, who was also a basketball player. She was good company, and we spent many long, cold Swedish nights playing cards and making love. I wasn't planning on getting serious with anybody, though. When Joe and I got really bored, we would venture out to the local discotheque to take in the scene. It was 1976, so ABBA was at their peak of success, and "Dancing Queen" seemed to be playing everywhere I went, on an endless loop. I was more into the Doors and Jimi Hendrix. ABBA left me cold. The Swedish women absolutely loved them, though, and whenever they heard an ABBA song, they would dance like crazy in their tight jeans and white clogs.

Joe ended up marrying a local girl and starting a family. He remained in Sweden, and we are still in touch. Many of the American players I met did the same. I really enjoyed my time there, experiencing a different culture and learning a foreign language, but it was still a lonely way of life for me. Although I'd established a good circle of buddies, I desperately missed my family and friends. It was time to come home.

I moved back to Philadelphia in the summer of 1977, living with my parents for a while. Dad especially loved having me home. He'd sold *The Gibbut* and bought a sailboat, which he kept at Barnegat Bay. Mom wasn't a natural sailor, so now that I was home, he could go sailing with someone who actually enjoyed it. I got a job in construction during the day, and after much thought about what I wanted to do, I applied for and received a scholarship to West Chester College. I planned to get a master's degree in psychology, taking night classes so I could continue to work construction during the day. I holed up in the library on weekends to catch up with my studies.

After everything I'd gone through in dealing with my depression over the years, pursuing a career as a psychotherapist made sense. I hoped to become the kind of psychologist who really listened to his patients, understood their issues, and genuinely cared about their well-being, joining my Buddhist-influenced beliefs to my intuitive feel for helping others. I was genuinely excited about going back to school now that I had found a path I was passionate about.

4

Breaking In to the Biz

"*Hi,* my name is Nathalie. Can I speak to you for a moment?" A beautiful young girl with lustrous brown hair almost to her waist sat down next to me in the lecture hall. My heart started pounding.

"I had a dream about you last night," she said, never dropping her gaze. "I believe we are somehow connected."

That was the day that Nathalie Gabrielli walked into my life. It was the last day of a three-day meditation conference with the Guru Maharaj Ji. I'd flown out to Denver alone to see my guru again, to enjoy a rare weekend off, and to reacquaint myself with Maharaj Ji's three key commandments: to meditate, to help others, and to speak the truth. When the conference was over, I would fly back to Philadelphia, where I was living with my girlfriend, Ruth, and going to school to get my master's degree. Ruth was a sweet, lovely girl, but we'd sort of drifted together through convenience more than any grand passion. More important, Ruth didn't share my interest in spirituality. I meditated regularly and went to conferences and seminars, but she remained resistant to that part of my life.

Despite our spiritual differences, Ruth and I had a good life together. School was going well, and I was planning to open a surf shop on the South Jersey shore in the summer. I was still working as a carpenter anywhere I could to help pay the bills. Overall I had nothing to complain about, but I was still searching for enlightenment, which was why I had come to the conference where this beautiful stranger had approached me so boldly.

"Can I write to you?" Nathalie asked me. I thought it might be nice to correspond with someone who shared my spiritual beliefs, so I scrawled my address on a piece of paper and left the conference hall. I flew home later that afternoon, never expecting to hear from her again.

A few days later, I received an exquisite and poetic handwritten letter from Nathalie. She told me she was attending New York's High School for Performing Arts, the school renowned for its starring role in the movie *Fame*. She was living with her mother and younger brother in an apartment in Manhattan. Her letter went into great detail about the spiritual connection she believed we shared. I was impressed and intrigued by the depth of her writing, especially for one so young. I thought it showed surprising sophistication. She told me she spoke two languages, was well traveled, and regularly spent her summers in Europe. It was obvious that Nathalie possessed a worldliness I had never encountered before.

A few weeks later, on a trip to New York to buy some merchandise for the store I'd leased on the Avalon boardwalk, I met Nathalie for lunch. I had no intention of cheating on Ruth, although I knew that our relationship wasn't going anywhere. Nathalie and I spent the day walking around the city, getting to know each other. Her parents were French, and they'd gotten divorced some years before. Her father owned a well-known clothing store on Madison Avenue. I told Nathalie about my own family and of my devotion to Maharaj Ji. I told her about the time I'd jumped on a plane and flown to England to see Maharaj Ji speak at the Albert Hall in London and how I had converted my mother—who, as a reaction to her strict Catholic upbringing, had always been against any form of religion—to the Maharaj Ji's path.

"Even my father, who's a Presbyterian and teaches Sunday school to adults, came along to a few sessions where I talked about meditation and my spiritual beliefs," I said. "He's been a public speaker all his life, yet he told me he was proud of me and how well he thought I'd conveyed my message."

Nathalie smiled. "I think I'd like your dad."

"You would, and he'd love you."

At day's end we were both exhausted, so we went back to her mother's apartment on East Seventy-Sixth Street to relax. We sat and talked for hours, this time about our meditation practices. I was entranced. Here was someone young, pretty, vibrant, and exciting, who shared my passion for all things spiritual. As we talked, the setting sun lit her from behind, giving her incredible hair a sort of halo.

Before I knew what was happening, I found myself taking her in my arms and kissing her passionately. As our lips touched, I felt electricity surging up and down my spine.

I left New York that night totally confused and madly in love. After just one kiss! I took the last train back to Philadelphia, my head spinning. Being with her felt comfortable, natural, and right. And being with Nathalie was all I could think about. I felt possessed.

I told Ruth about Nathalie right away. "I've met someone who is spiritually, physically, and creatively completely connected to me," I said, with genuine guilt and sorrow. "I honestly think I could spend the rest of my life with her. I'm so, so sorry, Ruthie, but I've never felt this way before. Please understand. I have to follow my heart."

Within a week I went back to New York to see Nathalie. We spent the day touring the city, talking and walking in Central Park. That night we had dinner with her mother and brother back at their apartment. By the time dinner was over, I had missed the last train, and so I asked Nathalie's mother if it would be okay if I crashed on her sofa.

"Don't be silly! You can sleep with me," Nathalie said, as if I'd asked a dumb question. I was taken aback, but her mother never said a word about it. I thought, *I guess this is how they do it in France.* That night Nathalie and I made love for the first time. It was as if I had found my spiritual mate, the woman I was truly meant to be with. In her arms I finally found the peace I'd been seeking.

I spent the next few months shuttling between my place in Philadelphia—the Fine Line Surf Shop I'd opened in Avalon with my lifeguard buddy Chris Gilday and a local surfer named Henry Peddle—and Nathalie's mother's apartment in Manhattan. I visited Nathalie every chance I could. We had intensely cultural and spiritual weekends together that were such a contrast to my other life.

Nathalie was going to graduate from high school soon, so she was thinking about where she might want to go to college. I suggested she consider schools in California, where I hoped to set up my psychotherapy practice and surf, but Nathalie decided to attend New York University so she could study dance there.

I was spreading myself thin between working, running the surf shop (which was a disaster, because we kept giving boards away), lifeguarding, going to school, and traveling back and forth to see Nathalie. After two and a half years of graduate school, I was also doing my practicum as a guidance counselor at a high school. My job was to sit in an office at the school and have students come in to talk to me about their problems. I liked the work. I really seemed to be able to relate to the kids, and when a few told me they were depressed or worried about the future, I felt I could draw on my own experiences to advise them.

I needed a B or higher from my supervisor to pass the practicum, the last barrier to getting my degree. When she gave me a C, I was genuinely shocked. I had been getting nothing but A's in my comprehensive exams. I went straight to my adviser at West Chester College to complain and was told that the supervisor gave me such a low grade because I had long hair and dressed sloppily. "It has nothing to do with your performance," he told me.

I'd done so much hard work and had come so close to achieving my goal, only to have it snatched from me because of someone else's prejudices. The low practicum grade meant I would have to go back and work another six months as a high-school counselor and come out with a B this time in order to get my degree. I wasn't sure I could motivate myself to do it.

When I told Nathalie what had happened, she could see how frustrated I was, but she said she had a solution for me. "Okay,

Bruce, now you really have to listen to what I've been saying to you all along," she said.

I shook my head. "Not that male-model idea again."

"Yes!" she cried. "I told you from the first day I met you, it's the perfect job for you! You can earn as much as a thousand dollars a day, which is a heck of a lot better than the eight dollars an hour you get as a carpenter. You're such a beautiful man, Bruce, and you're tall and thin, which is just what they want. Look at these guys!" she said, showing me a page of long-haired jocks lying around on a beach in Bermuda, shirts open to the waist, tanned and fit. "You easily could be one of them."

I was flattered that Nathalie thought I was model material, but I really didn't think I was in the same league as the slick-looking guys who were modeling clothes for big-name fashion designers like Calvin Klein and Giorgio Armani. I was a scruffy surfer from Philadelphia. "Sloppy," my supervisor had called me. I lived in old jeans, sneakers, and a T-shirt, with an army greatcoat thrown over the top. I rarely shaved. Nathalie, on the other hand, had an innate sense of style. She looked fabulous whatever she put on. I often wondered what she was doing with me.

"I don't know, Nathalie," I replied. "I really don't think this will work."

"Trust me," she said, smiling. "It will. And if it does, it'll give you the money you need to decide what you want to do next. That Ph.D. you keep talking about doing at grad school, for example. You won't have to work so darn hard. You can spend more time with me. We can fly to see the Maharaj Ji anywhere in the world, and when you've made enough from modeling, you can quit."

As I thought about it, I realized I didn't have much to lose. It wasn't as if I were making modeling a career, and I figured it would be easier than hammering nails all day. Nathalie got me a good haircut and sent me to her father's shop, where he kindly lent me some smart clothes—a blazer, a shirt, some pants, and a nice sweater. This stylish, silver-haired Frenchman must have thought his daughter was crazy. In the phone book, I found a photographer in New Jersey, just across the river from Manhattan, and reluctantly paid her three hundred dollars for a half-day shoot. She took my test shots in the backyard of her house.

"Yes, you could be a model," she told me confidently as she fixed me in her lens.

I was nervous during the shoot, but she walked me through it. I thought back to the time I had Carol take those photos of me in my dad's sweater and my mom's beret, and I tried to recapture some of that sense of cool.

"Yes, Bruce, that's good," the photographer said encouragingly. "Look left now, smile, lean back, that's it. Okay, and hold it."

When I went to pick up the photographs from her studio, I could hardly believe what I was seeing. They were by far the best pictures anyone had ever taken of me.

Feeling more confident, I stuck them into a book and took them around to the three agencies Nathalie had told me about. The first was Zoli Management in the basement of a brownstone on the East Side. As I walked into the office of a man by the name of Tom La Spina, I was confronted with a wall of *GQ* covers featuring close-up shots of male models. It was very impressive. My confidence began to ebb.

Mr. La Spina flicked through my photographs rather disdainfully, pausing now and then to look me up and down. He asked me a few questions. I could feel the sweat trickling down my back as I answered him. He leaned back in his chair and studied my features critically, as if he were examining a prize steer.

"Hmmm. Let me take this book and show it to Zoli," he said finally. "Come back in half an hour."

My hopes lifted. That meant I had a chance. I walked down the street, where I nursed a cup of coffee. Exactly thirty minutes later, I returned to the basement and knocked on Mr. La Spina's door.

"You have a good look," he told me, rubbing his chin thoughtfully. "There's definitely something there."

I grinned.

"But Zoli didn't really like you. He doesn't think you're *GQ* material. My advice to you would be to read *GQ* magazine, get some new clothes, have some more test shots done by a different photographer, and then maybe come back later."

I frowned. I didn't get it. If I had the look and all I needed was some different clothes and a different photographer, then why not send me to *GQ* and have them dress me and take the pictures to save me from doing it? It didn't make sense.

With a heavy heart, I went to the two other agencies Nathalie had recommended. They were Ford and Wilhelmina, and they both gave me flat rejections. "You are not model material. Go home. Forget it." So I did.

"I rolled the dice and I lost," I told Nathalie that evening. "I lost three hundred bucks."

Nathalie wasn't so easily discouraged, however, and secretly I was pleased by her stubbornness. Being rejected had fired up the competitor in me. I felt as though I'd been offered membership to an exclusive club but the gatekeepers had refused to let me in. I began to really study men's magazines, getting to know the designers, finding out who the best models, photographers, and agents were. I was encouraged by what I saw. *What do they know? I look just like some of these guys!*

Nathalie agreed, but she also understood that success in the fashion industry depended a lot on whom you knew. Fortunately for me, she had a friend who knew a man who had a contact—a French talent scout named Jocelyn, who worked for the First Agency in Paris. Jocelyn was the first overtly gay man I'd ever met—tall, black, beautifully dressed, and very flamboyant.

"Come to the Underground tomorrow night," Jocelyn told me after giving me the once-over. "It's a club off Union Square. *SoHo News* is hosting a party to announce the top five male supermodels of the year. It's the first time the mainstream press has ever given men in the business that sort of recognition. It'll be a good place for you to be seen. *Bon?*"

I was a stranger to the New York club scene, and I was completely out of my element in the noisy, dimly lit basement. I arrived early, bought a drink, and stood alone on the periphery, watching and waiting. Jocelyn eventually showed up with a couple of other hopefuls.

"There they are," Jocelyn said, pointing to a roped-off VIP area, surrounded by adoring female groupies. Five well-groomed men in dark suits produced dazzling smiles for the flashing cameras. "*Mon Dieu*, they're gorgeous! That's Todd Irvin, Michael Ives, Tom Flemming, Rick Edwards, and Jeff Aquilon."

I recognized a couple of the faces from magazines, but it felt weird to be ogling them along with everyone else. I'd never been exposed to this level of glamour and hype before.

"That could be you up there one day, *chéri*," Jocelyn whispered in my ear. At that moment I knew I wanted to be behind that velvet rope more than almost anything I'd ever wanted in my life.

I left the club that night feeling deeply confused. The sudden urge to be a model shocked me. The spectacle I'd just witnessed was part of a world that had nothing to do with me, Bruce Hulse. I was a lifeguard, a carpenter. I wanted to be a psychologist. I was a jock, a basketball star, a Buddhist who was searching for inner peace, a surfer from Philadelphia who just wanted to make enough money each year to maintain his low-key lifestyle. I'd even turned down the offer of a lieutenant's job at the lifeguard station so that I could stay with my buddies on the beach. I was happy crashing at my parents' house, or at Nathalie's. As long as I had enough cash to pay for gas and beer, that was all I needed.

But those glamorous men with their beautiful clothes, fabulous hair, and flawless skin had sparked something in me, the part of me that loved to be in the limelight on the basketball court, or posing for the art class at Cornell, or standing at the podium talking about meditation. I returned to Nathalie's in a pensive mood.

When nothing happened on the modeling front for a couple of weeks, I went back to banging nails, although construction work was tailing off for the winter now that it was nearly November. I knew I'd be going back to the beach the following summer, but I needed something to bring in some money until then. Nathalie and I had been dating for almost a year, and I was having a great time with her, although her mother began to complain about my hanging around the apartment all day, eating from her refrigerator. When I went home for a visit, it wasn't much different. My mom kept berating me to get off the couch and get a job.

As luck would have it, I was at Nathalie's when her mother told me I had a long-distance call.

"Bruce, baby? My name eeez Sophie Fraise," said a voice with a thick French accent. "I'm with zee First Agency in Paris, and Jocelyn sent us your pictures. We love you, baby! We want you to come model for us in France."

Nathalie was thrilled. "Oh, you must go!" she cried, clapping her hands together delightedly when I told her. "This is just the break you need."

"But it's France," I said uncertainly. "Can't you come with me? You speak French."

"I can't, Bruce! I'm in college. You'll be fine."

"You think? I don't know. I mean, it's nice to get some positive feedback, but I don't really want to go that far away on my own. Actually, I'm not even sure I want to go at all."

Nathalie smiled. "Listen, you should go and give yourself from now until Christmas to see how it goes, okay? If it works out, then I'll try to come and join you later."

Her words summed up our relationship. It was so loose and easy. I saw her on weekends when I could come to New York. She rarely, if ever, came to visit me in New Jersey or Philly. She was a free spirit who never tried to tie me down or seek any hard-and-fast commitment from me. We weren't living together, and we weren't married. I had no idea if she saw other people when I wasn't around (although I really doubted it), but I never asked, and she never once asked me what I did when she wasn't around. I'd never been with anyone so undemanding before. She was just happy if I was happy. It was as simple as that.

I scraped together enough money to buy the cheapest airplane ticket I could find from New York to Brussels, then hopped a train south to Paris. I arrived at the Gare du Nord with two hundred dollars in my pocket and a scrap of paper from the airline promising to send on my luggage, which they'd lost.

I walked into the ground-floor offices of the First Agency just off the rue de Rivoli. The place was buzzing. Models—men and women, French, English, American, and Italian—were walking in and out, asking question after question. "What am I doing tomorrow?" "What happened with that shoot in Africa?" "Who sent me to that asshole Pierre?" I felt like I was at the center of the modeling universe.

An attractive woman in her thirties jumped up to say hello.

"Ah, Bruce! You made eet! Good, darling." She picked up a ringing telephone and spoke quickly. "No, he's not ready. . . . Yes, you can have him, but you have to pay more money."

Putting down the phone, she said, "Now, we'll send you out first thing tomorrow, so get some rest tonight. How do you like Paris? Oh, you'll have lots of fun here. You'll do well for us, Bruce. Where are you staying?"

I looked at her blankly. "I have no idea."

Just then Jocelyn walked in and kissed Sophie three times, in true French style. "Oh, Bruce can stay at my place until he finds somewhere," he said flippantly. He introduced me to another young American hopeful named Michael Evans, who'd just flown in from the States with him.

"Um, thanks," I said, wondering just how beholden I was to Jocelyn for this opportunity.

Jocelyn seemed to read my mind. "Michael and another new model will also be staying. You'll be perfectly safe, *chéri*."

Outside, I heard the distinctive throbbing rumble of a large motorcycle over the general hum of the traffic. Agency staff exchanged looks and began darting right and left. A few moments later, a tall, slender guy sauntered into the office, carrying a helmet and wearing tight red leather pants. He had a rock-star aura about him. I recognized him from the night of the party at the Underground in New York. As I sat quietly on a sofa in a corner, someone

My first shoot in Paris with Paolo Roversi.

reminded me of his name: Todd Irvin, the current "it" boy of the male-modeling universe.

Todd made his way around the room, hugging and kissing agents and assistants. Everyone was at his beck and call, asking if he needed anything. "A drink, Todd? A cigarette? Would you like a coffee?"

An agent approached Todd and began to discuss his upcoming schedule, mentioning that he was booked solid for the next three months. I was shocked when I overheard him tell the booker that he didn't want to work that much. I would have done anything for a single job, let alone three months of work. The agent and his crowd of assistants then disappeared into one of the conference rooms to discuss which jobs Todd should take.

Sophie saw me watching. "One of zee reasons we decided to bring you here eez because we think you look like him," she said with a wink. I was taken aback. I honestly couldn't see any resemblance but figured that if she could, then I might get some work.

I stayed at Jocelyn's that first night in Paris, with Michael and another male model. When Jocelyn saw me sit down in a corner to meditate, he was horrified.

"You must give all that up," he said, tapping me on the shoulder and wagging his finger at me in that tut-tut French way. "I know about religion, and it's—how you say?—evil. If you want to be a model, *chéri*, then you'll have to put all that behind you. Fashion is a world of materialism and appearance and instant gratification. If you try to cling to things you believe in, you'll be in big trouble."

In my jet-lagged, vulnerable state, Jocelyn seemed like the incarnation of the devil. There was no way I was going to abandon my entire belief system just because I was pursuing a possible temporary career as a model. No way at all.

I finally curled up to sleep on the couch fully clothed, but I was awoken in the middle of the night by the sounds of two of the men in the apartment having sex. I've always been open-minded, and I've never had any problems with anyone's sexuality, but to actually have to listen to someone having sex, straight or gay, disturbed me, and I wanted to get the hell out of there.

The next morning I got up and put on my jeans, T-shirt, and old army coat. Jocelyn took one look at me and shook his head. "Oh, no. *Non, non, non!* You can't go to your castings dressed like that! *Vien!* Come with me." He took me to his closet and threw the doors open. I had never seen so many clothes so beautifully arranged. There were cashmere sweaters, jackets, shirts, shoes, ties—all color-coordinated. "I will dress you!" he cried, reaching for some pants, but I backed away.

"Thanks all the same, Jocelyn, but I think I'll just stick to what I'm wearing, if that's okay with you." I realized then that Jocelyn viewed me almost as his property, his investment, and I didn't feel comfortable with that. I didn't want to be rude to the guy who'd given me my first break, but until I found out exactly how much of a say he had in my future, I was going to play it cool.

Sophie helped me find another place to stay, a hotel called La Pension du Roc, where I paid a month's rent for a tiny room. I got friendly with the concierge, Pierre, and each morning I'd come down to the restaurant to eat an omelette du fromage avec pommes frites for breakfast, while reading the *International Herald Tribune* that he'd give me. There were about fifteen other models staying at the hotel, and the atmosphere was like a coed college dorm, with people coming and going all the time, most of them working. Not me, though. I went to three or four auditions, or "go-sees," every day, all of which ended in rejection. I had only my test shots with me—no editorials or "tear sheets" to show that I'd actually done any professional work yet—and my inexperience clearly counted against me. Some of the other models at the hotel were earning fifteen hundred dollars a day doing catalogs, and I barely had enough money for food.

To keep myself from getting depressed, I found a meditation class and a martial-arts instructor, and I spent my weekends visiting museums and flea markets. Wearing my army coat and a black military beret I'd picked up for a few francs at a flea market, I'd sit at sidewalk cafés drinking strong black coffee or vin rouge and reading Henry Miller's *Quiet Days in Clichy* or his *Sexus, Plexus, Nexus*—which weren't the best things for a lonely young man to be reading in Paris, as they were all about random sexual encounters. Jocelyn would invite me to parties or clubs occasionally, and sometimes I would go along, but I didn't like how much cocaine they were snorting or the way some of the younger models seemed to be screwing themselves up psychologically.

One guy, a surfer from California, confided in me that he was binge eating and then throwing up immediately afterward. This was before most people had ever heard the word *bulimia*.

"I'm all messed up," he told me. "I can't even look at food without wanting to gobble it all down and then vomit it all up."

I tried to counsel him as best I could. "You're going to make yourself really sick, man," I told him. "I think you should go home, go back to what you know. You need to get back to the surf. Get back to nature for a while. You need to get the hell away from this crazy scene." He eventually took my advice and did just that.

I quickly ran out of money, and Sophie gave me an advance of several hundred dollars, but still there was no work forthcoming. I figured that the advance must mean the agency had faith in me, even if no one else did. I tried to call Nathalie from a telephone booth about once a week, but the calls were short and expensive, with an annoying echo on the line, and sometimes she wasn't home when I called. I felt a million miles away from her, physically and spiritually.

When a pretty young American model, Terry, and her elder sister moved into La Pension du Roc, I couldn't help but notice. All the guys did. Terry had beautiful green eyes, long dark hair, and a fantastic body. Her sister was there as her chaperone. They were given the largest room in the hotel because they were sharing it, and then they unexpectedly invited me to share it with them.

"We don't know a soul in Paris," Terry explained a little fearfully. "We've never been to Europe before, we don't speak French, and we'd feel a lot safer if you stayed with us." The financial saving was attractive to me, and so, I have to admit, was Terry. I didn't have it in me to say no.

Everything was completely aboveboard at first. Terry, her sister, and I all slept in the same big bed, but nothing happened. As the days passed, however, Terry started wandering past me in her bra and panties when I was trying to meditate. Our eyes would meet, and it was clear that the attraction between us was mutual. Eventually we arranged to meet in the communal bathroom one night at midnight, after her sister—who was a heavy sleeper—had drifted off. Our encounter that night was amazing. Terry and I had an intense and explosive physical connection. I felt as if I were on a separate planet from Nathalie and New York and everything I'd been back there.

I never lied to Terry. I told her about Nathalie from the start. She told me she had a boyfriend back home, too. We were just two lonely people comforting each other in a faraway country, and it didn't feel like we were hurting anyone. Even so, I couldn't stop thinking about a Sir Walter Scott quote my father used to repeat when I was growing up: "Oh! What a tangled web we weave / When first we practice to deceive!" Though I didn't know it at the time, the relevance and significance of those words would shadow me for years to come.

The approach of Thanksgiving meant that most of the American models in Paris were going home to be with their families. It made me homesick to think of everyone sitting around the table in New Jersey with Mom and Dad: April and her husband and their kids; Carol and her children; Diane and her husband and their two boys. This would be the first Thanksgiving I'd ever missed at home, and the thought of missing out on all that love and laughter brought a lump to my throat. *Maybe I should just quit now,* I thought. Christmas seemed a long way away.

Fate must have been listening to my thoughts. The next time I walked into First Agency, Sophie was very excited to see me. "Oh, Bruce! I have some exciting news. *Vogue Hommes* has seen your pictures and wants to use you for a shoot with Paolo Roversi. Zis eez great, darling. Zis eez very good!"

A chance like this, I knew, could be a step on the path to success. First you have test shots, which I had already done; then you get an editorial; then you're asked to do a catalog; then you get an advertisement; then you're on the runway at one of the big fashion shows; and finally you're in commercials and into the really big money, traveling to exotic locations around the world. My mind began racing as I thought about where this could lead.

Sophie sent me to the huge studio where the Italian photographer Paolo Roversi worked. From the moment I walked in, I was thrown in at the deep end. There were dozens of people buzzing around—makeup artists, hairdressers, stylists, assistants. There were three male models, all in various states of undress, and I was quickly ushered in and stripped of my jeans and T-shirt. Someone fixed my hair, slicking it with gel. Someone else smoothed fake tan onto my face, neck, and chest. I was dressed in a shirt, a tie, a dark suit, and an overcoat and positioned in front of a wall of paper.

Paolo used giant movie floodlights to drench the set in light, and he shot with a huge Polaroid camera. For each shot I was led, eyes closed, to the spot where he wanted me. Then he counted, *"Un, deux, trois,"* and I had to open my eyes as he took the picture, then close them again, or I would be blinded by the lights.

As everyone got in tune with what Paolo wanted, there was a rhythm to the work that I hadn't expected. I was no more than a mannequin, really, being changed, then led forward, shot, then led back over and over and over again. People were tugging clothes off, putting clothes on me, shouting directions in French, Italian, and English. The intensity of the day made it feel completely surreal. It was as if I were watching myself from the corner of the room, observing, just as my father always had, with a wry smile on my face. *So this is what modeling's all about? Well, gee, whaddya know?*

It was incredibly hot under the lights, like being inside an oven, especially with all those winter clothes on, but I felt stupidly, childishly happy. The gates to that exclusive club had finally opened up, and I had been allowed inside. I was working at last. I wasn't hammering nails all day. I was in Paris, France. I was wearing the best designer clothes, working with an internationally renowned photographer, being dressed and preened and stitched in and snipped out. I was doing what I'd come here to do.

Against all odds, I had become a model.

5

In Vogue

Christmas at home that year, 1981, was all I'd imagined it would be and more. I hadn't realized just how much I'd missed my family. We all sat around the table as I told them my tales of Paris and they made fun of me, as they always had.

My cousin Lisa Marie, the pretty young daughter of my mother's brother Corky, had moved in with my parents when I went away to college. She was enthralled by my stories. "I want to be a model and see the Eiffel Tower!" she cried.

"Me, too. Why can't I be a model?" April whined.

"Because you're too short," I told her, laughing.

"I still don't understand why they picked you, Bruce," Mom said, serving me sweet potato casserole. "You're such a slob. You don't even own a comb!" Everyone laughed.

I'd flown home a week before Christmas, when Sophie and Evaline and the rest of the staff at First Agency packed up and disappeared for their annual ski trip, leaving me alone and rather sad. The *Vogue Hommes* shoot had been an amazing experience, but it had earned me only two hundred dollars for a full day's work. I could have earned almost as much banging nails. After a few more advances and a loan to get home for Christmas, I still owed the agency several thousand dollars.

Nathalie and I had been reunited in New York, and it was if I'd never been away. Paris and Terry felt like a distant dream, and now that I was back home, I just wanted to reconnect with Nathalie and focus on reality.

I applied for a job as a basketball coach and history teacher at St. Andrew's, a posh private boarding school in Delaware (where the movie *Dead Poets Society* was later filmed), but, not having any real teaching qualifications or my psychology degree, I didn't get the job. I was still dividing my time between my parents' house and Nathalie's apartment, sleeping where I could, exercising, meditating, reading, and waiting for something to come up. I went running a lot with Dad, which I loved. I knew I could go back to carpentry in the spring, but for now I had no money and couldn't even afford car insurance.

While I was home, Sophie phoned from Paris and told me she'd booked a couple of fashion shows for me in Germany in January. I needed the work, because I still owed her a lot of money, but I told her I had to think about it. Before I made my decision, I thought it would make more sense to go back to the New York agencies I'd tried before and tell them I'd now had some experience in Europe. Ford and Zoli wouldn't even see me, but Martha Paccione, from the Wilhelmina agency, agreed to. When I walked in, though, her face fell.

"Didn't I see you before?" she said, clearly disappointed.

"Yes," I said, trying to appear nonchalant, "but that was before I went to Paris and got an editorial in *Vogue Hommes.*"

"Oh." She arched an eyebrow. "Okay, then, let's see it."

"Um, well, it's not coming out for a few weeks."

Martha tilted her head and looked at me critically. "Well, then, why don't you come back to me when you have it?"

I managed a smile. "Right." I turned to walk away.

"Bruce," Martha called. "What are your plans? If this doesn't work out, I mean?"

I had to think about it for a moment. "I'll go back to the South Jersey shore to be a lifeguard."

Martha nodded.

I went back to Nathalie's and threw my photo book on the sofa dejectedly. This was hopeless. Even though I'd spent all that money on test shots and traveling to Paris and going into debt with the agency, I was really getting nowhere. Sophie's offer of work in Germany was only a couple of fashion shows that probably wouldn't even cover my airfare. I could go on chasing that carrot forever. It was time to quit this crazy business.

A few days later, however, the telephone rang.

"Bruce, it's Martha Paccione from Wilhelmina. Are you sitting down? Bruce Weber is looking for lifeguards to model for a spread in *GQ* magazine. I presume you'd be interested?"

Even with my limited experience of the world of fashion, I already knew that Bruce Weber was a god among fashion photographers, loved and respected by everyone in the industry, from the lowliest makeup artist to the most demanding art director. Meeting him would be like an actor meeting Martin Scorsese, or me—the former me who dropped out of an Ivy League school to go to live in an ashram—being granted an audience with the Dalai Lama.

"Are you kidding me? Tell me where I have to be, and when."

As I walked to Weber's studio on Twenty-sixth Street the following day, I tried to remind myself how many times I'd been rejected before—probably fifty times in Paris alone. This was no guarantee of work at all, just another go-see.

This will be a sign, I told myself as I walked down the street. *Bruce Weber knows modeling like nobody else. If he agrees to use me, then I'll stick with it. If he says no, then I'm giving it up.*

I walked to the fourth-floor studio and knocked nervously on the door. I was wearing my trademark look: jeans, T-shirt, sneakers, combat jacket, and my beloved French beret. Bruce Weber opened his door, and I saw a man with a bright smiling face above a little beard and a red scarf. I was reminded of Santa Claus.

"Come in, come in!" he cried. "Oh, my! You're great! You have an incredible nose. Oh, I'd love to photograph you!" Those were his opening words. He told me he had just booked a gig in Hawaii for *GQ* with Andie MacDowell, Joan Severance, and Jeff Aquilon, all hugely successful supermodels at the time. "I'd have loved to use you on that shoot," Bruce said, "but we've already cast the models."

Bruce Weber would love to use me on a *GQ* shoot in Hawaii with supermodels? The Buddhist in me wanted to believe him, but the cynical Philadelphia kid knew that it seemed too good to be true. I told Bruce I was headed back to Europe to model anyway.

"So where are you from? Tell me something about yourself," Bruce said. As I told him briefly about my life, about my family, about Cornell, and being a lifeguard, I felt totally embraced by him, really welcome. His exuberance was contagious, his personality a force of nature. I was probably there for twenty minutes or so, but it felt much longer, as if we'd been chatting for hours. Finally Bruce took down my contact details and promised to call. I shook his hand and floated out of that studio. Not only had the gates been opened to me, but I'd been invited to the inner sanctum. I felt truly blessed.

Now that Bruce Weber had shown some interest in me—and given that there was no carpentry work on the immediate horizon— I decided to accept Sophie's offer of work in Germany after all. I flew out a few days later for a week of shows, for which I was to be paid around five hundred dollars a day. My first editorial, the Paolo Roversi shoot for *Vogue Hommes,* had just come out, so I bought a couple of copies from a newsstand in Frankfurt. I flipped through the pages, and it felt weird but strangely thrilling to suddenly come across a picture of me, standing under those studio arc lights, looking like a strong, masculine version of the person I thought of as me. I sent a copy home to my folks and kept one for my files. Dad proudly pasted the photo into a scrapbook, as he would with all my subsequent editorials and cuttings, and he told anyone who would listen that his son was now a male model. Mom, on the other hand, wasn't so hot on the idea. "When are you going to come home to finish your studies and get a proper job?" she asked me.

My first German show was at the 1907 Kaufhaus des Westens in Berlin, the largest department store in Europe. I'd never done a runway show before and was distracted by all the naked women backstage. I tried to ignore them as best I could and walk out onto that runway with the confidence of a player walking onto a basketball court. I was the only male model, and I was the big "star" just because I'd done one editorial. We had to strut down the runway and back again for an audience of elegant German ladies all dressed to the nines. The contrast between the chaos and nudity backstage and the cool sophistication out front was a whole new experience for me.

The week progressed, and so did the catwalk shows. Gradually I got more comfortable with the pace. On our penultimate night in Berlin, all the models went to a nightclub after the show to blow off a little steam. Late that evening I found myself dancing with a six-foot-tall Chinese model, who was wearing a red miniskirt and a tight silk blouse. Electronic German disco music was blaring all around us, and somehow the two of us got locked into a rhythmic, sexual dance groove. We were throwing back champagne like it was beer, getting drunker and hornier by the minute.

The combination of the alcohol, the exotic European setting, and the feeling that I was in some sort of fantasyland lured me into believing that this night had nothing at all to do with who I really was or what Nathalie meant to me. Slowly and methodically, as our bodies pulsed in perfect sync with the music, the Chinese dancer drew me into the dream of what it would be like having her sitting on top of me as we made love. I was lost in the seduction of the night.

Back in her tiny cubicle of a hotel room, she began to kiss and grope me. It was unusual for me to be standing eye to eye with a woman when kissing her, and I liked the sensation. She stripped all her clothes off in a frenzy, and we started to make love. Halfway through our liaison, however, she stopped cold and pushed me back on the bed. In poor English, she said, "Thank you for choose me. Many beautiful women tonight. Why you choose me?"

Truth be told, I didn't choose her. I thought she'd chosen me. I'd just followed the path of least resistance. As I listened to her talk about the other beautiful women at the club, I realized she was terribly insecure about being the only Asian in the midst of all those blond Germans. At that moment I wanted to walk out, but I knew that if I did, she'd only be even more insecure. So we began this odd dance, where she asked me to demand whatever I wanted sexually. To every request she would reply, "Thank you." The role-playing was mechanical, and suddenly there was no connection between us anymore. I quickly got it over with so I could leave. She wanted me to stay and offered to massage me until I fell asleep, but I knew I couldn't spend the night with her. What had started out as an exciting sexual adventure in a German disco had turned out to be a passionless, almost clinical experience in a barren Berlin cubicle.

The next morning all the models met for breakfast, and the Chinese woman followed me around like a lovesick puppy. I felt ashamed of myself and sorry for her. We did our last fashion show of the week at the Frankfurt Fashion Institute later that night, in front of the largest crowd of the tour. The client was delighted and sent magnums of Dom Perignon champagne backstage so we could celebrate. I still felt ashamed about the night before, so I grabbed two bottles of champagne, jumped into a taxi, and left for the airport to see Nathalie, who was meeting me in Rome to attend a Maharaj Ji meditation conference.

Once again memories of my infidelity disappeared when I saw Nathalie. We spent the entire weekend making love, meditating, and hanging out together as if nothing had happened. I convinced myself that I had little reason to feel guilty about what I'd done. It was just sex. There was no love involved. I loved Nathalie. What we had was meaningful and true. We had the kind of connection that would be impossible with a one-night stand. I knew that Nathalie loved me, and I was grateful that neither of us ever spoke about our time apart. As long as things stayed that way, then surely we were both getting what we wanted from the relationship—and whatever else we needed in between. Surely everything would work out.

I returned to Paris and the First Agency after my Italian weekend with Nathalie, wondering what other work Sophie had for me. I walked into the office as usual, but this time everyone jumped up to greet me and kiss me hello. For the first time since I'd started modeling, I was generating income. Modeling is a ruthless business. When I was making money for the agency, I was the golden boy. When I wasn't, I'd be lucky to get anyone to take my calls.

I noticed a couple of young hopefuls sitting on the sofa in a corner, watching me in awe, just as I'd watched Todd Irvin on my first day. There was so much hope in their eyes. I heard one of the staffers telling them, "That's Bruce Hulse."

FRANCOIS GIRBAUD again takes off from the flight jacket, piloting it into a highly adaptable weathered leather blouson. There's a quilted zip-up inner vest, a removable contrasting leather over-vest and a detachable collar of shearling, about $1200. The leather pants have knit cuffs, about $700. Both by Francois Girbaud for Compagnie des Montagnes et des Forêts. Wool-cashmere scarf by Charvet, about $190. Wool gloves, Aris, about $6. Cuffed leather boots, Francois Girbaud by Unic, about $250.

THE ELEGANCE OF BROWN AND GRAY

Must reading. This page accessori mines whether this drop-shoulder, deep un jacket is dressy or playful, about $275. shirt, about $150, pleated cotton trousers Alt, Perry Ellis Men. (Her dress: Perry E $260, scarf: André Oliver, about $25.) Op silk, linen and wool forge an updated clas $385, cotton knit top, about $98, cotton-l about $100. All, Alexander Julian. (Her ja $500, trousers, about $290, both, Shamask Spluda, $90, bracelets, Bonwillum, about

Absolutely nothing is as classy or as versatile

New Orleans editorial.
© FABRIZIO GIANNI

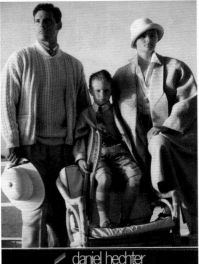

Right, top: *Gianfranco Ferré campaign, Rome.*
© HERB RITTS FOUNDATION

Middle: *Daniel Hechter campaign, Luxor, Egypt.*
© FABRIZIO GIANNI

Bottom: *Corneliani campaign, New Orleans.*
© FABRIZIO GIANNI

Italian Men's Vogue, *Barcelona, Spain.*
© FABRIZIO GIANNI

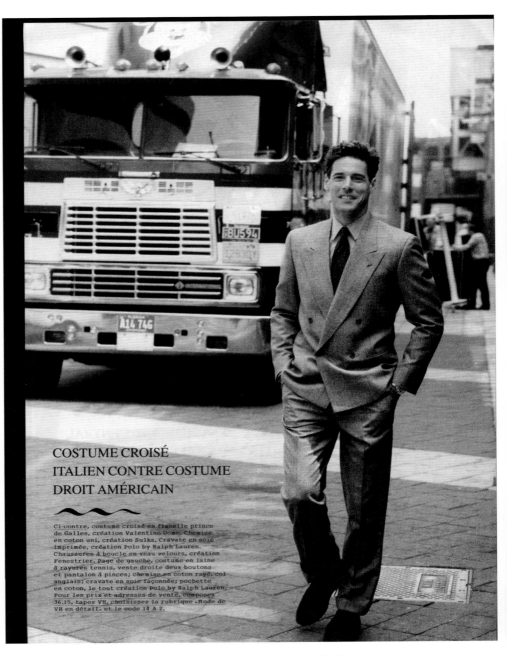

**COSTUME CROISÉ
ITALIEN CONTRE COSTUME
DROIT AMÉRICAIN**

Ci-contre, costume croisé en flanelle prince
de Galles, création Valentino Uomo. Chemise
en coton uni, création Sulka. Cravate en soie
imprimée, création Polo by Ralph Lauren.
Chaussures à boucle en veau velours, création
Fenestrier. Page de gauche, costume en laine
à rayures tennis, veste droite deux boutons
et pantalon à pinces; chemise en coton rayé, col
anglais; cravate en soie façonnée; pochette
en coton, le tout création Polo by Ralph Lauren.
Pour les prix et adresses de vente, composez
36.15, tapez VH, choisissez la rubrique «Mode de
VH en détail», et le code 14 A 2.

Italian Elle *shoot, New York City.*

© ULI ROSE

Italian editorial.
© FABRIZIO GIANNI

GQ *shoot in Italy.*
© FABRIZIO GIANNI

*Versace campaign,
Milan, Italy.*
© CLAUS WICKRATH

Why not run away from home—together

GQ shoot, Water Island, New York, with Julie Wolfe.

Miami Beach.

Big Island, Hawaii.
© KNUT BRY

Switzerland
GQ *shoot.*
© FRANK HORVAT

Big Island, Hawaii.

© KNUT BRY

Sophie introduced me to one of the young men. His name was Nick Constantino. She asked me if I would be willing to show him around Paris and escort him to his first few go-sees. He was a tall guy with piercing green eyes and jet-black hair. He was wearing a black Armani suit and carrying a little leather portfolio that looked like a man purse. At first glance we had nothing in common, but despite that we would soon become friends.

Now that I was moving into the big leagues, Sophie arranged for me to have my own third-floor apartment in a little side street near Montparnasse. It wasn't huge, but it was mine. I could feel a positive energy building in me. It seemed I could do no wrong. I started getting more and more jobs, even though none of them paid serious money, and I never quite understood the French tax system and how much the agency seemed to be taking out of my paychecks.

It wasn't long before Nick started working, too. Somehow he'd met Andy Warhol, who was also in Paris at that time, and Nick and Andy started hanging out. One night Nick invited me to dinner at a fancy restaurant with Warhol and a bunch of other people. Warhol had a way of sitting back and observing that seemed to bring out everyone else's worst insecurities. He also liked to take everyone's photograph, which just made people even more edgy. At one point in the evening, I ended up sitting next to him, and we had this wacky conversation about aliens from outer space, which Warhol seemed to believe in. My father had always been fascinated by UFOs and had saved clippings on reported sightings since he was a child, so I could keep up my end of the conversation. Here I was, sitting in a restaurant in the back streets of Paris, talking to Andy Warhol about my father, Bill Hulse from New Jersey, and his collection of UFO clippings. This new world I'd entered was getting weirder by the minute.

I walked into the agency one morning as usual and found Sophie jumping up and down. "Bruce Weber's office called!" she cried. "Zey want you to go back to New York. Weber eez shooting an entire issue for Italian men's *Vogue, L'uomo Vogue*, and he wants you for a shoot somewhere on Long Island."

I didn't care where the hell it was—I knew this was my big break. I'd finally passed the test. Working with Bruce Weber would be like being a high-school soccer player and going straight to the World Cup. It would also help pay off my debt to the agency and take me one step closer to getting home—and to Nathalie. Even though I'd have to pay my own airfare and pass on several editorials Sophie had lined up for me in Europe, I gave up the apartment in Paris in a heartbeat.

I arrived in Manhattan in the first week of March 1982, a week away from my thirtieth birthday, more excited than I'd been in years. Nathalie was over the moon for me. "See, my darling, I told you this would work!" she said, kissing me hello at the airport. I was still in a state of shock, and her French parents—who could both have been models themselves and had always regarded me as a typical scruffy American—clearly couldn't quite believe my turn of good fortune.

With no official agent in New York, I had virtually no guidance about going out on this, my first big shoot. I just had to trust that I was in the hands of a maestro. At dawn on the morning of the big day, a Lincoln Town Car picked me up from Nathalie's mother's apartment to take me on the ninety-minute drive to the picturesque seaside town of Bellport, Long Island, where Bruce Weber owned a home. It was a bleak, gray, drizzly morning.

Weber was already at work when I arrived. He had asked the lady who owned the little local antiques store to come and be a part of the shoot, along with a dancer he knew from New York. The other male model, Jon Wiedemann, was there, and Weber wanted Jon's father in the shots as well. He had all these disparate people lined up ready to be a part of what he was creating. When he saw me arrive, he stopped what he was doing and came over to greet me.

"Good to see you, Bruce!" he cried, flashing that megawatt smile and shaking my hand. "Thank you so much for coming. Look at you—you look great! Now, I just need to get your hair cut, so I'd like you to go over and see lovely Bob Fink, my hairdresser, if that's okay with you."

I'd have had my head shaved at that point if Bruce Weber wanted it, so when Bob Fink spent the next hour giving me an Elvis Presley rockabilly look, with short sides and a pompadour at the front, I didn't really mind. It was a far cry from the way I normally looked, with my hair long and disheveled. But it wasn't so different from the twenty-five-cent haircuts I'd gotten as a kid. By the time Bob had finished with me, I was a little taken aback, but what the hell—I was game. Jon Wiedemann, who later married the actress Isabella Rossellini, had gotten the same cut, and we joked about our appearance. By the time we were finished in hair and makeup, we looked like two guys who'd just stepped out of a Walker Evans photo of the Oklahoma Dust Bowl.

For the first few shots, Weber had me dressed in my old black beret and an Italian Armani military-style jacket. From the moment Weber began shooting, I could see how disciplined and impassioned he was and how different this would be from my experiences in Europe. He was an incredible coach and had the control and focus of a film director. There were about ten other models on the set, but Jon and I were the key players; the rest were supporting cast. It was freezing cold, and for several shots Bruce had me standing in the wind and the rain, my jacket open to the elements, wet right through.

Weber was tireless, and his energy and enthusiasm were contagious. It inspired me to raise my game, despite the physical challenges of the shoot. Weber's vision transcended mere photography, and I got caught up in it until I, the model, became the surreal character he could see through his lens. I think he was impressed that I stayed as stoic and focused as he was. There was little movement; I had to remain completely still as his eyes and his lens bored into my soul. He might step forward and move my chin a little or ask me to tighten my stomach or take a breath, but even his slightest suggestion was intense and intimate. I felt as if I were a model in an art class again; I didn't want to waver. I gave him as much as he gave me, trying to project my inner self outward, to become an equal partner in the unique dance that goes on between model and photographer. I was taking lessons in my craft from the greatest master of all.

Every now and then, Weber would lighten the intense atmosphere with a laugh or a gesture to let me know he was having as much fun as I was. We were simpatico from the beginning. His sincerity was real and surprising. "You look so handsome," he'd purr. "Oh, that's beautiful. Yes, just like that. Perfect." He'd make me feel like I was the handsomest man on the face of the planet. Weber had a wonderful way of conveying how much he appreciated taking your photograph—something I would later discover to be rare. Some photographers belittle models, especially male models, but not Weber. With every click of the shutter, he made me feel like an epic movie star.

And it was a click, not a whirr, because he used a huge Pentax 6.7 with no motor drive. It had a big wooden handle, and he had this dramatic stance, this way of dropping to one knee and doing a turn, wielding his machine like a big-game hunter brandishing an elephant gun. You'd hear the shutter click, and then you'd hear his

assistants loading his spare camera for the next frame. I've worked with photographers who don't even press the button themselves; they have their assistants do it for them. Bruce Weber was truly hands-on. At the conclusion of that day's shooting, he was as wet and cold as we all were.

As the light drizzle continued falling, a troupe of stylists and makeup artists stepped in and out of the scene to make sure everything was perfect. I sensed that something was being created that

day that would become more than just fashion photos for a magazine. We were making art. I knew that the photos would be nothing
short of spectacular.

By day's end I was exhausted. Whoever says modeling isn't
hard work has never worked with Bruce Weber. He will keep going
until the last glimmer of light fades from the sky. Despite being
physically drained, I still felt oddly bereft when he finally said,
"That's a wrap."

Later that night we hung out at an inn in Bellport. All the men
on the set shared an upstairs room, and we sat around drinking beer
and telling stories. I felt like a boy at Scout camp. Weber stayed there,
too, even though he could easily have gone home. He was interested
in hearing all about our lives. Jon Wiedemann had been to Harvard
and was headed for a life in movie production; I'd been to Cornell
and was a lifeguard who hoped to be a psychologist; and Bob Fink
shared some hilarious drunken anecdotes from his life as a gay hairdresser to the stars. We shared an extraordinary camaraderie that
evening that was unlike anything I had come across in modeling.

The shoot continued for two more days, and the friendships
only deepened. Dear Bob Fink began to confide in me, telling me
about his problems with drink and drugs, and I used my counseling
experience and my memories of my mother's battles to give him
what advice I could. He and I remained friends right up until his
death many years later, and I still miss him. Jon and I talked long
into the night about what we'd do when we got out of modeling.
The more I got to know Bruce Weber, the more I realized what an
extraordinary human being he was.

Everyone knew he was extremely pleased with the work we'd
done, because he was kind enough to keep telling us so. What I didn't
realize was quite how impressed he was with me. Just before we

wrapped on the final day, Weber pulled me aside and said, "I'd really like you to meet a buddy of mine. You'd be doing me a big favor if you did." I had learned that Weber loved to arrange meetings between like-minded people who might be useful or helpful to each other. I wondered whom he had in mind.

"Sure, Bruce," I replied. "Who is it?"

"His name is Calvin—Calvin Klein—and I think you'd be perfect to work on his new campaign."

My eyes opened wide. Calvin Klein? My God! I felt like I'd just won the jackpot in Atlantic City. I was so stunned I didn't know what to say.

"Just go as you are, be yourself, and wear your beret," Bruce said. "Don't bother to take any pictures with you. I know Calvin's going to love you. Tell him some of your stories, and let him take in what I saw in you when we first met. I'll take care of everything else."

At the end of the shoot, we hugged and said good-bye like old friends. During the course of that amazing three-day marathon, my life had been changed irrevocably. I had found in Bruce Weber a mentor, a friend, a spiritual adviser, and an advocate. *This is what modeling should be all about,* I thought as the Lincoln sped me back to Manhattan: creating beautiful images and having a good time doing it with super-talented professionals who have integrity and compassion and kindness. Jocelyn was wrong. This industry wasn't all about greed and materialism and instant gratification. Like any other large-scale human endeavor, it attracted good and bad people. And I had just been fortunate enough to form a connection with one of the very best.

6

Calvin Klein

Standing in front of the mirror two days before my thirtieth birthday, I checked myself over for the tenth time. I was wearing a white crew-neck T-shirt and an old pair of Levi's. Finally I pulled on my beret. "Okay, now don't blow it," I told my reflection. "Stay present and focused. This is it."

I walked the ten or so blocks to Calvin Klein's offices in the garment district on West Thirty-seventh Street and took the elevator to the fifth floor. I entered a large, modern reception area, where I was asked to sit down and wait. I couldn't help feeling nervous as the minutes ticked by. Calvin Klein was, with Ralph Lauren, atop the Mount Olympus of men's clothing. The actress Brooke Shields had been featured in the huge advertising campaign for CK Jeans, with the tagline "Wanna know what comes between me and my Calvins? Nothing." I'd seen the billboards in Times Square, and I knew that Calvin's shoots were some of the best in the fashion industry.

Five minutes passed. Then ten. Fifteen. Then twenty. My palms were sweating. My head felt hot under my beret. I knew that Weber had already made a strong case for me, which I knew would count for something. Bruce had once told me he found it almost impossible to use a model he didn't like. "Personality is everything," he'd said. So if Calvin Klein wanted to use Weber, he had to seriously consider the photographer's choice of models. But that still didn't mean I was going to get the job. There were plenty of other models whom Calvin and Weber could agree on.

"Mr. Klein will see you now." The secretary's voice roused me from my anxious thoughts. She escorted me through a double doorway into a large open-plan office, where one of the world's greatest fashion designers stood to greet me from behind a huge desk.

We did the introductions and shook hands, and then Calvin said, "Did you bring any photos?"

My heart sank. "Um, no."

"Never mind. I love your beret. Where did you get it?"

"At a flea market in Paris."

"Oh, I love those places. I like to find vintage clothing and use it as an inspiration for new designs. Now, please, sit down. Tell me where you met Bruce."

The meeting was relaxed, and we chatted for about ten minutes, but unlike Bruce Weber, Calvin Klein gave nothing away, either with his facial expressions or by anything he said. He was pleasant but impossible to read. There was no talk of any specific campaign he had in mind. He never told me he thought I looked good or would be suitable for his clothes. I felt unusually nervous in his company. He did mention an upcoming shoot in Greece for his menswear line but gave me no indication whether he wanted me for it. Suddenly he brought the meeting to an end by standing up and thanking me for coming in. There was no mention of working together in the future. I shook his hand and left, not knowing if I had pleased him or if he never wanted to see me again.

I went back to Nathalie's apartment and called Weber's office. He wasn't there, but I asked his assistant to convey to Bruce how the meeting had gone. I felt restless and homesick, so I called Dad. He was delighted for me and promised to pass the news on. We used to call Dad "The Pipeline," because you only ever had to make that one call to let the entire family know what was going on.

After I got off the phone with Dad, I reminded myself to stay focused on what was really important to me: lifeguarding at Avalon Beach that summer. I called a few of my buddies to make sure they were still doing it, too, and that they'd found a place for us to stay. While I had them on the phone, I updated them on my latest modeling adventures.

"You just met Calvin Klein?" one said. "You're shitting me, man! Calvin Klein doesn't even exist! You're so full of shit, Hulse!"

Friends like Pat Scullin, Glenn, and The Shoe wanted to know what France was like. "How were the chicks, Hulse? Are those French girls really hot?"

Doc X was the only one who really seemed to understand what I was achieving. "I know who Bruce Weber is, man! That's great!" he said. "And Calvin Klein? You made the big time. I'm so proud of you, B." Doc used to say we'd all end up getting old and fat on Avalon Beach. The fact that I'd broken away and was doing something different really appealed to the free spirit in him.

A few hours after I'd made all my phone calls, Weber called me back and asked me to tell him what had happened with Calvin Klein, word for word. As I described the meeting, I hoped I hadn't let Weber down, but he seemed satisfied. "Good, good," he said. "Now I have one more favor to ask you. I want you to go and see another really good friend of mine. His name is Donald Sterzin, and he's over at *GQ* magazine. If you're free, I can fix you up to see him tomorrow."

I could hardly believe my ears. Donald Sterzin, along with Bruce Weber and a few other key players, had transformed the way men were viewed in the fashion industry. Under Sterzin's visionary guidance as *GQ*'s fashion director, male models in magazine shoots had gone from the cool, classic, fully clothed look of the fifties and sixties to the virile, athletic look, where a man could be naked and proud of his physique.

Condé Nast, which owns *GQ*, had its offices on Madison Avenue, and this time when I got off the elevator on the *GQ* floor, I was seen almost immediately. There was no sitting around for hours as there had been on previous go-sees. A little firecracker of a man introduced himself to me as Donald Sterzin. He looked me up and down with a wry smile.

"So *you're* big Bruce Hulse," he said, one hand on his chin, the other on his hip. "What does Weber see in you? I mean, I don't get it. Look at you! You're a skinny, lanky, *okay*-looking kid."

I wasn't sure if he was being critical or playful, but he didn't give me a chance to think about it. With a wink and another smile, he grabbed my arm and led me back behind the reception desk and into the bustling offices of the Holy Grail of men's magazines. "Let me show you around," he said. "This is where it all happens. This is where we make the next star. Although, God knows, we're not feeding the poor in India. It's only male modeling."

Donald had a quick wit and a sarcastic take on fashion models and the business in general. I told him a little bit more about my background in the hope that something would connect us. I really wanted him to like me. Clapping his hands together, he called over some stylists and asked them to fix me up with some clothes. "Let's see how you look in these. Oh, my, those abs! Do you work out? Do you do sit-ups? Oh, that's right, you were a lifeguard. A lifeguard from Cornell! Then what *are* you doing here, darling? You're one crazy, mixed-up kid."

The stylists quick-changed me into several outfits as Donald looked on happily, never failing to rib me. "I *still* don't get it. What does Weber see in you? I hear he's going to use you for Calvin Klein. Well, I'm going to use you for *GQ*, whether you like it or not."

GQ was going to Switzerland to do a spread for the September 1982 issue. Donald had hired Frank Horvat, a famous photographer (although one I'd never heard of), to do the shoot because Donald was intrigued by his work.

"Let's meet up in Paris at the end of April and go on to Switzerland for the shoot. Okay?" He said it so casually, as if we were just making an arrangement to meet for lunch a few blocks away.

I shook Donald's hand and told him I'd be there. "Thank you. I won't let you down." I'd just booked my first *GQ* gig!

The next day was my thirtieth birthday. For as long as I could remember, my father had called me early in the morning on every birthday, making sure he was always the first to wish me happy birthday. This time I was finally able to tell him that I was earning good money. And I told him I might be about to hit the modeling jackpot.

"I'm so very happy for you, son," he told me. Hearing the pride in his voice was the best birthday present anyone could have given me.

Once Sophie and her agency heard that I had worked with Bruce Weber and was booked for the *GQ* job, they really began to get behind me, pushing me as the next hot model in the business. They encouraged me to come back to Paris to work until the Swiss job came around, which I did, taking up lodging in my old apartment again.

Sophie booked me a ten-day job in Madagascar to shoot an advertisement for a French department store. To my delight, my friend Nick Constantino was also booked on the shoot. We took a twenty-six-hour flight to Africa, along with the photographer, the art director, the stylist, the hairdresser, three gorgeous female models, and a host of additional crew members. Madagascar was beautiful but plagued by poverty, and it wasn't always easy working there.

The photographer wanted us to look tanned, so we spent the first few days sunbathing and snorkeling the amazing coral reef. The girls always seemed to need some suntan lotion rubbed in somewhere. I was strongly attracted to one model, Patricia Pillotti, but she had a boyfriend and I was trying to stay true to Nathalie, so neither of us did anything about it. I took Nick under my wing and showed him the ropes. We became even better friends, lollygagging around in the tropical sun, getting to know each other and the island.

Shortly after I returned to Paris, Donald Sterzin arrived to arrange additional casting for the *GQ* job in Switzerland. Once again he ended up booking Nick as the other male model, but he told me he was still trying to find the female models. When I went to Donald's luxurious hotel overlooking the place de la Concorde, I was astonished to find a lineup of beautiful girls in miniskirts in the corridor outside his room waiting to enter and meet him.

I walked in, and Donald greeted me by saying, "Bruce. Look at you. You're a big-shot model in Paris. I knew you when were you were nothing—a lowly lifeguard from the Jersey shore."

I smiled.

"Sit down. Order up some food and champagne—we're in for a long afternoon. I need you to pick a model to work with. Now, do you like blondes or brunettes?"

I thought I'd died and gone to heaven. All those girls were out there waiting for me. The hottest models in Paris—and I had to choose just one! If this was a dilemma, then it was one I was glad to face. I'd come a long way from practicing Twenty Questions with the tourist girls at Avalon.

Each girl walked into the hotel room alone. They would pose for Donald and try to charm him, but he'd point to me, pass me their portfolio, and say, "He's the one you'll be working with, so you'd better make eyes at him, honey. You're wasting them on me."

After a while the models began to look pretty much the same, which is to say that they all looked fabulous. I just had to decide which one would be best for the shoot and which one I thought I could really click with. Sex sells, and chemistry between models is just as important on a fashion shoot as it is between fellow actors in a movie. When you have to spend hour after hour staring into someone's eyes as if you really want to make love to her, there has to be some attraction there for it to really work.

Finally I recognized one of the girls, a statuesque beauty named Annette Rask. Two weeks earlier a buddy of mine had shown me some stunning photos of her that he'd taken when they were on vacation together in Ibiza. Now here she was, standing in front of

GQ *Switzerland shoot with Annette Rask.*

me. Better still, Annette came from Borås, the Swedish town where I'd played professional basketball after college. We knew a lot of the same people, which would make working with her easy and comfortable.

I leaned over and whispered to Donald, "She's the one." He didn't seem to see it, but then again he hadn't seen her photos. After she left the room, I begged Donald to book her. He resisted, telling me I'd owe him big time if he did, but I pleaded until he relented.

Just before I left for Switzerland, Sophie received a call from Calvin Klein's office. He wanted to book me for his shoot on the Greek island archipelago of Santorini. I could hardly believe my luck. In the space of just a few weeks, my fortunes had completely turned around. After a lifetime of making little more than minimum wage,

I was being offered fifteen hundred dollars a day for the ten-day Calvin Klein shoot. That would be more than enough for me to buy a beach house near Doc X in Avalon and retire there one day.

As excited as I was by the prospect of working for Calvin, I'd been consulting with the brotherhood of other male models in Paris and listening carefully to their advice. They warned me to get the best deals I could. Every model's career was relatively short-lived, and it was in the model's best interest not to leave all the negotiating in the hands of the agents. Experienced models advised me to ask for more and see what the client said. If they really want a model, they'll pay more than the first offer. Some clients also offered to pay their models with free clothes from the shoot, and that had already happened to me a few times, but I wasn't interested. Modeling was a means to an end for me, and that meant I needed hard cash.

Trying not to sound as nervous as I was, I told Sophie to counter-offer with a request for three thousand dollars a day. I don't know where I got the balls.

"You're crazee, Bruce!" Sophie cried. "If you ask for zat kind of money, you'll lose zee job!"

I didn't think so. Something in my gut told me Weber and Calvin wanted me more than she realized. I insisted she make the call. After some negotiating we settled for two thousand a day, and I arranged to fly to Greece immediately following the *GQ* shoot. I didn't know it at the time, but those next few weeks would prove to be the most important time in my fledgling modeling career. All the photos from those shoots would be coming out in September. By the end of the year, I would be established as the new top male supermodel.

Two days after getting the call from Calvin Klein, I met up with Donald and his team at Charles de Gaulle Airport in Paris to board our flight to Geneva. I was high from excitement. When we landed in Switzerland, we drove to Lausanne and checked into the five-star Hotel Lausanne Palace, on the banks of Lake Geneva.

Nick and I invited Annette Rask and the other girl model to my room for a dinner to celebrate my news and our good fortune at being in Switzerland together. We feasted on lobster, caviar, and champagne—all on *GQ*'s dime. Annette was even prettier in person than she had been in her photographs. After dinner Nick disappeared with his model, and Annette and I began to embrace. She kept whispering that I knew nothing about her. I told her I didn't want to know anything about her, I just wanted to make love to her. That's exactly what we did until she finally fell asleep in my arms. We made love again the following morning as we waited for room-service breakfast. I felt as if I were on an all-expenses-paid honeymoon.

When Donald and I met up in the lobby to check out, he looked as exhausted as I felt. "You *really* owe me, Hulse," he told me. It suddenly occurred to me that my bed was up against the wall of his room. He was a good sport about it, even after he got our bill. "Look at you!" he said, waving the bill in my face. "You used to eat hamburgers on the beach, and now you're eating lobster in fancy hotels!"

We caravanned to a picturesque mountain village and spent the next week taking exquisite pictures of the latest French collections. The location was straight out of *The Sound of Music*, with sheep in the meadow and snowcapped mountains for a backdrop. Donald thought that Horvat, our photographer, was "a grump," but he was fantastic at what he did, and we quickly got into the rhythm of creating beautiful images. Donald's constant banter kept us all laughing.

We stayed in an old mountain chalet with even thinner walls than at our hotel in Geneva. Every morning Donald complained about our noisy lovemaking. "I know, I know," I'd say, grinning. "I owe you!" I'd told Annette about Nathalie from the start, and I convinced her—and myself—that we should just enjoy the moment. I was caught up in the idyllic beauty of our surroundings, the pleasure of the work, the fun of laughing my ass off with Donald, and the joy of making love to this statuesque Swede. Perhaps it was the Buddhist in me, but all I could think of was the here and now. Carpe diem!

I left Geneva and flew straight to Athens and then on to Santorini to do my first shoot for Calvin Klein. A photo assistant picked me up at the tiny airport and drove me to the north end of the island, where an entire village had been commandeered for the shoot. It was spring, so there were no tourists, and the mountains were dancing with flowers.

The pretty white village perched on the edge of the hillside was practically a ghost town; I had no idea where the locals had gone. Winding steps ran like arteries to the town square. The photo assistant took me to my "room," a cavelike white stucco house built into the rock wall formed by one of the world's largest volcanic eruptions. The interior was as spartan as a monk's cell, with a couple of beds, a table, two chairs, and a bare lightbulb. The simplicity of my lodgings inspired me to meditate every day. I was sharing the room with Didier Malige, Bruce Weber's French hairstylist. Didier watched from his bed as I meditated and practiced yoga every morning before running down the steps and jogging on the black-sand beach.

There was a restaurant in the town where we could go literally whenever we wanted and ask for food. I loved it, especially the Greek salad and the local shrimp, which I devoured in huge quantities— sometimes twenty or thirty in a sitting. On my first night there, we all gathered around a long table under the stars to get to know each

Donald Sterzin and me on a GQ *shoot on Water Island, Long Island, in the summer of 1983.*

other. Calvin was there, of course, and Bruce Weber and his partner, Nan Bush, plus the supermodel Iman, who was nice enough but a bit aloof. Also part of the group was the model Joan Severance, who went on to be an actress, and Kelly Rector, Calvin's assistant, who would later become Mrs. Calvin Klein. There was Zack Carr, a brilliant young designer with Calvin, plus about fifty crew members, including stylists, assistants, and everyone else associated with the shoot. We dined well on calamari, vine leaves, shrimp, salad, and baklava, washed down with plenty of cold beer, Greek wine, and ouzo.

"How come you can eat so much and stay in such good shape?" Calvin asked, watching me gorge on yet another plateful of food.

"I work out," I said.

"So Donald Sterzin tells me!" said Bruce Weber. "He slept in the next room on their last shoot." Everyone had a good laugh at my expense.

The following day I was allowed to relax and sunbathe, so I could acclimate myself to the island and the heat and get to know my way around. Weber likes his models to look naturally tanned, not painted, but you have to be careful not to burn yourself, or the shoot could be ruined. Didier gave me the longest haircut of my life—two hours!—snipping here, cutting there. He was such a perfectionist that I kept fidgeting in the sun, asking, "Aren't you done yet?"

I was to be the only male model for the first four days, and then Tom Hintnaus, a former world-class pole vaulter from Brazil, was being flown in for the underwear shots. Secretly, I was a bit put out. *I'm in as good shape as he is,* I thought. *I could do the underwear, too.* But I had to remind myself of the age-old modeling joke: "How many models does it take to change a lightbulb? Ten. One to change the bulb and nine to stand around saying, 'I could have done that job!'"

There were also some children to be used in the shoot, and it turned out they were the sons of Anthony Perkins, the actor from the film *Psycho*. I have no idea how they came to be involved, but if I was learning one thing about Bruce Weber, it was that he liked to bring all sorts of disparate people together and throw them into the photographic mix.

The sky, bluer than any I'd ever seen at Avalon, hung above whitewashed walls, giving the place a stark quality that Weber was eager to use. When it was time for my first day of shooting, I was dressed in some of Calvin Klein's amazing men's collection and placed in a corner, hemmed in by the white, white walls to provide contrast to the sleek, dark lines of the suits, shirts, and jackets.

Within minutes I knew that this was going to be a much tougher assignment than I had realized. The light bouncing off the walls was so dazzling it hurt my eyes. I was accustomed to bright sunlight from my years of lifeguarding, but this place really required sunglasses. Without them it was going to be very difficult to stand there all day and pose. But this was my big chance—my first big shoot for Calvin Klein—and I didn't want to let anyone down. Focusing all my inner strength on the task, I felt like a yogi in India who stares at the sun all day as a form of worship. In a way I was doing the same for Calvin and Weber.

Everyone around me was wearing sunglasses, and no one seemed to notice the agony I was going through, as the sun grew stronger and the light became brighter and brighter. Finally, when Weber was happy with our morning's work and called for lunch break, I had to confess the truth.

"I can't see," I told him. I extended a hand into the red-spotted blackness that was all my eyes could now register. "I'm sure it's just temporary, and I'm really sorry, but someone will have to help me back to my room."

Weber was mortified. He was also genuinely concerned that he might have damaged my eyes permanently. Zack Carr led me to my dark room and became my nursemaid, laying me down and placing cold compresses on my now-aching eyes. Not only were my eyes swollen, but I was nauseous and had heatstroke, so I was out of commission for the rest of the day, which set the shoot back badly. Everyone seemed more concerned about my well-being than about the loss of time. Zack said Iman and Joan Severance hadn't had the same problem because their shoots had been against black canvas backdrops.

Weber came to see me and was so caring and nurturing. I said, "I feel like I got injured and let the team down. Sorry, Coach." Part of me wanted him to put me right back to work, but I knew there was a chance I could ruin my eyesight if he did. Weber told me he was thrilled with the photos he'd already taken and that I wasn't to worry. Fortunately, after I'd spent a day in bed, my sight was fully restored, although my eyes were still puffy and sore. Weber worked around the problem by having me led to the white walls with my eyes closed for each frame, telling me to open them on a count of three, just as for those Paolo Roversi studio shots in Paris. He thought I was heroic to keep going under such duress.

"Wonderful," he'd coo. "Perfect, Bruce. You look like Montgomery Clift in *A Place in the Sun*. You're an actor, Bruce, a movie star. Look at you! You could be Richard Burton as a young man!" Bruce Weber was a devotee of all the old movies and probably Elizabeth Taylor's biggest fan. He'd seen all her films and had met her several times. He loved to regale us with stories about her or tell us about his favorite scenes in *National Velvet* or *Cleopatra*. I had never felt more beautiful or loved than I did during those days in Greece. It was as if I were living inside a bubble of praise. I felt like a mythic hero channeling the spirits of the ancient Greek gods.

A few days into the shoot, people on the set began talking about supermodel Andie MacDowell, who was on her way out to model Calvin Klein jeans for the campaign. The guys spoke of her extraordinary beauty, which, they said, was matched by her sweet southern manner. I was so green to this business that I hardly knew any of the female models. I'd only just become familiar with the names and faces of the men. My sole experience of women models in the past had been my father's subscription to *Sports Illustrated,* which published a swimsuit edition every year, featuring the likes of Cheryl Tiegs and Christie Brinkley.

Andie was arriving on my first day off from shooting, so I volunteered to pick her up from the airport, eager to see this goddess everyone was talking about. I borrowed one of the open-top Jeeps and sped off as the Greek sun beat down and the breeze blew in from the Aegean. When her plane landed, the door opened and out stepped a vision of loveliness that snatched my breath away. She had wild curly black hair, above a pretty little blue and yellow floral sundress, and she had the sweetest smile.

"Andie?" I ventured.

"Yes, who are you?"

"Bruce. Bruce Hulse. I'm one of the models on the shoot. I've come to pick you up."

"Oh, it's so nice to meet you." Her voice, her smile, those brown eyes, that hair flying in the breeze—everything they'd said about her was true. We set off in the Jeep. I was unusually nervous. We chatted a little about the shoot, but mostly we just took in the beautiful day and the gorgeous scenery all around us.

At one point Andie asked if I could stop the car for a moment. "I'd like to pick Calvin some wildflowers," she said. I parked the Jeep, and she got out, walking into a nearby meadow with an innocence and feminine grace I'd never seen before. I watched as she stooped to pick the flowers, selecting each one carefully, smelling them and stopping occasionally to look around and arrange her bouquet. Eventually she returned to the car and pulled a single flower from her bundle. "Here," she said with a smile. "This one's for you." I was speechless.

When we reached town, Andie was welcomed like returning

royalty. She hugged and kissed those who knew her. Those who did not received a radiant smile and a warm hello. I stood in the shadows and watched the way she moved through the adoring crowd. This was the closest I had ever been to stardom, and it was incredible to see the effect firsthand.

Andie was given a day to get acclimated, and I went back to work. A couple of times I saw her watching from afar, and she'd smile and wave. Then, when she started work, I couldn't help but sneak a peek. She looked so amazing in those tight black jeans she was modeling, as Weber sat her on a white wall, with a white top against her tanned skin so that her dark hair and the dark jeans made a striking contrast. She was such a professional, I could only watch in awe.

A couple of nights later, we all went to a restaurant in the adjacent town for dinner. There ensued an unspoken game of musical chairs in which everyone wanted to sit next to Andie, but I made sure I got a seat next to her. I listened attentively to her stories as I was drawn further into her world. She told me she lived in a brownstone in New York but had a French boyfriend in Paris. I told her, briefly, about Nathalie. She spoke of growing up in the South and said that her father was almost as tall as I was. She was about to get her first break as an actress in *Greystoke: The Legend of Tarzan, Lord of the Apes.* She laughed and said, "You'd make a great Tarzan. It's a pity the part is already cast." She was so self-effacing and genuine that I was utterly smitten.

After dinner Andie said she wanted to walk back to our end of the island. It was a couple of miles away, and everyone else wanted to drive, so I offered to escort her. We walked along the old cobblestone streets under the stars, trying to shake off the ouzo buzz. Near the edge of our village was a funky one-room discotheque with no one in it except the owner and his wife. We wandered in, and Andie turned and asked, "Would you like to dance?"

"Absolutely!" I replied. I handed the owner a few drachmas and asked him to play some music. As the Bee Gees came on, the solitary disco glitter ball began to spin, and we whirled across the dance floor, laughing while I made funny monkey moves and fooled around.

An hour later we were both exhausted, so Andie suggested we go home. "We really should get some sleep if we want to look good for the shoot tomorrow," she said. I knew she was right, but I didn't want the night to end. We strolled hand in hand, and when we reached the point where the winding steps led up to my room or down to hers, I couldn't bear to leave her. There was a secluded promontory above us, where I knew we could look at the stars. I suggested we head up there, and she agreed. We stood close at the top of the stairs, with the sounds of the waves crashing below and the warm breeze lifting her hair. My hands were trembling. I felt like a high-school kid out on my first date.

Turning to her, I worked up my courage. "You're so beautiful, Andie. Is it okay if I kiss you?'

She smiled and said, "Why, yes, of course."

Now I was surely in Bruce Weber's world, for this moment felt like a scene from one of his favorite movies—*Gone With the Wind*—given Andie's southern charm and grace. We kissed and embraced passionately until I whispered, "Let's go to your room." She agreed.

Arm in arm, we walked to her room, which was just as bare and unglamorous as mine. The table lamp she turned on was way too bright for us both, so I gallantly took off my T-shirt and threw it over the top of the lamp to try to create some ambience. I stepped out of my jeans, pulled her dress off, and laid her down on the bed. Just as we began to kiss again, the smell of something burning broke the

spell. My shirt was on fire! Andie giggled as I yanked the shirt off the lamp and stomped it out on the floor with my bare feet. Then she pulled me back down onto the bed, and we made love all night long.

I left Andie's room at dawn and returned to my room and a gently snoring Didier. I hardly slept; an hour later I got up as usual for my meditation and yoga. The events of the night before already seemed like a fantastic dream. I went down to the shoot wearing the clothes I was to model that day, but Weber announced that he probably wouldn't need me until later. Happy to continue my daydream, I sat on the sidelines as the other models were used, and I pondered the events of the previous night. The weather had cooperated, bringing us another perfect day in paradise. Zack came by to chat, and we drank a couple of beers. The alcohol gave me a nice, mellow buzz, and I felt as if I were back at Avalon, sitting by the beach. I sank another couple of beers, happy and sleepy in the hot sun.

The sun had begun to dip below the horizon when Weber appeared and said he needed me on set. As I got myself into position in front of his lens, I suddenly thought that I might be too buzzed to work. Sitting in the sun, I hadn't felt drunk or out of control, but here in front of Weber's camera I just wasn't present. My head was spinning, and I couldn't focus. Weber took only a couple of frames before he told me curtly, "I'm done with you. You can leave now."

I had a terrible sinking feeling in my stomach as I walked off the set. I hoped Weber hadn't noticed—maybe there just hadn't been enough light to work—but I feared the worst. Sure enough, Weber found me a few minutes later and pulled me angrily to one side. My basketball coaches had reamed me out in the past, but this lecture was far worse.

"Do you need so much attention that if you don't get it, you have to draw it to yourself by getting drunk?" Weber asked. "Do you think you're so important now that you're exempt from being professional?" He told me that I'd never work for him again, and he stalked away, leaving me alone. By that time I was stone-cold sober and about two inches tall. I feared that everything I'd achieved up to that point had been destroyed by one moment of stupidity. I could not believe I'd been so irresponsible. I wandered down to the beach alone to consider my future and think about ways to rectify the situation. Then I went back to my room to lick my wounds. I didn't sleep a wink.

I knew I had to speak with Weber and try to make things right. Early the next morning, I went to his room and asked if we could talk. He could see the sincerity in my eyes and agreed to hear me out. I told him that everything was happening so fast; I admitted that I wasn't handling my sudden success as well as I had hoped I would. I confided in him what had happened with Andie and confessed that it had thrown me even further off balance. I wasn't making excuses; I just wanted him to understand why I wasn't thinking straight. He listened, and eventually he softened. He told me it was a tough shoot for him, too, and that he'd had a few artistic differences with Calvin. We talked for an hour, like old friends. In the end we hugged, and all was forgiven. I knew I could never—and would never—let him down again.

Andie and I played it cool for the rest of the shoot. We were friendly, but there were no more opportunities for us to be alone together. On our last day at Santorini, when the entire crew was down at the beach, I asked her if she could come back to Paris with me, but she told me she had to get back to New York.

"I don't want this fantasy to end," I whispered with genuine sadness. I truly believed I was falling in love with her. But Andie was far more seasoned than I. She understood that this was just a fling. Location romances weren't the same as real relationships; they were part of the fantasy created by the photographer, the art director, and the models during the few days they spend working together in the most exotic locations. The message sent by the photographs created on the shoot is that at any moment all these beautiful people are going to strip off their fabulous clothes and have deliciously uninhibited sex. In a situation like that, it's easy to buy in to the fantasy, even if you're helping to create it.

To my delight, Andie did agree to spend one last night with me in Athens, after the shoot was over. We met at a hotel away from the rest of the crew, and we hardly left our room. Those precious few hours together were magical. The following morning we parted reluctantly, promising to stay in touch, and for a while we did. Soon afterward she sent me a beautiful poem about our night together in Greece, a mythical time that neither of us would ever forget.

7

Cover Boy

I flew home to the States, looking forward to a return to what I knew and loved: Nathalie, Avalon, and another summer on the beach as a lifeguard. The Calvin Klein and *GQ* shots would be coming out in the fall, so I knew this would probably be my final opportunity to just be "Hulse" or "B" with my buddies, drinking beer and pretending that the world beyond New Jersey didn't exist.

I'd signed with the Wilhelmina Agency in New York, negotiating them down to just 5 percent commission instead of their usual 20. "Zoli, Ford, and Elite have offered me five," I lied to Martha Paccione. "Take it or leave it." She took it, but she was eager for me to do the rounds immediately to get more work. I wasn't interested. I knew that my world would go crazy come September, and the clock was already ticking. Right now I needed a break.

I had to wait for my break, though. Before I left for Avalon, Donald Sterzin set up a *GQ* shoot for me with Andie MacDowell at a studio in downtown Manhattan. They needed some pictures to fill an empty slot for the September issue. Seeing Andie again was wonderful, of course, but this time we were on home territory, and the fantasy world that had surrounded us before no longer cocooned us from the harsh truth of our deceptions. We worked the shoot, which went well, and then she invited me to her apartment later. She knew I wouldn't refuse. I rode my bike across Central Park from Nathalie's mother's apartment to Andie's place, wondering what on earth I was doing. How could I possibly hope to recapture the magic we'd known in Greece when we were now just a few blocks away from the woman I professed to love? The guilt and the hypocrisy of what I was doing almost made me turn around and ride back, but I didn't.

To this day, though, I am glad we spent one last afternoon together. Although I haven't seen Andie since that day, I've followed her life and career with interest, and mutual friends have conveyed her good wishes to me. I, too, wish her nothing but happiness in return.

My final full summer lifeguarding in Avalon was bittersweet. I savored each moment. My pals had rented a beach house, but as I was the last to arrive, I only got the closed-in porch to sleep in. The usual suspects were there: Big Pete, Stoover, The Glenn, Shoe, Rob Graham, Pat Scullin, and, of course, the one and only Doc X. There was a new recruit, too, a college All-American swimmer named Ed

Flory. He was a great guy, although the one big complaint about Flory was that he ate food from the communal fridge without replacing it.

I invited Nathalie's kid brother, Laurent, to come join us, and Nathalie came out a lot that summer, too. She was such a New Yorker that it was wonderful to see her out of her normal environment, running on the sand and swimming in the surf. My parents, my sisters and their kids, and my cousin Lisa Marie all came to visit, too, and we had fun family picnics on the beach.

I was still "The Guru," the one who grew the vegetables and led the meditation classes. Avalon Beach Patrol was still the champion team among the lifeguards, winning all the swimming races, and I was still teaching the surf grommets to respect the water, but I knew in my heart that this was the end of something special. Whether I liked it or not, my life was becoming more complicated. Avalon would always be an integral part of my life, but it would never quite be the same.

Even the time-honored ritual of chatting up the girls on the beach had lost a bit of its charm. I'd just been with some of the most beautiful women in the world, so the girls at Avalon no longer held the same appeal. I was more aware of how a woman moves, stands, holds herself—all things I'd never even noticed before. I worried that I was beginning to judge people for their external appearance rather than their personalities. I'd eaten fancy food all over the world, so the basic cooking served up by my buddies sometimes left me uninspired. Plus, I now had money in my pocket, lots of it, and with it came guilt. To compensate I bought my stand partner, Chris Gilday, a brand-new surfboard for his birthday, and I constantly treated the rest of the guys to meals or to the movies. Big Pete used to say, "The good thing about Hulse is he didn't give a fuck about money when he didn't have it, and he doesn't give a fuck about it now that he does." I hoped that would always be true.

What I hadn't realized until that last summer was that life-guarding was good preparation for being a model. The similarities were uncanny. In the eyes of the world, you're a god. Everyone admires you. It's your job to stay connected, focused, and undistracted by the many temptations that surround you. Also, you have to be comfortable with your own company, because you spend a lot of time waiting around for something to happen. The best similarity of all, though, is that your ego can never run away with itself, because your buddies won't allow it. Mine used to tell me regularly, "So you're a model? Big frickin' deal! I could do that if I wanted!" And the truth was, lots of them could have.

That's exactly why I called up Bruce Weber with an idea. I'd talked to Weber for hours on end about life at Avalon, about Doc X and all my friends, the races, the waves, and the amazing cama-raderie that existed among the lifeguards living and working on the beach. Weber was always so interested in other people, and he'd tell me, "Oh, they sound so great, Bruce, I'd really like to meet them one day." He was fascinated by how authentic the lifeguard lifestyle was. So when I suggested he come up and do a shoot with the people I'd been telling him about, he jumped at the chance.

I went back to New York briefly to set it all up and meet with Donald Sterzin, who'd agreed to run the piece in *GQ*. Then Donald, Weber, and I drove back down to Avalon in a big black limousine. I'd never arrived at the beach in such style. I'd persuaded Scarhead to give us permission to do the shoot, and I'd even asked him if he'd agree to be in a couple of the shots. "Oh, I dunno," he growled, frowning. "Maybe. I guess."

Our limo pulled up outside the Doc X Mansion, where we

From left to right, Donald Sterzin, me, and Bruce Weber outside the Doc X mansion.

found a huge homemade banner stretched across the front of the house: WELCOME BRUCE WEBER AND DONALD STERZIN! Doc X came running out with a camera I'd recently bought him and started taking photos of us arriving. Then the four of us went to a fish restaurant I knew in Cape May for lunch. Doc X was the best companion I could possibly have chosen for that lunch. He was such a great conversationalist and knew all the right things to say and the best stories to tell about Avalon, "his beach." Weber and Donald were by turns enthralled and entertained, as was everyone who came within Doc X's orbit.

As we were leaving the restaurant, Donald pulled me to one side. "Are you sure Doc X isn't gay?" he asked. "He's in love with you, Bruce. I can tell by the way he looks at you."

I laughed. "No, X isn't gay," I said, thinking of all the girls whose hearts he'd broken. "He just never had a dad or an older brother, and I guess he looks up to me that way."

Weber set up his crew on the beach and asked all seventy-five lifeguards to get in line so he could choose the ones he felt would be best for his shots. I watched my buddies stand in line and realized they were actually nervous. He chose about fifteen of the most muscular with the most interesting faces and then took photos of them posing on the stand, rowing, running, and swimming. He selected Big Pete, Ed Flory, the brothers Steve and Danny "The Dog" O'Malley—who were on our rowing team—Jim "Rono" Ronin and a football player named Jeff Jones. He asked Scarhead to step into a couple of the shots, and we all watched in amazement as the Cap's hard-nosed resistance melted under the brilliant dazzle of Bruce Weber's smile.

I savored every moment of this event, the first time my two worlds, old and new, had collided, and it was happening in that most holy of places for me. It was also the first time my friends had ever seen me working as a model or watched the unique dance that takes place between a professional model and the photographer. I think they were fascinated as I held those poses for minutes on end, keeping my concentration as Weber's huge Pentax zoomed in on my features, one shutter click at a time.

"Hey, look at Hulse!" I heard one of my buddies say with genuine astonishment, halfway through the shoot. "He's fricking beautiful!"

The shots Bruce Weber took of the Avalon Beach Patrol that day remain some of my all-time favorites. They are so heroic: muscular young men at the peak of their physical powers, up on the lifeguard stand, looking out to sea. The spirit of that magical beach and that last special summer for me are forever captured in photographs. I wasn't the only one affected by the wonder of that day. Ed Flory went on to have a successful career in modeling following that shoot. He was a natural, and Weber loved him. The Cap so adored the shot featuring him in command of some of his finest lifeguards that he had his copy of it framed, and he hung it in the middle of the wall at the beach-house HQ for everyone to admire. For all I know, it still hangs there. My copy hangs on my wall, too, a treasured memento of a bygone—and much-missed—era.

After that golden summer came to an end, I returned to New York City and rented a loft apartment on Twenty-ninth Street between Sixth and Seventh avenues. This was my first real home in Manhattan, and taking that step made me feel more grown up than I wanted to feel. Nathalie was still going to NYU and living with her mother, and she expressed no desire to move in with me. I didn't want to live on my own, so I invited a few of my beach buddies to come to the city. Fortunately, Rob, Stu, and Big Pete, who had no immediate obligations in New Jersey, jumped at the chance. The words *rent-free* were all they needed to hear.

I grew up in a big family, and I've always enjoyed being surrounded by people. The more chaos, the better. I like being able to go to my room, shut the door, and read a good book, but it's also comforting for me to know that other people are around. Some might say I'm afraid to live on my own. Maybe it dates back to the time my mother went to the hospital. Maybe not. But I believe that humans are social animals, and I'm happiest when I feel myself to be a member of a tribe. It took me a long time to understand that I could get married, have kids, and create my own tribe.

We dubbed the apartment the "Lifeguard Shack," and it became the ultimate crash pad for anyone I knew. The deal was that I paid the rent and the guys chipped in whenever they could. The guys all tried to find work, with varying degrees of success. Rob was good-looking, with the same outdoorsy style I had, so I helped get him signed to my agency, and he did a few catalog shoots. Since he didn't work that often, he sat around the apartment building model airplanes. Stoover got a job working as a suit salesman for Nathalie's father, at his Madison Avenue clothing store. Big Pete spent most of his time hanging out at Gleason's, the famous Brooklyn gym, boxing and lifting weights. Occasionally he'd pick up work as a bouncer at a nightclub, which meant we'd all get in for free that night.

When I wasn't working, I'd come home and hang out with the guys, drink beer, meditate, or play chess. The apartment was in what was then an unfashionable area of Manhattan, so it was a big space for the money, with hardwood floors and bars on the windows. It was a large loft apartment that had been created by putting a divider wall down the middle of a huge space. The landlady was an artist

Tommy Preston and Rob Graham at the "Lifeguard Shack," New York City, 1983.

who occupied the other half of the loft. She was always out of town, so we often used her side of the loft to hang out in. As long as we got her rent to her on time, she didn't seem to mind.

Because I paid the rent and my name was on the rental agreement, I laid claim to the largest bedroom. My one rule was that whenever I was in town, I got to sleep in my own bed. When I was gone, I didn't care who slept there. Everyone had a key, so you never knew who was going to show up at any given moment. Guys slept in any space available. There was even a walk-in closet that we turned into a tiny bedroom for Big Pete. Our ingenuity took our landlady by surprise when she came upon him one day. "There's some guy living in that closet!" she told me. " He looks crazy." I assured her he was harmless. I had to laugh, though, thinking of Big Pete unfolding out of that tiny space and scaring her half to death.

My cousin Lisa Marie was commuting into the city to study dance. When she asked if she could stay with me, too, I had no hesitation about saying yes. Lisa Marie was a gorgeous sixteen-year-old who'd had a tough childhood caring for her father—my Uncle Corky—and my Czech grandparents. She deserved a break. She looked like a younger version of the German actress Nastassja Kinski. She fit right in with the guys, sometimes cooking and cleaning for us, and I'm sure they all lusted after her.

One day I came home to find her dancing around the apartment like a little hippie chick. I grabbed my video camera and filmed her laughing and twirling in the kitchen. I sent the tape by messenger straight to Bruce Weber's office. Later that afternoon he called me up. "Who is this girl, Bruce?" he asked excitedly. "She's beautiful! I want to photograph her! I want to see her! Can she come to a shoot tomorrow? I'm using a new model named Uma Thurman for an Italian magazine spread, and they'd be perfect together." Despite being only five feet five inches tall and a little too busty for a model, Lisa Marie was immediately signed by Click Models. For a while she became the daughter Weber never had. She also modeled for Robert Mapplethorpe, and before I knew it, she had become the face of Calvin Klein's Obsession perfume. She did some acting, appearing on *Miami Vice* and in *Planet of the Apes* among other projects, and she eventually ended up as the fiancée of Academy Award–winning film director Tim Burton for almost ten years. All because I grabbed my video camera that day!

On one crazy shoot in New Mexico, she and I even ended up working together as love interests on a commercial for director John Stember, which was kind of weird, especially when I, as a rough, dust-covered cowboy, was supposed to take her in my arms and give her a passionate kiss. "I can't do that, man!" I told John, looking down at Lisa, dressed in a sexy western dress. "She's my cousin!"

"Of course you can," he scolded. "It's just an act, like all the rest of it." Lisa Marie and I looked at each other and shrugged. We somehow got through it, although the memory still gives me the creeps to this day.

The guys who lived with me in the Lifeguard Shack kept me sane in those early years of my modeling career. That apartment was the place where I felt most comfortable when I wasn't with my family or on the South Jersey shore. I guess it was the closest I could come to replicating those hot summer nights in Avalon. We all shared the same philosophy: Give when you have it and take when you need it. Above all we had the same goal: Do whatever it takes to find a job that will get you through the winter and back to the beach in the summer. It didn't matter if it was banging nails, bartending, or modeling for Calvin Klein. Being a schoolteacher was ideal, because it was one of the few jobs that gave you summers off. The plan was to get back to the beach as early in the season as possible and stay as long as you could. That had been my routine for thirteen years. But now that my modeling career was taking off, that routine was coming to an end.

Once the Calvin Klein campaign and my *GQ* editorial spread came out in September, work really took off for me, as I'd known that it would. I was traveling and working and making big money. Bruce Weber put me in touch with his accountant, and I had him handle all my income, pay all my bills, and make sure I had enough cash to play around with. I felt like I'd really hit the big time.

On one of my earliest jobs, I was flown to Washington, D.C., for a catalog shoot. Waiting at La Guardia Airport, I spotted a tall, good-looking guy in the departure lounge, and I guessed he was the other male model flying down from New York. That was my first introduction to Tommy Preston, who has remained one of my closest friends. We sat together on the flight, and when he told me he'd been a football player and pulled out *Meditation in Action,* a book I was familiar with, I knew we'd hit it off. Tommy was ten years younger than I was and had been discovered at a University of Florida model showcase. Like me, he was on his own spiritual search.

"Dude," he'd say, "I'm just gonna do this for a while until I make enough cash, and then I'm gonna go on a motorcycle trip to South America or something, or maybe buy a property in Hawaii and sit and meditate and find God." I knew just how he felt.

We male models had a strong brotherhood. Guys would happily make friends with other guys, offering advice when it was needed and doing their best to get along on a shoot. I'd often call up Bruce Weber or Donald Sterzin with the name and number of a guy I'd met who I thought would be ideal for *GQ*. If anyone became too arrogant or demanding on a shoot, the rest of the guys would take him to task. If a new kid came along, we'd be sure to tell him how important it was to negotiate his fee with his agent and to push back when bargaining with clients. There was a real kinship among us.

The only time that rivalry did begin to bite a little between the men was when it came to cover shots. My career was going well, and I had nothing to complain about, but I soon came to learn that being on the cover of *GQ* was every male model's dream, the male equivalent of a *Vogue* cover. There were only twelve models selected for this honor each year, making it one of the most coveted bookings in the industry. The exposure received from having a *GQ* cover was big money in the bank. On top of what you made from the cover itself, you could make an additional hundred thousand dollars in catalog and designer ad campaigns that would come to you as a result.

Donald Sterzin often teased me about my chances of making the cover. "I don't know if you're ready, Hulse," he'd say. "I'm not sure you're good enough. You're fine for the editorials, but the cover? I don't know." As usual, it was hard to tell if he was being serious. Regardless, I knew I was ready and I wanted a *GQ* cover more than anything.

Whenever I worked on any *GQ* shoot, the photographer would usually pull each of the models aside at the end of the day to do a "cover try." We all knew the importance of these photos, so no matter how tired we were, we'd give them every ounce of energy we had left. A special sort of ceremony would take place. The stylist would come along with a special shirt or sweater made by the designer who'd paid the most for advertising that month, the hair and makeup people would step in and try to make you look your best, and then the camera would move in for the close-up. Maybe I was just too nervous about it, but the more I tried to put my spirit and soul into those shots, the further I seemed from getting the cover.

After three or four cover tries with various photographers, in-

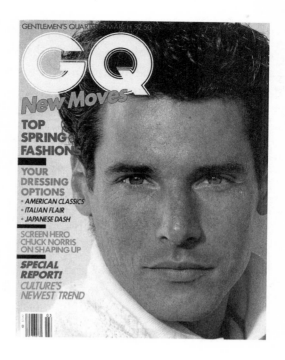

cluding Bruce Weber at Water Island (which I really thought would be a slam dunk), I still couldn't break through. Even if Donald liked the photos, he still had to get them approved by the head of Condé Nast, *GQ*'s parent company. "I don't know what to tell you, Hulse," Donald said. "I'm trying as hard as I can here. You've gotta give me something more."

This time I knew he meant it. I tried not to be discouraged and remained confident that sooner or later I'd be chosen. As far as I was concerned, I deserved the cover. Modeling is, after all, a business predicated on selling an illusion—not just to consumers but to the models as well. For more than a year now, photographers had been telling me, "Bruce, you're so handsome," "You're gorgeous," "You're a god," and it had all gone to my head. I looked at some of the men who'd made the *GQ* cover, like Todd Irvin (the model I'd first seen at the agency in Paris), Tom Flemming, and Jeff Aquilon, and I honestly didn't think they had anything I didn't. I mean, I was Hulse; I was Bruce Hulse, one of the top ten models created by Bruce Weber and Donald Sterzin in their bid to create a Hollywood-style royalty of male supermodels to rival that of the women.

I wasn't sure how many more chances I'd be given, however, so when photographer Rico Pullman took a series of close-ups of me for a cover try at his studio one day early in 1983, I really put everything I had into those shots. You could almost hear my muscles straining. After the shoot I didn't hear a single word from anyone for two whole days, even though I bugged Donald every chance I got. Then, about a week after the shoot, he called. "You owe me big time, Hulse. It looks like your ugly mug is finally going to be on the cover. March issue."

I was overjoyed. I thanked Donald, and I immediately called my parents and Nathalie to tell them the good news. Martha, my agent at the Wilhelmina agency, was ecstatic. She wanted to throw a huge party in my honor at a nightclub and invite hundreds of people, but I resisted. Instead I asked for a small dinner for my family and close friends in a private room at a restaurant on Twenty-third Street.

A few days before the party, I'd bumped into Andy Warhol on the street somewhere near Central Park. "I made the cover of GQ," I told him excitedly. "Why don't you come to the party they're throwing for me and meet my family? You could talk to my dad about UFOs." He said he'd love to and said he'd take some pictures for his *Interview* magazine.

The night of the party, he pulled up outside the restaurant in a long black limousine, stepped inside, took a few photographs, and said hello to everyone. Then he told me there was someone in his car who wanted to meet me.

I followed Andy Warhol outside, as did my buddy Nick Constantino, ever curious. When the limousine door swung open, we found Bianca Jagger sitting inside with Halston, the iconic clothes designer. Bianca pleaded with us to jump in and go to another party with them. I was sorely tempted, but I graciously declined, saying that I couldn't really leave my own party. Before I could utter another word, Nick cried, "I'll come!" He jumped right in, and they all drove off for what was apparently a wild night.

I'd hoped my party at the restaurant would be low-key, but Martha had placed a six-foot poster of the cover on a stand at the end of the room for everyone to see. I brought the poster back home with me to the Lifeguard Shack. The following day I left town for a week to go on a shoot; when I returned home, I discovered that while I was gone, my face on the poster had been adorned with a thick black mustache. My friends had also decided that it would make a great dartboard. My precious poster was completely destroyed. I had to laugh. Thank God for my buddies. I could always count on them to keep me grounded.

8

Shooting Star

When I first introduced Bruce Weber to Nathalie over dinner in New York one night, I could tell he was very taken with her. They chatted animatedly about everything from movies to food, and I saw that this was truly a meeting of minds.

A few weeks later, Weber called me up and asked if he could book me for an editorial shoot for British *Vogue*. "It's an unusual concept shoot," he told me. "I want you to be the thirties photographer Edward Weston, and I want Nathalie to be his muse, Tina Modotti. I know Nathalie's never modeled before, but she's studied acting in school, and I think she'd be great for this." He paused. "There are only two problems. Some of the shots will be nude, and I'll need to cut off her hair. Do you think she'll do it?"

Nathalie's lustrous brown hair cascaded all the way down her back; it was the striking feature that had first made me notice her at that meditation conference in Denver. It was her trademark look. "I dunno," I said. "But I'll ask."

I should never have doubted Nathalie's free spirit. She jumped at the chance. These shots would be the first time any nudes had appeared in British *Vogue,* and she loved the idea of our being part of something so groundbreaking, even if it cost her her hair. Weber sent us several books on Edward Weston so we could learn more about his unique photographic style. I studied them carefully, because I knew I had to be well informed and mentally prepared. Bruce Weber expected nothing less from me.

The shoot took place in the backyard of Weber's beautiful old country home in Bellport, Long Island, not far from the duck farm where I'd had my first big break. It was an amazing property out in the woods, with tree houses and a pool and a rich sense of history and character. Soon after we arrived, the hairdresser cut Nathalie's hair to her shoulders, and then we got started. It felt like we were filming a silent movie. Weber gave me one of his big Pentax 6.7 cameras, and I, as Edward Weston, began taking pictures of my Tina Modotti.

As Weber took each shot, frame by frame in that great-white-hunter style of his, he directed us from behind his Pentax, telling stories about Weston and Modotti's relationship. I soon became completely immersed in my role, until I *was* Edward Weston, taking amazing photographs of a girl I was madly in love with, in the most spectacular setting. Nathalie was a natural, posing as if she'd done it all her life. When Weber asked her to take her clothes off, she just stripped down, completely uninhibited by the crew around us, and lay on a drop cloth laid out in a field, twisting her body into amazing shapes as he stood over her.

Toward the end of the day, as the sun was setting, Weber moved us out onto a beautiful old wooden Chris-Craft boat on the bay. He brought in another model, a young Puerto Rican girl named Talisa Soto, to add intrigue to the shots by showing that Weston was such a ladies' man that he had not one but two lovers. One of the most famous photos Weber ever took of me was with Talisa toward the end of that shoot. It's a thoughtful, moody, black-and-white shot of the two of us on the back of the boat, me in 1930s-style pants and shoes, smoking a cigarette. That shot has appeared on countless postcards and has been used in art and photography books worldwide.

When Weber finally announced a wrap, he suggested we celebrate by jumping nude into the water. Nathalie and I did just that, but poor Talisa, who'd refused to do nude shots earlier, cowered in the boat and covered her eyes. Weber kept on shooting, photographing Nathalie and me jumping off the boat, taking incredible candid shots of us.

As soon as the British *Vogue* spread appeared, everyone wanted to know who the new beautiful dark-haired model was. Nathalie quickly signed up with Click Models, and her unintentional career took off. It didn't occur to me that modeling might not be right for someone whose goals in life were to dance, to teach dancing, and to find spiritual enlightenment. Of course it didn't occur to me that modeling might not be right for me, either. That moment still lay in the future. For now, Donald Sterzin booked Nathalie and me right away for a *GQ* shoot at Jackson Hole, Wyoming.

"We're trying out a relatively new face on the scene," he told me. "Some Peruvian photographer named Mario Testino. Tell me what you think." Nathalie and I loved Mario from the moment we met him. Every time he took a shot, he'd say, "Fabulous," or "Wonderful, darling." Like Bruce Weber and all the best photographers, he exuded only positive energy and made you feel so good about yourself that you gave him the best possible look. "Bruce," he told me, "that Paul Smith shirt looks so good on you, you simply have to buy it!"

The other models on the shoot were Terry Farrell, who was dating Sean Penn at the time, Matt Norklun, and Joe Kloenne. We were out in the heat in the middle of a prairie with the Grand Teton mountains in the background, modeling all these cool English clothes, when I looked over and saw Nathalie's eyes flicker just before she fainted. I ran over to where she had fallen, as did Mario and the rest of the crew. Nathalie was fine, just dehydrated, and she came to almost immediately, but Mario was kindness personified. "Take her to the shade, get her some water. We must stop the shoot," he told his assistants. I worked with Mario many times after that, and it was always a pleasure and a privilege.

The year 1983 was a very busy one for me. I worked so much that for the first time since I was a teenager, I wasn't able to return to Avalon to work as a lifeguard. I did get there for a week or so in July, but The Cap saw that I wasn't really focused on the job. When I had to leave for a runway show in Milan, he told me not to bother coming back. "I need someone I can rely on, Hulse. Saving lives isn't some hobby you can dip in and out of when it suits you." His words cut deep. I knew he was right, but I'd hoped to hold on to my job for longer than that. My buddies were all still there, hanging out, surfing, drinking, and getting laid, but I wasn't part of that lifestyle anymore.

There were many times during that long, hot summer of '83 when I was stuck in an even hotter studio, sweating under lights, or in a smoky fashion show with all the usual noise and cameras clicking and photographers calling out, that I'd be wistfully thinking about sitting on the stand at Avalon, with the sun on my back while I waxed my surfboard, waiting for my turn to paddle out into the surf. Instead I was doing the Dior campaign and a lot of catalog work in Europe, spending weeks traveling back and forth across the Atlantic. The workload was dizzying. I had agents all over the world who would call me up and beg me to fly in for an editorial, a catalog, or a runway. I was still signed with Sophie in Paris, but she and her assistants, Evaline and Patricia, had left First and were now with an agency called Passion.

"Bruce, baby, come and do zee runways. It'll be good for you," Sophie said to me on the phone one day. " You'll really be seen here!"

"But how much will it pay?" I'd always ask. Runways never made me much, and I resisted them when I could, except for big names like Donna Karan or Perry Ellis. The majority of the big runway shows were in Milan, Paris, London, and New York and took place over a period of a few weeks each year. The agencies would typically fly in a group of models a week prior to the shows to go on go-sees and castings. The designers you were already booked with would be available to see you for fittings. The idea was to book as many shows as possible to maximize the time spent abroad.

Milan was always the craziest. The streets were packed with hundreds of models scrambling to get to their appointments, while the novice models were willing to sell their souls to the devil just to get one booking. Fortunately, I had an advantage because of the work I'd previously done for *GQ* and Calvin Klein. People within the industry recognized me, and designers often requested me. Unlike other models, I didn't have to wait in line for a fitting or a casting; I'd show up and be escorted straight in. I received preferential treatment, but that was still no guarantee I'd be booked for the show.

I attended meeting after meeting with designers such as Versace, Valentino, and Armani. I'd walk into the studio, and the designer or one of the casting agents would look at my book before ushering me over to racks of clothing. All garments would be tailored to each model, because the fit had to be flawless. A typical male model is anywhere from five feet eleven inches to six feet four inches tall, with a neck measuring fifteen and a half to sixteen inches and a thirty-two- to thirty-four-inch waist. Models with bodies outside these measurements were rare, because the clothes wouldn't fit them properly. I fell right in the middle of the size ranges across the board. My only problem was my feet. Typically the designers carried only up to size eleven and a half or twelve in shoes. There wasn't much I could do about it, other than learn to live with the discomfort of a shoe that was at least one size too small.

Once I was selected for a runway show, I'd have to strip down to my underwear, while my body was closely scrutinized. Then the comments would begin. "Oh, Bruce, you look a little too big. Have you been lifting weights?" Or "You really must eat, honey. You're too thin." I'd be handed a rapid succession of garments to try on: pants, jackets, shirts, and shoes. It was a race to make it through all the outfits in the shortest time possible, because I always had another fitting scheduled back-to-back.

I much preferred doing ad campaigns to walking the runway for a fashion show, which reminded me of a three-ring circus. Backstage was always so chaotic, with everyone doing quick changes and people screaming at one another. Then there would be the Greek chorus of seasoned male models hanging out, drinking too much free champagne, flirting with the girls, and not taking anything too seriously. I soon joined their ranks.

My appointed dresser, who'd be responsible for dressing and undressing me during the show, would have the rack of my clothing with my name on it and would quickly provide me with a rundown of each outfit. Without a personal dresser, there'd be little or no chance of managing all the swift clothing changes for the night. As showtime neared and the music began pumping out front, the backstage area would become more and more frenzied. The music would get louder in preparation for the eruption of sound that always began every show. The louder the music, the higher the energy. A receptive, buzzy audience could really raise the show's intensity. A quiet audience was much harder to read and could kill a show.

Behind the scenes, production managers and set assistants would be running around, talking loudly into headsets, and making last-minute adjustments. Rows of makeup artists and hairdressers would be hurriedly working on all the models, calling for sprays and mousses and curlers and tongs. It was like being trapped on a fast-moving conveyor belt in a factory: You were pulled off it, you had something done to you, and you were thrown back on again. People usually tried to remain calm and professional, but some found it hard to keep their cool under the mounting tension. Many seemed to thrive on it. There are extreme personalities in any industry, but the fashion world has more than most; the trick was to stay out of their way. My only obligation was to do the job and get to my next show. Sometimes the shows were set up in the same general location, making it easier to do several a day. Other times it was an adrenaline-pumping race against time and traffic to make it across a crowded city to get to the next one.

Even when all the elements came together—I made it across town, I was dressed in the right clothes, and I was out on the runway—I didn't usually enjoy the experience. In fact, I always felt a bit self-conscious about putting myself on public display like that. The whole experience felt so awkward and artificial as people gawked and snapped pictures. I never minded having my photo taken by a single photographer on a studio setting or out on a shoot, but multiple flashes from every angle made me uneasy. Still, it was an important part of the business and something I had to endure to get all-important bookings with the big designers.

I once did a show for an Italian designer who wanted us to remain completely motionless, like mannequins. Half an hour into this gig, most of the models had broken out of their poses and were off bullshitting with one another in the corner. The designer was furious and ran around screaming, "Do not talk! Ssssh! I want mannequins! Mannequins!"

At another show, for Versace, I worked with supermodel Janice Dickinson. We were the last two models to walk out together for the finale. I was wearing a tuxedo, and she was dressed in a sumptuous wedding gown. During the walkthrough earlier in the day, Gianni Versace had been up front yelling, "I need you to be like a god, Bruce. Be like a god!" Only Versace could say something like that and make it sound genuine. I didn't work with him often, but I loved his energy.

Unfortunately, I found Janice to be quite dark. She had a negative aura, and I didn't like the way she kept staring over at me. I've always been very sensitive to people's energies, and Janice's was unsettling. She came across as a ticking time bomb. There was no way to tell when she would explode, and I certainly didn't want to be there when it happened. She claimed in later years to have had sex with more than a thousand men. I'm here to tell you I wasn't one of them.

The best thing about fashion week in a given city was that everybody was in the same place for once, which rarely occurred in the modeling world. Normally we were scattered all over the globe working different shoots and shows. This meant we could catch up with friends we hadn't seen in a while, like at a giant class reunion. I had some riotously late nights with buddies like Nick Constantino, Tommy Preston, and other male models who'd become friends along the way. Another guy I'd come to know was Doug Myers. He'd been a lifeguard at Avalon on my last year at the beach. After one look at him, I knew he'd go far. I took some photos of him and sent them to Bruce Weber. "I think this guy might really have something," I wrote. I was right. Within a year Doug had secured a six-figure contract to model Ralph Lauren, and now here he was in Milan.

The strangest part of doing the fashion shows was coming face-to-face with my fans for the first time. Whenever I left any of the big shows, there'd be a crowd outside waiting for their favorite models. As soon as I emerged, people would press forward and ask for my autograph or to have their photograph taken with me. Although

I had no idea how most of these fans knew who I was, they all seemed to know my name and most of the work I had done. My days of playing basketball had prepared me to handle the collective focus of a crowd, and I was always careful to be gracious and kind, but deep down that was never really my scene. Although it was lovely to have fans, I knew that outside the elite fashion circles, male modeling was a bit of a joke. It wasn't as if I were a successful actor or an esteemed politician. I hadn't really done anything to deserve the accolades. And while I might have been the man of the hour, I knew there'd be a slew of new young models next year who could steal my crown. I never doubted for one second that my career could take a downward turn at a moment's notice.

At the peak of my success, I was making around a hundred fifty thousand dollars a year—and blowing it just as fast. I remember racking up a thousand-dollar phone bill calling friends from a hotel room in London over the course of just two or three days. I was paying rent on the New York apartment, and I rented a lake house in the Adirondacks for the summer for my folks and my sisters and their kids; I tried to join them when I could. I'd buy jewelry and Hermès scarves for my mom and sisters in Paris, and I flew buddies like Big Pete out on shoots with me to Jamaica and other places, so they could surf and hang out at my hotel. I also started making contributions to an Indian reservation in South Dakota. While sitting up late in a hotel room one night, flipping channels on TV, I even ended up underwriting the cost of raising an African child, who subsequently wrote to me for years.

But it was Avalon where I'd left my heart. I did try to invest my money there once, by buying a beach house not far from the Doc X Mansion. But my representative screwed up the deal, and, sadly, I lost the property. Stupidly, I never tried again. And I never followed the lead of my smarter male-model buddies who were investing their money in fledgling Apple or Microsoft, or properties in run-down areas of Manhattan that were about to experience a value boom. Doc X tried to get me to save and invest, but his words fell on deaf ears. As long as I had enough in the bank to put me through college by the time I was finished with modeling, that was all I cared about.

Juggling work and play with business was getting harder by the month, as the pace of my modeling career became increasingly difficult to maintain. I seemed to be flying off to another shoot every few days. I felt permanently jet-lagged, but I always had to stay focused and look good. There were times when I was double- and triple-booked, and then there were the few occasions when my phone wouldn't ring, and I would panic. But it never failed: Whenever I didn't work for a short period of time, a sudden onslaught of offers came flying in all at once. I was learning about the insecurity of the freelance life. I had to pick and choose which jobs I went on. Sometimes I'd take the less lucrative gig just to avoid having to take a long flight to Europe, which always screwed with my body clock.

Cocaine had long been a feature of the fashion industry, just because the work was so draining. It was often provided to models by the hairdressers, stylists, and makeup artists. At first I usually turned it down, but as time went on and everyone around me was getting high and having fun, I found it more and more difficult to resist. I was never one of those guys who needed booze or drugs to feel invincible, but the occasional line of coke did help me get through the day sometimes. And when the rest of the crew was taking it, and teasing me when I didn't, I felt I had no choice. I always regretted it the next morning, though. A cocaine hangover often meant that I couldn't get up and meditate, and it usually brought with it some sense of depression that I feared might signal a return to that deeper darkness.

I also hated what cocaine did to other people. I'd be at a party and everyone would be hovering around the guy with the coke, stroking his ego, bringing him drinks, all waiting to be fed. And the guy with the coke would often use the drug to gain access to the female models, many of whom began to use coke to keep their weight down, which was becoming a growing obsession among them as the current look moved away from the more voluptuous, full-busted, athletic women of the seventies and early eighties.

Then there was the politics of cocaine, the fact that it was pro-duced by the South American drug cartels. People were being mur-dered down in Colombia just so idiots like me could get high or stay thin. It didn't make sense.

One of the worst experiences I had with coke was on a shoot for a high-end cosmetics company in Palm Beach. The hairdresser laid out big fat lines while we sat around drinking piña coladas, waiting for the rain to stop. John Stember, the award-winning photogra-pher, was hoping for the perfect sunset so he could get his one shot. I could hardly believe I was getting paid all that money to drink and get high.

As the day wore on, though, and the drink and drugs started to take effect, I began to shake from doing too much blow. The worse I felt, the more disgusted I was with myself. I kept thinking, *This is not me. This is not who I am. Who the hell am I? I'm being paid thou-sands of dollars to do this work, and I don't even have enough respect for my colleagues to do it right. What would Weber say if he saw me like this? What would my parents say?* I hated what I had done to my body and was disgusted with how I had handled myself that day.

Another time, while shooting for *GQ*, the female model I was working with was so coked up that I felt as if I were holding a zom-bie in my arms. The photographer attempted to capture some usable images. He tried to direct her to move this way or that, but she was practically unresponsive. I couldn't wait to get away from her and back to my room.

The last time I ever used coke was on a Victoria's Secret shoot in Palm Beach, when I snorted so much during the day that I ended up curled up on the bed in my hotel room in a fetal position, shaking uncontrollably and cursing myself. *Doc X would kill me if he saw me now,* I told myself. *This has got to stop.* And it did. I never took cocaine again.

Nathalie was almost as busy as I was that summer, and we hardly saw each other, which wasn't good for either of us. So when she was booked for a December shoot for *Mademoiselle* magazine in Barbados, with an up-and-coming photographer named Herb Ritts, I decided to go meet her and surf while she worked. Then we planned to stay on for a Christmas vacation together. I had seen Herb's work, which featured largely black-and-white photographs of models and actors in the style of classical sculpture, and I'd heard good things about him, but our paths had never crossed. We met at the crew hotel, and Herb recognized me immediately. He said he'd love to photograph me on the shoot, and he got the editor to agree to it, so suddenly Nathalie and I were working together again. We had fun, although it meant I didn't get to do as much surfing as I wanted with the Bajan boogie boarders, who were absolutely fearless.

Herb was a quiet, soft-spoken man, quite different from Weber. He didn't have that same infectious enthusiasm for every aspect of life and was much more interested in the fashion world and who was working with whom. There seemed to be no limit to his knowledge of photographers, designers, and models. He was incredibly passionate about photography and extremely precise in his picture making, so I was eager to experience his creative processes firsthand. I soon discovered that Herb's sets were structured and organized, with every detail and nuance worked out in advance. His sense of lighting was most important. He was meticulous about the way light fell across the body. He positioned Nathalie and me exactly how he wanted us, naked and in the water. We had to hold specific poses for twenty minutes or more, which forced me to draw on my experience of modeling in art class back at Cornell. It wasn't easy to stay focused amid the big waves that kept crashing us against the rocks.

After half an hour, Herb would say, "That's fine, Bruce, now move your chin one inch to the left." I was used to Weber, who was much more of a free spirit, encouraging spontaneity and creativity, allowing me to act out a role and bring his vision to life. Because of Herb's demand for precision, the Barbados shoot was tedious and unbelievably exhausting, but Nathalie and I remained determined to endure it so we could provide Herb with everything he needed to get his shots. If I'd been working with any other photographer, I think I might have been less patient. Deep down, though, I knew that the finished product would be nothing short of brilliant. I was right. The photographs were gorgeous. Herb had masterfully conveyed his distinct and unique vision.

One aspect of that shoot that was new to me, however, was the fact that I had to do sexy, intimate pictures with someone I was romantically involved with. The joke among models was that you could never do "hot shots" with a girlfriend, because you didn't want to show the world the intimacy you shared with someone you really cared about. Herb's lens zooming in on the two of us kissing felt invasive, even voyeuristic, which was a strange feeling. I had to try really hard not to let it bug me. Our shots with Weber as Edward Weston and Tina Modotti had been less intimate and therefore easier to do.

Barbados shoot with Nathalie for Mademoiselle *magazine.*

My job in advertising was to make consumers believe I that I'd just had—or was about to have—wild, crazy, swinging-from-the-chandelier sex with the woman in the photo, and that if they bought that product, they could, too. I was selling romance. Often when I was on a shoot with a model I'd just met, I was the first to buy in to it. There I was, in those beautiful settings with gorgeous women I couldn't help but be attracted to, whose job was to undress, then nuzzle and lust after me. If the chemistry was right, the illusion created in the images soon transcended fantasy and became a reality.

When I was working with Nathalie in Barbados, however, the energy never came off as romantic or sexy. We knew each other too well, and it had been a long time since we'd felt that instant animal attraction that ignites a passionate encounter. Herb didn't seem to notice, but I could feel the difference. As I fondled and kissed Nathalie, I wondered which male model would be next in her arms and how he and she might respond.

I wasn't the least bit surprised when Herb quickly ascended the ranks to become one of the top photographers in the industry. He participated in a long-term collaboration with Madonna and took wonderful photographs of the Dalai Lama and Elizabeth Taylor, to name but a few of his famous subjects. He also directed many prize-winning commercials and music videos. We maintained a solid relationship and continued to work with each other over many years, shooting international ad campaigns for major designers such as Gianfranco Ferré and doing lots of magazine editorial work together.

I once spent a tedious week with Herb Ritts and a crew of twenty in Rome, during which we took half a day getting just one shot of me in one outfit. His fastidiousness only enhanced my respect for him. Anytime anyone like Ritts or Weber called and asked me to work with him, I'd say yes before he'd even finished the sentence. I loved working with such brilliant and creative minds. They inspired me to do my best work, and I will always remain grateful for the lessons those incredibly talented artists taught me. And when we lost Herb, years later, to the disease that snuffed out so many bright lights in our industry, the world seemed a far duller place.

As much as I already respected Bruce Weber, a shoot for Maxwell House coffee in Sacramento, California, made me respect him even more. Another male model and I sat in the back of a four-man river raft and ran white-water rapids while Bruce sat up front facing us, taking shot after shot.

That shoot was difficult enough for the other model and me, when we could see where we were headed and anticipate when the falls and rocks were coming. But Weber had no idea what we were going to hit or when the camera was going to smack into his head. Soaked to the skin, he endured run after run for four straight hours, until he was satisfied and we finally brought the raft in to land. We peeled off our wet clothes, put on some dry flannels, sat by a fire, and gradually began to warm up.

"Man, you've got some balls!" I told Weber, shaking my head at the sight of him, ashen and still dripping. I knew he'd be covered in bruises the next day.

Weber beamed back at me. "Well, this is a lot nicer than being on that boat, that's for sure," he admitted. When he finished his shots of us all relaxing by the fire and drinking coffee, he seemed pleased with the day's work. Later he told me he had something to say to me. "I've always seen you more as an actor than a model, Bruce," he said. "You take on any role I give you so well. You completely become that person. That's why I'd be so grateful if you'd go and see a friend of mine." When Weber had put me in touch with people in the past, it had always worked brilliantly to my advantage, so even though I didn't really think I had much acting potential (despite having taken a few acting classes at Cornell), I agreed to hear him out.

"His name is Ed Limato," Weber said. "He's an agent with William Morris in Beverly Hills, who represents Richard Gere and Mel Gibson. Fly out to L.A., check in to the Beverly Hills Hotel—it's the best place—and when you go see him, wear that beret of yours and just be yourself, okay?"

I did exactly as Weber told me. I hated Beverly Hills; it all seemed so phony to me, but I figured I had nothing to lose. I put on my signature accessory and took a cab to Ed Limato's offices, where I was ushered into a large, wood-paneled office. A huge, silver-haired bear of a man rose to meet me. My immediate impression of Ed was that he was distinguished, intelligent, and gracious. His baritone voice was bright, and he had an incredibly commanding presence. He shook my hand firmly, asked me to take a seat, and we talked at length about films and television. He asked me about my life and how I'd come to be a model.

When I'd finished telling him about my family, Avalon Beach, Doc X, Cornell, surfing, Paris, *GQ*, and Calvin Klein, almost an hour had passed. Ed just sat there listening and nodding and asking more questions. He seemed in no hurry. Finally he smiled broadly at me.

"Bruce Weber is right," he said. "You're a big, strong, good-looking guy, and you have a lot going on beneath the surface. Too many Hollywood actors these days don't. We need a few more heroic types like you." He told me he wanted to represent me and asked me to move to Los Angeles as soon as possible, so that he could get me enrolled in some acting classes and introduce me to some people.

"I see great potential in you, Bruce," he added. "There's no reason I can't eventually help get you to the top of this profession."

I was completely taken aback. I hadn't expected him to make any such sweeping statements, and I certainly hadn't expected things to move so quickly. He was basically asking me to give up New York and my successful modeling career to chase a dream I didn't even know I wanted. "Isn't there any way I could stay in New York and take acting classes there?" I asked.

"That wouldn't work," he said, shaking his head. "You'd have to be here so I could develop you."

I told him I was honored by his offer and thanked him, but I said I'd have to think about it. "This would be a huge step for me, especially since my career is firing on all cylinders right now." He said he understood and asked me to get back to him.

I didn't know what to make of the whole situation. I think part of my problem was an overwhelming fear of failure. I was doing well as a model, and I didn't want to submit myself once more to the rigors of casting calls and auditions. Moving to Los Angeles, turning my back on modeling, and throwing myself into something that might or might not pan out was more of a risk than I was willing to take. I never did get back in touch with Ed Limato.

I did enroll in acting classes in New York, though, under the tutelage of a woman named Kate Stewart. Big Pete came along, too, and helped me with some of the parts I had to play, which we'd practice over and over again in the Lifeguard Shack. Because he looked so much like Marlon Brando, he was considered to play Brando's part in a local production of *On the Waterfront,* and he would have been great in it. I got parts in a student movie called *The Doomed* and in a small feature film called *Mile Zero,* but that was as far as my acting career went, despite numerous private lessons with Kate. She eventually told me she couldn't do anything more for me because I was too "stoic" and couldn't open up to my darker emotions.

Looking back, I don't regret not making a commitment to pursue acting, but I do believe I could have taken the time to check into it further. I should have at least called Ed Limato back. Would I have been any more content with my life if I had become a successful actor? Maybe. But what if I'd been a big flop and had become even more miserable? In retrospect, I can see that an acting career might have been possible for me back then, but now there's no way I'll ever really know now, and I'm at peace with my decision. I did what I thought was best at the time.

After all, my life then was pretty good. I was working, earning good money, and having a blast in the Lifeguard Shack with my buddies. It was such a comfort to know that when I returned from a photo shoot in some far-off place, after weeks of working with strangers, I'd have my friends to greet me. My place might not have been fancy, but it was home. Trouble was, there was never enough time to settle back into it. Just as soon as I had adjusted to being back in New York, the phone would ring and I'd be whisked off to another job. This transient existence was creating an ever-increasing gap between me and everyone else in my life. I hadn't seen Doc X in months. I was certainly straying from my relationship with Nathalie more than I wanted to. There was little I could do to end the cycle unless I chose to stop working, which would mean finding a new career—something I wasn't even prepared to entertain while things were going so well.

I was trapped by what models call the "golden handcuffs"—they were valuable, although not worth enough to keep you for the rest of your life. And, most important of all, they were handcuffs, locking you into an industry and a way of life that you just couldn't escape. As long as the calls kept coming, promising the chance to make lots of money, travel to exotic locations, and spend time with amazing women, I would always be a prisoner.

Like everyone else in the business, I convinced myself that this was just temporary, a chance to make enough money to get me where I wanted to go. In my case I was being paid to study, I reminded myself, as I endlessly wrote in journals and read textbooks in the long hours spent waiting during shoots. Whenever models complained to me how bored they were, sitting around all day, I'd say, "Read a fricking book!" If I had a spare, I'd lend them one.

My plan was clear. I'd keep modeling. I'd study hard. I'd make enough to set myself up for life, and then I'd put all I'd learned on this extraordinary journey to good, practical use. Maybe I'd even write about it one day. This was the life I'd somehow created for myself, and this was the way I'd lead it, for now. I was one lucky son of a gun. I was traveling the world at somebody else's expense, and I still had Nathalie, plus the pick of the world's top models. What could possibly go wrong?

9

A Tangled Web

"*Nice* ass!" A voice with a New York accent uttered its approval from behind me as I slipped off my clothes, ready to get dressed for yet another Paris ad campaign.

I turned around and smiled at a gorgeous young model named Patti Hansen, who also happened to be the new wife of the Rolling Stones' Keith Richards.

"Thanks," I said. "That's because I screw a lot."

Patti, just twenty-six years old and already a veteran of the Wilhelmina agency, laughed out loud.

"Just kidding," I said, although I wasn't. The ice was broken.

Patti and her fellow model Paulina Porizkova, a gorgeous young Czech, were going to be my colleagues on the shoot, which was for the Italian designer Enrico Coveri, whom I'd met at a runway show immediately after I did a shoot for Stella Artois in the south of France. Fortunately for me, Enrico liked me so much he asked me to stay on and be the male model for his campaign.

I'd first seen Paulina Porizkova at Coveri's runway show. With her long brown hair, big blue eyes, and standing almost five feet eleven inches tall, she was perfect model material. I called hers "The Body of Death," because I knew it would kill any willpower I had if I ever got near her. When we met, it was early in her career, long before she was voted one of the most beautiful women in the world or became its highest-paid model, with a $6 million contract for Estée Lauder cosmetics. Backstage at the show, she repeatedly stripped naked in front of the rest of us, not caring at all that we could see her amazing figure. I could hardly keep my eyes off her.

Until Patti and I started joking, both she and Paulina had been rather cool to me, probably because they regarded me as just another random, stupid male model. I didn't really mind; I was getting to understand the psyche of the female model more and more as I journeyed through this industry. It seemed to me that many models who had been dubbed "divas" were only projecting that persona out of self-protection. Otherwise they'd be regarded as fair game for the rich, famous men who would troop backstage to pick off the weak and the unwary.

These wealthy men with their fancy sports cars waiting outside wanted trophy girlfriends and were willing to lavish diamond jewelry or expensive gifts on them to get what they wanted. If a model had a coke habit, much the better. These playboys could easily afford to feed it. Few of the younger, more inexperienced models stood a chance against these predators. Those who had been around for a couple of years, and who knew how the game was played, soon developed a tougher hide. That was when being a diva came into play. Only by being seen to be aloof, demanding, or pretentious could they maintain their independence in the face of this onslaught.

I remember meeting Naomi Campbell in London when she was just starting out. We spent an evening with friends at a nightclub. She was a young, sweet, lovely English girl who had no idea of the incredible demands that were about to be placed on her. In this industry people want their buck, their pound of flesh. Impossible pressure is often put on a model to make sure he or she meets expectations, regardless of the impact on the model's life. The professionals understand this. They're ready to work, no matter what. The more chameleon-like models can be, the more work they can get. Drug problems, jet lag, relationship turmoil—none of that matters, as long as the advertiser loves you. You can behave any way you want, as long as the photographer gets his picture. And if playing the diva helps a model get through it with her sanity intact, then what the hell.

Paulina wasn't a diva; she just wasn't interested. We took some photos together and then separately. Between setups she undressed right in front of me, as before, with a look of total disdain on her face. Her whole demeanor conveyed that she wanted nothing at all to do with me.

After the shoot I got dressed and wandered outside. I spotted Paulina in a market across the street, buying some fruit. I walked over to her and struck up a conversation. "Is it okay if I walk with you?" I asked.

"I guess," she said.

"That was an interesting shoot today, wasn't it?" I said.

"Work is work," she said. I kept walking and talking with her, hoping she'd warm to me. Persistence has always been one of my strengths. Eventually we started getting along, even smiling and joking. After a while I asked her if she would like to join me for dinner.

Paulina laughed. "Are you crazy?" she asked. "I would never go out with a male model!"

"Come on," I said. "It's better than eating alone in the hotel."

"You're too good-looking, Bruce," she said, suddenly serious. "I hate good-looking men."

I refused to give up, explaining that I was really a nice guy and that I was only doing modeling to make some money to go back to college. After thinking it over, Paulina finally agreed. I took her to a little French café I knew just off the Champs-Élysées. We sat down, and I asked her about her background and how she got started in the industry. I learned that she was born in Czechoslovakia but that when she was little, her parents fled to Sweden because of the Russian invasion. Poverty-stricken and a political refugee, she got her big break when a photographer sent some photos of her to the Elite agency, which invited her to Paris.

I was fascinated by her story. We drank some wine and talked for hours. I soon discovered that this beautiful girl had a surprisingly sassy sense of humor. Her vast reserve of dirty jokes included a trick in which she folded her napkin in such a way that it suddenly looked like an erect penis. Before dessert I knew I didn't want the night to end. When we stepped outside the restaurant to hail a taxi, I asked her, "Stay with me tonight?"

Paulina looked back at me and smiled. "That would be nice."

Whenever I was paying for my own accommodation in Paris, I was in the habit of checking in to the Pension du Roc, the cheap little hotel Sophie had first put me up in when I was a newcomer in town. It wasn't the best place to stay, but it reminded me of my humble beginnings and made me feel grounded. I knew the concierge, Pierre, and I liked the fact that it felt like a home away from home, where I could eat my cheese omelette for breakfast every morning. It was only a bed for the night after all, and I hated wasting money on fancy hotels.

Paulina and I strolled back to the Pension, and I took her up to my room. As soon as I shut my door, the attraction we'd felt for each other exploded into the open. We were all over each other, and we tore that room apart. It was like a professional wrestling match. I'd never had such energetic, wild sex with anyone before. We didn't fall asleep in each other's arms until we were completely exhausted.

Paulina had to leave early the next morning for New York, but she promised she would call me later that night. I couldn't wait to see her again. The vision of her standing naked in the middle of my room was floating around in my head for most of the morning.

Once again my commitment to Nathalie felt like a distant dream. She was somewhere on the other side of the world, modeling, being a free spirit herself for all I knew. We were consenting adults, enjoying the moment.

Later that afternoon I was in my room when I received a telephone call. I wondered if it was Paulina, but it wasn't. It was an

English model named Liddy, whom I'd just been working with on the photo shoot for Stella Artois in the south of France.

"Hi, Bruce. I'm in Paris for a few days. Can I come over?"

Talk about terrible timing. I liked Liddy a lot. She was a pretty girl with reddish brown hair, big blue eyes, and freckles. She introduced herself as "Liddy from City," because she was signed with the City modeling agency. We'd hooked up during our photo shoot together, and we'd had a lot of fun making love in her room during a rainstorm with the rain beating against the windows. I caved in and told Liddy to come over. Could I possibly have made this any more complicated? I rushed down to the front desk and asked Pierre to screen my calls for the rest of the evening. "But if a girl named Paulina calls," I told him firmly, "put her straight through to my room, okay?"

Liddy arrived, and we wasted no time getting to know each other again. I didn't receive a call from Paulina, so I assumed she must have had a problem getting through to me from New York. The following morning, though, I found out that Paulina had missed her flight and had decided to come back and see me again. When she called to arrange it, the concierge not only didn't put her through, he made it clear I was "busy" with someone else.

Paulina was understandably upset. I tried to explain and lay the blame on the concierge, but she wasn't buying it. I'd blown it. She flew off to her next booking, and I returned to New York for Christmas and New Year's with Nathalie and my family, never expecting to hear from Paulina again.

A few weeks later, Nathalie's mother was planning a birthday party for Nathalie at my apartment. Nathalie's birthday was January 1, but we often celebrated it a little late because everyone usually felt so exhausted after New Year's Eve. Nathalie had asked me to drop by the bakery and pick up a cake her mother had ordered. I was just about to leave the Lifeguard Shack when the telephone rang. It was Paulina. I was surprised to hear her voice and even more so to learn that she was in the city, staying at a nearby hotel. She had the afternoon off and wanted to see me. I look back now on the young man I was then in wonderment, and more than a little shame. I should have told Paulina that I had another engagement. I ought to have come clean and told her I was about to host a birthday party for my girlfriend. But . . . "Sure, I'll be right over!" The words flew out of my mouth before I could stop them.

From the moment I hung up the phone, I tried to justify how it was fine to stop by and say hello. I tried to tell myself there was nothing wrong with seeing an old friend who was in town and hardly knew anybody. According to my convoluted logic, I could pick up the birthday cake, have a quick chat with Paulina, and zip back to Nathalie's party.

I arrived at Paulina's hotel room with the birthday cake in a box, only to find her wearing next to nothing. I was doomed. Within seconds we were all over each other again. As in Paris, we completely tore up the hotel room, leaving clothing and debris everywhere. Somewhere in all that the commotion, the box with the birthday cake in it got squashed.

As I stood there naked, staring down at the crushed cake, I was immediately overcome with guilt and shame. It was one thing to be in an exotic location having sex with a beautiful model, but this was different. This was far too close to home. My two worlds were colliding, and I had breached a boundary. I should have been preparing for my wonderful girlfriend's birthday party, not screwing some woman in a hotel, even if the woman was Paulina Porizkova. I saw what I was turning into, and I didn't like it.

I quickly got dressed and told Paulina I had to go. I scooped up what was left of the cake, hoping Nathalie and her mother would buy some story about its getting crushed in the cab. Before I left, I told Paulina I had a girlfriend.

"Is that who the cake is for?" she asked.

I was too disgusted with myself to respond.

I had always seen myself as one of the good guys. Now I felt like just another jerk. If my sexual immorality was repugnant to me, what would others think? People I respected, like my parents, or my sisters, or friends like Doc X, or Tommy Preston? I was an addict who couldn't stop myself from chasing my next fix. And with each step I was taking down this selfish, hedonistic path I was stupidly choosing, I was heading closer and closer to the abyss.

Doc X had always been a great leveler in my life, someone I could turn to in my darkest moments. He liked New York, and if I couldn't get out to see him at Avalon, he would often jump at the chance to come see me.

Whenever I invited him to the city for a few days between modeling jobs, I always had an ulterior motive: I needed to talk to my buddy about what was happening in my life. I needed to tell him about Paulina, Liddy, Andie MacDowell, and the numerous other models I'd been infatuated with. After the incident with the cake, Doc sat and listened in silence to my emotional outpourings, his legs tucked under him on my couch, a mug of herbal tea in his hand, pondering the full catalog of my crimes. Rubbing his chin, he shook his head before giving me that wry smile. "Doc X doesn't blame you for your indiscretions," he told me. "Doc X, too, is drawn to this lifestyle. This world sounds like a true heaven on earth to any man. You shouldn't be so hard on yourself. B is only human. Doc X would also not have been able to resist all those beautiful women."

"Really?" I said, my heart lifting. "You don't think I'm totally fucked up?"

He frowned and raised a hand. "Doc X loves Nathalie. She has a pure heart and a good spirit. She is the best thing to ever happen to you. Doc X doesn't think you should risk losing her. Doc X thinks you and Nathalie should decide what you both want."

Doc X and Nathalie had hit it off from the moment they met. He knew that I loved her, so he loved her, too. Life was that simple for X. He had an appalling track record for breaking women's hearts himself, but he worried that if I lost Nathalie, I might somehow lose part of myself. He also made me see that because neither of us had ever formalized our relationship, we'd both been left to float along in our own little bubbles for too long. She'd stayed in Manhattan all that time I'd been out in Philly and Jersey, with me just visiting on weekends, and then when I'd gone to Europe, she came to visit only when she wanted to attend a meditation conference. Now that she was a model, too, our paths crossed even less frequently, and what relationship we had was fragmenting still further.

I loved X for always making me see how life truly was. And I loved having him in the Lifeguard Shack. Whenever he came to the city, something amazing always seemed to happen. Once I got him a job as an assistant with Bruce Weber for a day in his studio. I'd bought X a camera a few years earlier, and that had really opened his eyes to photography, so he loved spending the day with Weber and watching him work. I sneaked into the studio that day and took photos of Doc X photographing Weber. I still have them.

Another time X turned up back at the Lifeguard Shack black and blue.

"What the hell happened?" I asked, leading him inside and putting some ice on his swollen lip.

"Some asshole stole a woman's purse, so I chased after him," he told me, still breathless. Doc X was one of the fastest sprinters I'd ever seen. He also hated any sort of injustice. "He ran down into the subway, and I almost had him, but I tripped and fell. I picked myself up, though, and went after him. I rounded a corner, and he was right there!"

"Shit! What happened?"

"The asshole pulled a gun and pointed it at my head. He told me to back off or he'd blow my fricking brains out."

"Jeez, man. What did you do? I hope you ran like hell."

"I stared him down, B. I told that son of a bitch that he was fricking lucky that he had that gun, or I'd have kicked his butt."

That was the Doc X way.

My agents knew that whatever I was doing, wherever I was in the world, if Bruce Weber called, I would make myself available. So when I got a call asking me to do a jewelry shoot with Weber for *Vanity Fair* in the Adirondacks, I jumped on a plane from Europe without a moment's hesitation.

Weber had this terrific idea to shoot me as a Native American chief, my face smeared with war paint, surrounded by models—including Nathalie—dressed as Indian maidens. Only instead of wearing traditional Indian adornments, we would be wearing the amazing designer jewelry that was the focus of the shoot. Weber had his assistants light a huge campfire at the edge of a lake and encouraged me to act out the role completely, until he had me screaming and hollering at the top of my voice, dancing around the fire in all the heat and the smoke, beating my bare chest and making primitive gestures at the women, who were by now thoroughly unnerved.

"Great, Bruce, that's fantastic!" Weber called, the *click-click* of his Pentax barely audible above the crackle of the fire and the noise of my demonic cries.

"Now strip off the rest of your clothes, Bruce—-that's it—and when you're ready . . . leap over the flames!"

And so, fired up by the moment, the wood smoke, and the spirit of the Indian chief that had somehow taken over my persona, I leaped naked into the flames, giving Weber perhaps one of his wildest shots yet.

My next job was far less taxing, thankfully. It was in the Bahamas—always a favorite with models. I was booked for a job down there with photographer John Stember for Pan Am Airlines, who kindly flew us there first class. I was working with another male model named Billy, whom I'd done some catalog shoots with before, and a couple of female models, one of whom was a French girl called Sophie Billard. I actually felt relieved when I first saw the girls, because I wasn't immediately attracted to either one of them. *Thank God*, I thought. *I can just take it easy and concentrate on the work.* All I wanted was to do my job, study, and behave myself. I felt like I needed a break from the constant chase. I was tired and didn't want to play the game on this trip.

We arrived in Nassau and were driven to a beautiful old Colonial hotel. It was right in the middle of town, with a big garden and a gorgeous pool out back. Everyone was introduced to one another and said polite hellos. Sophie, who commanded any room she walked into, came across as rather reserved and sophisticated. She wasted no time in telling everyone she had a boyfriend, which was fine with me. I figured I'd just hang around with my friend Billy and chill out.

For this ad campaign, we models were supposed to be two wealthy couples on vacation. During the day we did shots of us frolicking on the beach and swimming in the ocean, which was perfect.

Put me anywhere on the beach and I'm a happy man. Whenever I wasn't needed, I spent my free time jogging up and down the beach or bodysurfing. The water was a lot warmer than at Avalon. Later in the afternoon, we went back into town, where John took some shots of us shopping in the markets and sampling the local cuisine at a restaurant. In the early evening, he wanted Sophie and me back at our hotel pool alone for a sunset shot.

They dressed me in a tuxedo and Sophie in a tiny black bikini. John's idea was that she was going to swim to the side of the pool, where I was to kneel and pour us a glass of champagne to share. We both did as instructed, and John was thrilled with the images he was capturing, so he encouraged us to go one stage further.

"Great, now drink the champagne together," he said from behind his lens. "Good, good. Now kiss her, Bruce. . . . Okay, that's good, now kiss her some more." He directed and we obeyed, dutifully engaging in several tender kisses.

The combination of the taste of champagne on her lips, the sunset behind her, and the beautiful French model in the little bikini had my head spinning. Until that moment Sophie and I had barely spoken to each other. Her beauty hadn't blown me away, as had been the case with Paulina. But something had changed. The more I kissed Sophie, the more I became convinced she was the best kisser ever. Everything else disappeared: the clicking of the camera, the lights, the assistants hovering around us. It was just Sophie and me, locked in a passionate embrace. In my mind we had actually become the lovers in the photograph.

"Okay!" John finally shouted. "Thanks. I think I've got everything I need."

Sophie pulled back abruptly. My fantasy romance was over. She twisted away from me and swam to the pool steps, where she emerged dripping and was handed a robe by her dresser. I remained motionless, staring after her as she walked off toward the hotel.

"Let's take a break, everybody," John said. "Are you good with that, Bruce?"

I couldn't answer.

The crew wandered off in various directions while I remained locked in my trance. Instinctively I followed Sophie like a zombie. I caught up with her just as she was about to enter her room. "Sophie," I said, "can I come in?"

She looked horrified. "Are you crazee? I told you, I 'ave, how you say, a boyfriend!" Her sexy French accent only made me feel crazier. Before I could say another word, she slammed the door in my face.

For the remainder of the shoot, she wouldn't talk to me or even glance in my direction. I, of course, remained completely infatuated. But, respectful of her wishes, I tried to focus on my studies and the work we had to do for the campaign.

On the morning we were flying back to New York, I was sitting having breakfast alone when she approached me in the hotel café. "What are you reading?" she asked. I looked up, amazed she was actually talking to me. I showed her the book, *Cutting Through Spiritual Materialism* by Chögyam Trungpa. I began explaining how easy it is to lose your way and get caught in the trappings of spirituality by not working on your inner being. And boy, did I know what I was talking about!

I was a little taken aback when she pulled up a chair and began telling me a bit about herself. She asked me how I'd come to be interested in spirituality, so I explained that I went to Cornell and had a degree in Buddhist studies. I think I even ended up apologizing for my behavior earlier in the shoot. "I got completely carried away," I said. "You're a great kisser, by the way."

"*Oui,* I understand, but I 'ave a boyfriend, François," Sophie replied. "I love him *très* much."

On the flight home, we sat next to each other in first class and continued our conversation. At one point the stewardess offered us some champagne. I thought, *Oh, no, here we go again.* It wasn't long before the alcohol took effect and we were right back at it, making out in our seats. I couldn't stop staring into Sophie's beautiful brown eyes. We were all over each other for the entire flight back to New York. It felt so surreal. Once we'd landed at JFK and taxied to the gate, the flight attendant came up to us and said, "That was the best public display of affection we've ever seen. You two definitely had a good flight." She gave me a wink.

As we were getting off the plane, Sophie grabbed my hand and said, "I want to spend zee night wiz you. Take me to your place."

"Okay!" I said. I was so excited that I almost forgot about my buddies at the Lifeguard Shack. For the first time ever, I didn't want them there when I returned to New York City after a shoot. I told Sophie, "I have to make a quick call."

Looking for a pay phone, I suddenly remembered Nathalie, too. What I was thinking? I had promised her we'd have dinner. As I dialed Nathalie's number, Sophie whispered in my ear, "Zere's something about you, Bruce. I have to be wiz you tonight." I knew I'd have to get out of seeing Nathalie.

I kept my phone call brief, afraid Nathalie might hear Sophie in the background. I told her I was completely exhausted from my trip and just wanted to head home and crash. She said she understood. That was Nathalie: always supporting me, even when I was lying.

Dinner's waiting at a candlelit inn, but it's such fun to dawdle. Ivory silk-knit turtleneck—actually ski underwear by Orvis—$22, tucks into very full-legged evening pants in cream silk. By Gene Ewing BIS, $164. Man's cashmere union suit, Malo Tricot.

Sunday came so soon—let's do it again!

My buddies weren't so agreeable. I virtually had to plead with Stoover. "Please, man, can you and the other guys just duck out of the place for the night?" I whispered into the receiver. "I'm with this French girl, and I want to bring her back."

Stu was laughing before I could finish my sentence. He told the other guys, and I could hear them hooting and hollering. "Fuck you, Hulse!" he said. "We're not leaving. This is *our* place, too."

"Yeah, but I pay the rent." I tried to reason with them, but it was futile.

"Yeah, but we're playing chess, and Rob's in the middle of putting together one of his airplanes. Go get a hotel room or something."

I tried to explain that I wasn't with just any girl. "She isn't a hotel-room type, Stoover. She wants to come see where I live."

There was silence on the other end of the line. I knew I'd have to up the ante. "Listen, there's a wad of hundreds in the top drawer of my dresser. Grab five hundred bucks and take the boys out for the evening, and don't come back before two in the morning, okay? My treat."

"Five hundred? That's all?"

Sophie looked like she was getting restless. "Five hundred is all you guys are getting!" I yelled into the receiver.

"All right, all right," Stu told me. "Calm down."

Sophie and I hopped in a taxi. By the time we arrived at the apartment, though, the champagne had worn off. I led her toward my bedroom, but she suddenly stopped me in the doorway. "Bruce," she said, shaking her head. "I cannot do zis. I cannot cheat on François."

Realizing there was no way I could change her mind, I called her a taxi. She left without another word. I sat alone in the apartment, feeling like crap. I figured that was the last we'd see of each other. Still, I couldn't get her out of my mind.

The following day I was hanging around my apartment, cleaning and catching up on phone calls, when the apartment buzzer went off. "Who is it?" I asked into the speakerphone.

"Bruce, it iz Sophie. I must talk to you."

I couldn't let her in fast enough. I whipped open the front door to find her standing there in heels, full makeup, and a little red leather miniskirt.

"I thought about you all night," she said. "I *must* be wiz you, Bruce."

My mind was trying to process what was happening. But before I could, she pushed through the door and we embraced. We shuffled into the kitchen, kissing passionately and tearing each other's clothes off. I pulled up her skirt and saw she had a garter belt on. I had never been more turned on in my life. We ended up having incredible sex right there on the kitchen floor. It was everything I'd fantasized that it would be.

"When can I see you again?" I asked her as we lay on the couch afterward, holding each other.

"I needed to do zis," Sophie said softly, "but we cannot see each other again. I am leaving for Paree tonight. I must go back to François." And with that she was gone.

I couldn't have been more confused. I got together with Nathalie the next day, I hung out with my buddies for a few days, I went to visit my parents and my sisters and all my little nieces and nephews with gifts I'd bought in Europe, and I threw myself into as many modeling jobs as I could book. I did everything I could to forget Sophie, but nothing helped. No matter how hard I tried, I just couldn't get her out of my head.

10

Unraveling

More than a month had passed since I'd last seen Sophie. Still reeling from our encounter, I had been in and out of New York working, trying to clear my head and pushing away the hope that we'd ever be together again. I was stunned when the phone rang one day and I heard her unmistakable accent.

"Bruce, I need to see you. Can you come to Paris?"

I didn't stop to ask questions. "Of course," I said. As soon as I put down the receiver, I called the airport to book the next flight to Paris. The ticket agent told me the only remaining flight was on Air Pakistan, which stopped in Paris before continuing to Lahore. I bought a ticket, jumped into a taxi, and rushed down to JFK. I didn't think twice about it.

I had a rough flight to Paris. There was heavy turbulence for most of the flight, and I was seated in the middle of a group of screaming babies. Without a doubt it was the most torturous flight I had ever endured. Halfway across the Atlantic, I began asking myself, *What the hell am I doing? I'm taking the Screaming Baby Express to Paris to sleep with a French girl who keeps messing with my head.*

I finally arrived in Paris and called up my agent, to see if she could get me into any nice hotels. I didn't want to stay at the Pension du Roc this time.

"What are you doing here?" she asked, surprised.

"Oh, just vacationing," I said. "Listen, if you can book me a job while I'm over here, too, I'd be really grateful."

"I'll see what I can do," she said. Fortunately, she was able to find me a room at a small, chic hotel in the city center. As soon as I checked in, I called Sophie. She asked me to meet her at the Jardins des Tuileries, just off the rue de Rivoli, so we could go for a drive. This was the Paris I had first gotten to know, the city I first arrived in when I came across from the States on the cheapest flight I could find. I'd walked past these beautiful gardens toward the offices of the First Agency, wondering if I was crazy to think I would ever get work as a model.

Sophie pulled up in a green MG convertible. I jumped into the passenger seat, and she leaned over and wrapped her arms around me. "Oh, it iz good to see you, Bruce," she told me, her breath warm on my face. "But I decided I *can't* see you."

"What?" I asked, incredulous. "I just flew all the way from New York. What are you talking about?"

She stared at the steering wheel in silence. After a moment she said, "I don't know. I am so confused."

She was confused? "Don't you want to come back to my hotel with me?" I asked. "I want to be with you, Sophie. I want to kiss you. I want to make love to you."

"I can't. I'm still in love with François," she said, and then she began to cry.

I could hear my buddies in the back of my mind: *You're freaking crazy, Hulse. Look at you!* It wasn't that long ago that I could barely afford the train ride from Philadelphia to New York. Here I was hopping a plane to Paris to try to sleep with this woman who was still in love with her boyfriend. I didn't know what to think about anything anymore.

I stared into the distance. I watched the cars racing around the place de la Concorde, where I'd strolled with the lovely Annette Rask that first night after choosing her for the Swiss *GQ* shoot. At the Egyptian obelisk in the center, I had once kissed beautiful Terry Cole, the model whose room I'd shared so happily at the Pension du Roc. I looked across at the pont de la Concorde across the river Seine, which I'd crossed to get to Jocelyn's apartment that first night in the city, when he'd told me I'd have to abandon my beliefs if I was going to stay in this industry.

There was nothing more to say between Sophie and me. I left her at the park and returned to my hotel alone. I was mentally and physically exhausted by the time I got back, so I lay down on the bed to get some much-needed rest. Just before I drifted off, the telephone rang. I stared at the receiver ringing in its cradle and thought, *Do I even want to know who this is?*

It was my agent in New York. "We've got a job for you tomorrow," Martha said. "How quickly can you make it back?"

I told her I'd be on the next flight out.

Herb Ritts called me one day to talk about an upcoming photo shoot he wanted to use me for. He explained that it was going to be a casual but challenging assignment.

His request was one I might not normally have accepted, but I knew that Herb would take exquisite and tasteful photographs that would be seen by the world as art. I also didn't want to pigeonhole myself as being homophobic. I wanted to be receptive to any and all ideas, as long as they involved the right team and the best photographers.

When it came to casting my counterpart, I had to put a lot of thought into the decision. I'd have had no problem selecting the right woman for a shoot, but I'd never before been asked to cast a male model for such an intimate shoot. It had to be someone I got along with, but, more important, someone who would be as comfortable with the theme as I was. I also didn't want to leave any room for confusion, so it had to be a model who was also straight. In the end the choice was obvious: Nick Constantino. He was sleeping on my couch, anyway, so I knew he was up for anything, especially if it would give us the chance to work together again.

Nick and I decided to have fun with the shoot. From the outset we recognized the humor in embracing and allowing ourselves to be shot so close together. Nick laughingly quipped, "Hey, sailor, let's go to work." Herb took us up to the rooftop of a building in New York, stripped me to the waist, placed a gold chain and a medallion around my neck, and had me smoking a cigarette. I draped

my arm over Nick's shoulder as if we were recovering from a wild night on the town. At first it was hard for both of us to keep a straight face, because our poses felt so ridiculous, but as the day wore on, our professionalism kicked in and it became just like any other shoot.

The photos were spectacular, as I'd expected. When Nick saw the finished product, he was furious. He grabbed the photos from me and ripped them to shreds. "None of our buddies are ever seeing these, Hulse! Do you hear me? I mean it!" All I could think was, *I hope these aren't worth a lot of money someday.*

On a similar shoot, Bruce Weber brought me in to work with a male model at a hotel in Santa Monica, California. He wanted to do some ambiguous sex shots for a book of photographs he was publishing. I had never met the model before, but I did my best. Halfway through the shoot, Weber stepped away from the lens and wiped his hand across his forehead.

"I know you're trying, Bruce, but it just isn't working," Weber said with a heavy sigh. It was the first time he'd ever said that to me on a shoot. I felt crushed. I had thought that the shoot was going well, but obviously something looked wrong to Weber's well-trained eye.

Of course Weber knew exactly how to fix the problem. Without missing a beat, he said to one of his assistants, "Can we get a girl in here, please?"

Within a month of our disastrous meeting in Paris, Sophie came back to New York to stay for a while. She told me that she had broken up with François and wanted to reconnect with me. Even though all my alarm bells were ringing, and even though Nathalie was still a big part of my life, Sophie and I started seeing each other.

Being with Sophie was like driving a new sports car: thrilling and exciting. I was addicted to the rush of something new and intrigued by her unpredictability. Soon I was spending more time at Sophie's apartment on the East Side of midtown Manhattan than at my own. My buddies noticed my absence and told me they missed me. I missed them, too, but I was in thrall to this crazy Frenchwoman, and I didn't seem to be able to break the spell. Nathalie was away a lot working, so I didn't have to deceive her too often.

It wasn't long before Sophie wanted more from me. She demanded that I make a choice between her and Nathalie. "It eez her or me," she declared petulantly. "I have give up everyzing for you—François, Paree, my whole life. Now it eez your turn."

I couldn't argue with her logic. Fair was fair, and I knew I couldn't keep up this charade forever. For some time now, I'd been dreading the thought of ending my relationship with Nathalie, but Sophie was forcing the issue, and in many ways it would probably come as a relief. I had betrayed Nathalie too many times, and I wanted to make a fresh start, with a clean slate.

The following weekend Nathalie and I drove to the South Jersey shore in my car, a 1971 Buick Centurion I'd bought a few years back, to stay at the Doc X Mansion. As we whizzed along the Garden State Parkway, all I could think of was how I was about to destroy Nathalie and how she didn't know yet. At some point during the weekend, I would have to find the courage to break the news that our four-year relationship was over.

That weekend we spent our time relaxing on the beach and surfing. Nathalie had come to love the ocean almost as much as I did. At night we cooked dinner and invited some friends over. It felt so relaxed and familiar; I never wanted our time there to end. I thought of all the years I'd been coming to Avalon and how Nathalie had fit right in. I thought back to the summer when her brother, Laurent, had lived with me on the beach, and she'd taken up running down the wide expanse of sand, waving and smiling at my lifeguard buddies at their stands all the way. I thought about how well she got along with my parents, especially my mom, always helping out in the kitchen and chatting happily with her about the books they'd read. Or how my sisters adored her and how their children loved to sit on her knee.

When I told Doc X about my plan to break up with Nathalie, he was visibly shocked. All he could do was shake his head and roll his eyes at me. "Are you nuts?" he cried. "You're jumping off a cliff! Nathalie loves you. You are making a big mistake, B."

"There's no other way," I insisted. "I have to tell her about Sophie and make a clean break, man."

"You don't have to tell her. Just stop fucking around. It's your guilt you should be facing up to, not Sophie or Nathalie." Once again Doc X had a way of boiling complicated situations down to their simplest elements. I heard him out, but I wasn't really listening. How could I face my guilt unless I told Nathalie about all the women I'd cheated with? Besides, I was in too deep with Sophie. It was time to make a change in my life, and Sophie was the reason for that change.

I felt sick to my stomach the whole weekend. By the time we waved good-bye to X, I still hadn't broken the news to Nathalie. During the drive back to the city on Sunday night, I sweated madly. The old Buick didn't have air-conditioning, so I rolled down the windows, but it made little difference in the summer heat and humidity. There was silence between us, broken only by the sound of the cicadas chirping outside. As we approached the Holland Tunnel under the Hudson River, connecting Jersey with Manhattan, the traffic started to slow, and we soon came to a standstill. My moment had arrived.

"We have to talk," I said, turning to Nathalie with my heart pounding. Those are four words that everyone understands.

There was a long pause. I choked up a bit as I looked into her eyes. I couldn't believe I was actually going through with it. I felt like an executioner, about to destroy the happiness of a beautiful girl who had always been there for me and had loved me unconditionally for years.

"I've been having an affair," I finally told her, blurting it out. "She's a model. She's really gotten under my skin. I need to see it through, Nathalie. I need six months to figure this whole thing out." I didn't know why a six-month trial separation popped into my head. I now think I was attempting to soften the blow. I also think I unconsciously wanted to maintain some sort of attachment to Nathalie. Perhaps on some level I figured that if things didn't work out with Sophie, Nathalie might still be there for me at the end of the six-month break. Needless to say, I was being incredibly selfish.

At first Nathalie listened calmly. I had expected some kind of violent reaction from her, but she was accepting and understanding, which made me feel even worse. Then her emotions bubbled to the surface and tears started streaming down her face. "I love you, Bruce. Why are you doing this?" she asked.

I had no good answers for her questions. All I knew was that I had to end our relationship, at least for the time being.

We drove the rest of the way into the city in silence. I dropped Nathalie off at her apartment and continued home alone. I collapsed into bed and fell asleep. The following morning Nathalie came to my apartment to talk. We had the same conversation we'd had in the car the night before. The words weren't any easier to say the second time around. I could see the pain in Nathalie's eyes. It was almost too much to bear, but I knew I had to see this through with Sophie or I would regret it for the rest of my life.

When Nathalie finally left, I called Sophie to tell her it was done. To my horror, Sophie immediately launched into me. "Poor girl. How could you do that to her? Why should I think you won't do the same thing to me one day?"

I couldn't believe what I was hearing. I did what she'd asked, and now she was questioning my intentions? Talk about a no-win situation! I had to spend the next few days and nights trying to convince Sophie that my feelings for her were true.

Doc X in front of the X mansion.

Looking back, I realize now that being with Sophie was a status kick for me. She was quite high-profile by then. Although she was soulful, we came from very different backgrounds. The Lifeguard Shack wasn't up to her standard of living, so I spent most of the time at her apartment. While Sophie loved upscale restaurants, I was happy eating at home. While she preferred going out with friends, I'd rather hang in the apartment, reading and relaxing, working on my meditation and yoga. We were polar opposites, and yet we were wildly attracted to each other.

One weekend some months later I took Sophie to my sister's place in Mays Landing, New Jersey, a house I'd helped build. It had such a quiet and relaxed atmosphere. April and Tom were laid-back people who grew their own organic fruits and vegetables; Sophie, with her miniskirt and high heels, just didn't fit in. I couldn't wait to get her out of there. In the car on the way home, we decided to smoke some pot. After a few pulls on the joint, a wave of anxiety hit me, along with a feeling of total paranoia. For a few minutes, I was terrified that I was having some sort of acid flashback. Thankfully, back at Sophie's apartment, I felt better.

A few days later, I woke up in the middle of the night with a feeling of angst that I didn't understand. I had a sudden, uncontrollable urge to make love to Sophie, and I woke her from a dead sleep. Unfazed, she reciprocated. She seemed turned on by my dominance, and we went at it until we both were completely spent. Afterward we drifted off to sleep on the sweat-soaked sheets.

After a few hours, I awoke again, this time in the middle of a full-blown panic attack. I knew with frightening clarity that my relationship with Sophie was wrong. It was all about sex and status, not love. All the emotions I'd been holding back for the past six months came rushing over me at once. What had I done? I realized that I didn't even know Sophie. We were strangers. My buddies like Doc X and Tommy Preston had told me how wrong she was for me, and it was suddenly and painfully obvious that they were right.

Sophie and I were headed for a place that offered nothing but loneliness. I'd been blinded by this French fantasy, but now I had to open my eyes. I had to take responsibility for my choices and live with the repercussions. My selfishness and lies had caught up with me. I felt more awake and alert than I had been in months. I saw that I had betrayed myself. What had happened to the mission of speaking the truth and being kind to others that I had taken upon myself when I joined the ashram in Ithaca? Somewhere along the trail, I had lost my way.

In the days immediately following my sobering realizations, I could feel depression closing in on me. I was trapped, boxed in by my own actions. I couldn't sleep or eat. I felt like a zombie, walking around in the ruins of my own life. The only thing left to do was to come clean with Sophie.

"I don't know what I'm doing with you," I finally told her. "This is totally messed up."

Sophie seemed not to understand what I was saying. I don't know if she lacked the compassion to have a real meeting of the minds, but we couldn't even communicate clearly around breaking up. All I wanted to do was talk to Nathalie, so I called her.

"I want to come back," I said. "I need you." I begged for her forgiveness. I confessed that I had become stuck in an endless cycle of self-deception.

Nathalie was shocked. It had been about six months since I'd broken up with her, and she was seeing someone new, so my call was confusing to her. Also, since we'd been apart, her friends in the industry had let her know about some of the other women I'd slept with. "I might be able to accept one, Bruce, but *all* those women? How could I ever trust you again?" She was right.

I felt so empty inside, which made me all the more desperate to patch things up with Nathalie. I seized on the idea that if I could somehow bring both Sophie and Nathalie together, I could make myself whole. I was clutching at anything that might put the shattered pieces of my world back together. In retrospect it was a crazy idea, but I convinced both of them to meet me at a coffee shop in Greenwich Village.

I felt like I was walking to the gallows that day, but I had this feeling that maybe we could all become friends and live happily ever after. To me, Sophie represented the new life I had chosen, and Nathalie represented my grounded spiritual side. I thought I needed them both in order to survive.

The two women in my life were already seated together at a table when I arrived. Elegantly dressed, they were in the middle of a deep discussion when I shuffled up in worn jeans and a wrinkled T-shirt, sporting two days of stubble. I hadn't eaten for days, so I was a rail-thin mess. Sophie and Nathalie were both visibly upset. I sat down with them, but they kept right on talking to each other as if I weren't there.

"What are we going to do about Bruce?" Nathalie asked Sophie. "I have never seen him like this before."

"I don't know," Sophie replied, shaking her head. "He is acting crazee."

I began wishing that I hadn't come. Then they turned to me and asked a lot of questions I didn't have the answers to. How could I behave like this? Who did I think I was? The trouble was, I knew exactly who I was: a selfish bastard and a liar, with no one to blame but myself.

In the end we all went our separate ways. Nathalie headed off to her family, and Sophie was making plans to return to Paris. I watched them go and then walked alone up Sixth Avenue in the bitter December air, wondering what to do next. It was nearly Christmas, so none of my buddies were at the Lifeguard Shack; they were all back in the bosom of their families. I couldn't face mine.

I lay down on my bed and spent the rest of that day and night curled up in a ball. I had destroyed everything I cared about most. I'd never felt more alone in my life.

11

The Hungry Ghost

In Tibetan Buddhism "hungry ghosts" are spirits with enormous bloated stomachs whose necks are too thin to pass food and whose mouths are too small for eating. They represent the futility of those who constantly attempt to fulfill their physical desires. As I struggled with the aftermath of losing Nathalie and Sophie, trying to find the path back to who I used to be, I felt the full impact of what my "hungry ghost" had cost me.

My friends and family were wonderful, rallying around, trying to help me as best they could, although we all knew this was something I was going to have to work out for myself. Keeping busy helped, so I booked as many jobs as I could, in between intensive meditation and studying. Fortunately, few photographers ever wanted me to smile—they preferred me chiseled and moody—so I rarely had to force my features into a rictus of joy.

I was booked to do an ad campaign for Bloomingdale's and an editorial for *L'uomo Vogue* in Italy that summer, but the idea of getting on a plane and crossing the Atlantic alone terrified me, so I asked Mom if she'd accompany me. She was delighted by the idea. Since she had never been to Europe in her life, I decided to make a vacation of it, renting a car and traveling around Italy to show her Rome, Florence, Siena, and Pisa, before heading up to St.-Tropez in the south of France.

"I'll come, too, buddy," Big Pete said, so I flew both of them to Rome with me. While I sweltered in the August heat, modeling suits and shirts by the hotel swimming pool, they took off sightseeing. I could just imagine the two of them walking around the Colosseum, the Forum, St. Peter's, the Vatican, eating gelato and getting along like mother and son. I was almost jealous. They'd come back to the hotel in the evening and have dinner with me, then take off again the next day, full of plans for new adventures. I was suffering from anxiety attacks and even occasional suicidal thoughts, but keeping my focus on the job at hand really helped—just as it had at the basketball tournament when I was a teenager.

One day Mom decided to come and watch me work in a beautiful Tuscan hill town called Montecatini. She was excited about seeing a fashion shoot. Unfortunately for her, the photographer was Herb Ritts, whose careful attention to detail didn't provide onlookers with much excitement. After an hour or so, Mom said, "Boy, this is way too boring for me!" and disappeared with Big Pete to walk around the town.

Tommy Preston showed up unexpectedly in Montecatini on his motorcycle. I had no idea he was booked as a model for this shoot, too, and it was really great to see him. He was shocked at how depressed I had become. "B, you gotta pull yourself out of this, man," he told me. "Life's not about women, it's about God realization. You need to come climb some rocks with me."

I appreciated everyone's attempts to help me, but I knew I needed to find my way out of this psychic darkness myself. I was frightened of my own shadow half the time, and part of me wanted to kill myself just to escape the mental torment, but the Buddhist in me knew that I would visit a heap of bad karma on myself if I did. When I returned to New York, I went to see a psychiatrist whom a model friend of mine had recommended. He listened carefully to what I had to say and inquired about my family history, my experiences with depression as a teenager, and my recent struggles.

"You have the classic symptoms of clinical depression, which means you have two choices," he told me. "You can take antidepressants or you can take up running. It's up to you."

Remembering how I'd felt the last time a doctor prescribed antidepressants for me, I chose the latter course. Even when I could barely get off the couch or put one foot in front of the other, I dragged myself to Central Park and forced myself to run around the path that circled the reservoir. For the first week, I could hardly run a few hundred yards before having to stop, but I persisted.

Come on, Bruce the Moose, I heard my father telling me. *Pick up the pace.* After a couple of weeks of running every day, I began to get my energy back a little, and I started to have moments when the endorphins kicked in and actually made me feel good. Then, in about the third week, my chemistry suddenly shifted. The depression slowly began to lift. I began to feel normal again.

I knew I needed something still deeper, though, something that would help me pursue a more spiritual path. Before Sophie left for Paris, she'd urged me to contact a man named Dwight Wilson, a martial-arts master who'd been raised in a Buddhist monastery in Japan. She said he specialized in overcoming fear and had worked with many other models in New York. So I called and made an appointment, not knowing what to expect.

Dwight's apartment was in an old industrial building not far from where I lived. I stepped over the winos and homeless guys camped out front and took the rickety freight elevator to the fourth floor and rang the bell. A huge, muscular black guy in his mid-fifties appeared, wearing only a tight red wrestler's tank suit. "Welcome," he said calmly. "I have been waiting for you." He beckoned me inside.

His dark, quiet loft apartment was a large open space with little or no furniture. There were two rows of floor-to-ceiling columns and a small kitchen area along the back brick wall. The floors were hardwood. There were no padded mats and no workout equipment. The temperature was sweltering, and the air smelled of sweat. It was like entering a portal into another place and time. Dwight made me uneasy, but I told him Sophie had referred me and explained how I felt I had lost my courage and that my fear was consuming me.

"You've come to the right place," he replied. "Life is about fear and power. To gain power you have to overcome your fear." He took a step toward me and put a hand on my shoulder. "Turn around and look at the column," he said. I did as I was told. Suddenly he grabbed the sides of my neck with both hands and squeezed. I must have lost consciousness. When I came to, Dwight had me on the floor in a choke hold. "I could kill you right now," he whispered in my left ear.

My body was frozen, and my mind was attempting to process what had just happened. I'd been practicing aikido and various other martial arts for ten years, yet I knew of no strike that could render someone unconscious with such speed. I said nothing, but Dwight put me out again with a choke hold. When I came to once more, he whispered, "In the beginning of time, when there were two drops of rain; you were one, and I was the other. We have been together through many lifetimes, Bruce."

Panic surged through my body like an electrical storm. I tried to remain calm, but all I could think was, *Get the hell out of here! This guy is going to kill you!* Finally Dwight relaxed his grip and let me sit up. I remained on the floor, dazed and bewildered. I did my best to remain calm. I didn't want to do or say anything to set him off again. If I bolted for the door, I was convinced he would break my neck.

Dwight stood up and loomed over me. "You are my student now, Bruce," he said. When he began to explain his teaching methods to me, my breathing slowed some, but I only fully relaxed when I realized that he didn't intend to kill me. Dwight's methods were unorthodox, but I was so desperate I was willing to try anything. Maybe his strange energy was exactly what I needed.

I started attending Dwight's weekly classes, hoping to find answers to my problems. He would stand at the front of the room, leading a group of us through various exercises. He had us do incredibly slow push-ups; if done properly, a single repetition could take up to a minute to complete. It required incredible focus, determination, and patience to do the exercise. Dwight drove us until every muscle was at the point of collapse.

After class one day, I pulled one of the other students, a fellow model, to one side and asked, "Did Dwight ever knock you out using a choke hold?"

The guy seemed surprised by my question. "No, why?"

On a few occasions, Dwight asked me to stay after class. We'd spend hours talking about deep meditation practices and fighting techniques, or about Morihei Ueshiba, considered the greatest martial artist of all time. Ueshiba was the founder of the discipline called aikido, which, literally translated, means "the art of peace." Even though he was said to possess limitless physical power, Ueshiba was a man of peace who believed that pointless violence was the worst sin a man could commit. The true way of the warrior was about resolving conflict, discovering the power of love, and achieving harmony with your surroundings. Those principles were what initially drew me to the practice, because they meshed perfectly with my Buddhist beliefs.

Dwight, however, was attracted by the power of aikido and something he called the "touchless strike," a technique that supposedly would render someone unconscious from across a room without physical contact. He said he saw something special in me and wanted me to be his next disciple, but I just needed to find a way to get through my panic. I soon came to realize that I wasn't getting what I needed from Dwight. In fact, after going to some of his classes, I felt emptier than ever. I still had trouble sleeping, and I had no sense of inner peace or contentment. I told Dwight how I was feeling, but he just told me to keep practicing the exercises.

"What about the love?" I asked.

"It isn't about love, Bruce," he said. "It's about fear and power."

That answer was a red flag to me. I wasn't willing to follow someone whose mind-set was so different from my own. I'd spent my entire life searching for love, and I wasn't going to abandon that quest in favor of Dwight's obsession with power. It was time to move on. At the end of the next class, I told Dwight my decision and explained that I needed to continue on my spiritual journey.

When I was done, Dwight stared me in the eye. "If you leave me, Bruce, you will end up going crazy," he said. There was a long pause. Without another word, I gathered my things and left. It was all about control for Dwight. He was trying to live by an ancient samurai code in twentieth-century America. The cultlike atmosphere surrounding him didn't feel right for me. Dwight died a few years later from a heart attack, which was hastened, I'm sure, by the prodigious quantities of ice cream he used to eat after class.

Unfortunately, I felt that nothing had changed for me. In fact, I felt I had taken a few steps backward, and I was more confused than ever. I knew only one way to handle it: I threw myself into work again.

When Macy's booked me to do a swimwear shoot with a photographer named Michael Halsband in a New York City studio, I was delighted. I wouldn't have to get on a plane; in fact, it was just three blocks from the Lifeguard Shack.

I walked to the job on the first day of the shoot, trying to keep a positive attitude and remind myself that there was still so much to be happy about in my life. I was still working and earning good money as a model. I had the love and support of my family and friends. I was running and building my energy, and I was finding solace in meditation and my Buddhist studies. Life sometimes conspired against me, though. Everywhere I looked, I seemed to see Nathalie or Sophie on billboards or in magazines, catalogs, or fashion bulletins. It hurt me terribly to see their perfect faces, those beautiful bodies that I had once caressed. I had lost all libido over the past six months, thanks to my depression, but my soul ached for their company and especially for Nathalie's spiritual succor.

When I arrived at the studio, I went inside, introduced myself, and quickly got undressed. I put on the swim shorts I was to pose in, then I stepped in front of Michael's camera and was introduced to my female counterpart. She was a ravishing six-foot-tall Australian beauty named Elle Macpherson, who lit up the room with her smile. I held Elle in my arms as we took our positions. She nestled against my naked torso in a skimpy swimsuit and looked lovingly into my eyes. I felt completely dead inside, and I noticed with an almost clinical detachment how holding a beautiful woman no longer stirred anything within me.

The shoot continued for several hours, with many changes of outfits and numerous different poses. The longer it went on, the more tired I felt, but the more animated and frisky Elle became. She was so charismatic and friendly, and all the crew seemed to love her. Michael seemed fixated on her; I couldn't have cared less. When we'd finally finished and put our clothes back on, Elle wandered over to where I was pulling on my coat and started chatting with me. She was rather boyish in her manner and extremely open, with an incredible sense of humor—a real guy's girl.

"Do you live in Manhattan?" she asked.

"Yeah. Just a few blocks around the corner."

"Oh, really? Can I come over and see your place?"

I hesitated. "I live with a bunch of lifeguards," I said.

"Oh, that's great, mate," she said in her Australian twang. "I love a lifeguard!"

When we got back to my apartment, it was unusually quiet—there was no one home. To my surprise, Elle stripped down in front of me. I looked at her in open appreciation, and a part of me wondered if I could still function sexually. We started kissing, and she was wonderful to be with, but I felt nothing at all except the sadness and despair that had dogged me for months now.

I pulled away from Elle. "I'm sorry," I said to her, "but I've been going through this major depression lately. I seem to have lost my sex drive. I'm all messed up over this girl I was dating for four years. I'm just really confused right now."

She was so understanding and kind about it. "No worries, Bruce," she said, kissing me playfully on the nose. "Let's just be friends, then." We started hanging out socially after that, meeting for coffee or dinner when we were free. She came over for a few group meditations at the apartment, and the guys absolutely loved her. I desperately wanted to feel something for her when we were together, but I was still going through the motions. My depression had too firm a hold on me.

Elle told me she loved the beach, so one weekend I took her to Avalon. On the way we stopped at my parents' house to have dinner and spend the night. When we walked into Mom and Dad's kitchen, I felt as if I had just brought an exotic animal into the house. My father was nearly speechless. Elle and I shared a bed that night and slept soundly, though we ended up having discreet but fun sex the following morning—a development that surprised us both. The trouble was, in my fragile state it was only a fleeting moment of bliss for me. Elle was wonderful, but I wasn't capable of being in the moment when we made love. I was there in body, but not in spirit.

Elle had just done her *Sports Illustrated* swimsuit cover, and she was riding a huge wave of success. When we arrived at the Doc X Mansion, word had gone out that she was coming, and the local guys were in awe. Doc X, who by now was taking photography lessons, shot some wonderfully candid photos of Elle and me frolicking in the surf for my portfolio. Avalon was predominantly a conservative Catholic town, and it could barely handle the sight of Elle in her G-string swimsuit as we jogged down the beach together. All weekend long, random guys began showing up at Doc X's house, hoping to catch a glimpse of her.

Though we had a wonderful weekend together and continued to see each other as friends for months afterward, I think Elle eventually grew impatient with my inability to be present for her. I understood how she felt, and I couldn't blame her for moving on. A year or so later, she married Gilles Bensimon, a leading fashion photographer and the creative manager of *Elle* magazine. She will always have a special place in my heart.

Still trying to work through my depression, I booked myself into an eight-day silent meditation retreat at the Mount Tremper monastery, which was run by the Mountains and Rivers Order of Zen Buddhism. The monastery was located on 230 acres of forest preserve in the Catskill Mountains in upstate New York. My good buddy Tommy Preston offered to come with me. I couldn't imagine the garrulous Tommy being able to keep silent for more than a few hours, but I was glad to have his company, so off we went. "This is going to be hard for T," Tommy said, "but T will do it for B."

By day three of the retreat, I was in emotional and spiritual agony. Sitting still, silently meditating, connecting with my breath—it all only conjured up the ghosts of Nathalie and Sophie. Later that day Tommy and I were given a silent work detail, digging the vegetable garden together. After a few minutes, Tommy couldn't take it anymore.

"Hey, B!" he whispered. "I've gotta get out of here, man. This silent shit is driving me crazy! Let's go climb a mountain or some-

Tommy Preston in Barbados.

thing!" I took one look at him, one look back at the monastery, and nodded. Dropping our tools, we jumped over the wall and into his car, and we drove away. For the rest of that week, we hiked around the beautiful Shawangunk Mountains outside New Paltz, New York, where he taught me how to rock-climb. I was terrified my first time, clinging to those sheer rock faces with all my fingers and nothing between me and death several hundred feet below, but Tommy was completely fearless, standing up on a narrow ledge above me, his shoelaces untied, taking in the view.

"Tommy!" I'd yell. "Get back against the wall, you idiot! If you fall, I'm gonna be stuck up here on my own, with no one to get me down!"

"It's cool, B. Get on up here and look at the red-tails. Man, those hawks are amazing. It's all about the space, B. This is where you'll find God."

Tommy had taught me a lot over the years, but one of his most important lessons was what he called "the way of the rock." It's a philosophy Tommy lives by. He believes that rocks have an energy that communicates. The way of the rock is learning to feel that energy so you don't have to muscle your way up a climb—you *Zen* your way up a climb. The way of the rock involves breathing and processing your fear, staying fully in the moment as you make your way up a cliff.

Unlike Dwight, Tommy was a natural teacher. He understood that nature offers us many lessons. He was never afraid to take risks or push limits. Tommy was the type of guy who would gladly agree to do a fashion shoot ten stories up a building in the middle of Manhattan's garment district. He'd open a window, climb out onto the twelve-inch-wide ledge, and walk it as if it were a runway in Paris or Milan. He'd freak me out with his madness, and yet I was always inspired by his willingness to reach beyond the realm of the expected. It is Tommy, more than anyone else, who has helped me conquer most of my fears. I'm not the man he is on the rocks, but I've learned to strive for his courage in everyday life.

When the two-year lease finally expired on the Lifeguard Shack and our landlady grew tired of all our comings and goings, she decided not to renew it. I had to find somewhere else to live.

Giving up that apartment was an emotional wrench, but it was also a big step toward shedding my past and leaving my mistakes behind. Rob moved to Paris to continue modeling, Stoover went back to New Jersey, and Nick Constantino decided to move to Los Angeles to try to pursue a career as an actor. I found an apartment in a brownstone on East Sixteenth Street and Third Avenue, near Union Square, and Big Pete moved in to sleep on my couch. I was finally beginning to feel a little better and thought I might even be open to dating a bit again.

I kept working, as usual. I went down to Atlanta to do a Macy's catalog job, when who should I run into but Todd Irvin, the first male model I'd ever seen in person, standing behind a velvet rope at the Manhattan nightclub Jocelyn took me to. Then I'd seen him in Paris, at the First Agency, when he walked in off the street in red leather motorcycle pants. Over the years that I'd been in the business, we'd bumped into each other in passing, but we hadn't had much direct contact. On this catalog shoot, we found ourselves stuck in a hot, stuffy photography studio for three days. There was nothing for us to do but talk and pass the time clowning around.

Todd reminded me that years earlier, when Sophie from the agency had found me my first apartment in France, they had arranged for him to stay there for a few days while I was out of the country working. "Man, I have never seen such a disorganized apartment," Todd said. "That place was a mess!"

"Hey, at least I let you stay there," I said. I reminded him of the first time I'd seen him in Paris, when all the agents were swarming around him, and I razzed him about his tight red leather pants.

"I would never wear red leather pants!" Todd protested. "They were green."

I told him the agency had initially brought me in to be the "next Todd," and I said, "I think I've far surpassed you, though."

"There's only one Todd Irvin!" he said.

"Yeah, the poor man's Bruce Hulse."

It turned out we had a lot more in common than I thought. Todd had been on the wrestling team at Duke University and graduated magna cum laude with a degree in psychology. He practiced tai chi and hoped to one day become a therapist. Like me, he started modeling immediately after college and had also done extensive work with Bruce Weber and appeared on the cover of *GQ*. Todd, a year younger than I, was another brother to me.

We had one other interest in common: women. We discovered that our encounters with models overlapped more than once. I shared the long story of my breakup with Nathalie and my rocky relationship with Sophie, who'd always had a crush on Todd. She had insisted that Todd was a god among male models. Ever since then I'd always referred to him as "Todd the God."

My motive for telling Todd about Sophie's attraction to him was twofold, I think. I knew he'd be flattered, but I was also hoping Todd might contact her the next time he was in Paris. Part of me was still captivated by Sophie and wanted to know what was going on in her life. More important, I wanted to know what she thought of me. In my skewed logic, I figured if Todd saw her, he might be able to discover her true feelings.

Todd called Sophie as soon as we returned to New York. They even went out on a date. The following day I called Todd and pressed him for information. "Did Sophie say anything about me?" I asked.

"Yeah. She said you're screwed up," Todd answered.

"That's it?"

"Pretty much."

It wasn't exactly what I wanted to hear. My plan had backfired. In retrospect, I don't know what I expected Sophie to say. Maybe I was hoping she'd confess she was still in love with me. Maybe I just needed to hear that there was no way back. Then, to my surprise, Todd and Sophie started really dating. He even took her to meet his parents in Canada. Initially he was infatuated, as I had been, but then he began to get bored, and after a while they split up. Todd the God and I remain good friends to this day. Sophie and I have never seen or spoken to each other since that time. Something about Todd's dating her released me from her spell.

For the first time in my adult life, I was single and on my own in New York. My depression still had a powerful hold on me, and I now realized that it probably always would in some form or other. Once my libido returned, it seemed that the only time I felt some respite from my depression was when I was making love to a woman. Sex filled me with joy and made me feel rooted. I became consumed with sexual desire again, that need to feed my hungry ghost, but I also knew I didn't want my life to amount to nothing more than a series of loveless sexual liaisons.

Even when I tried to behave myself, resolving not to seduce any of the models on my next assignment, I would arrive only to discover that the models wanted my scalp to add to those already dangling from their belts. Some even told me, "My girlfriends say you're great in bed, but I'd really like to find out for myself." I had neither the willpower nor the maturity to turn such offers down.

If I'd had an office job where I worked nine to five every day with the same people and came home each night to my wife, I would never have had these temptations, but my life wasn't like that. My life was all about sex—selling it, having it, and persuading others to want it, too. I knew that these mindless encounters wouldn't lead me to the place I was seeking, but they were hard to resist. In fact, I began to think that if having a little sex made me feel good, then sustained sex would make me feel even better.

I'd heard about a Chinese master who taught tantric sex as a vehicle for enlightenment, so I attended a lecture in Chinatown by the Taoist master Mantak Chia. He taught us that tantric sex involves a man using his stomach muscles and willpower to repeatedly delay orgasm, in order to conserve the energy that an orgasm would expend. The idea was to masturbate to the point of climax, then lock yourself down right before orgasm and breathe the energy up from your genital chakra up into your higher chakras. As that orgasmic energy ascended through the higher chakras, your consciousness would be elevated and would get closer to God.

I began practicing immediately. It was an intense experience. Just as Mantak Chia said, when I would feel myself about to reach orgasm, I would abruptly stop, lock down my body, and try to recycle the energy up into my higher centers. When I finally released, it was incredible. The tantric master also claimed that the spiritual charge would increase dramatically if I could practice tantra in the sun. Ultraviolet rays were supposed to impart solar energy to the body. I was eager to give it a try. While shooting a Diet Coke ad in St. Barthélemy in the Caribbean, I decided to put my lunch break to good use. I hiked to a secluded place on the beach, made sure I was directly in the sun, sat down in the sand, and started masturbating. I was only a few minutes into it when I heard a rustling in the bushes behind me. I immediately leaped up and pulled up my pants, terrified that someone from the crew had busted me jerking off on the beach.

"Hello?" I yelled into the woods. There was no answer. My heart was pounding. "Hello? Anyone there?" Then an old iguana strolled lazily out of the bushes and onto the beach. I just had to laugh, standing there with a hard-on. That was the last time I practiced tantra outside.

Once I'd mastered the solo technique, I began practicing tantric sex with women, for whom the practice was a win-win situation, because it also encouraged them to have multiple orgasms while I held back, allowing me to harness their energy, too. Whenever I was making love to a girl, I would inform her of the finer points of tantra, explaining how I was attempting to help both of us open up our higher centers. I quickly discovered that the explanation alone was a turn-on. If you do tantra with the right person, you can prolong the sexual experience for hours, because the act is a continuous stop-and-go. Every time I got close to orgasm, I would have the girl lock herself down on me until I became flaccid, but the act of doing so often induced an orgasm in her. Then we'd begin to make love again, with me holding back as long as I could, stopping and starting, to avoid orgasm. This practice of making love can get you high, as your body builds up a charge of energy that's aching to be released. Once I gave in, I had the most powerful sensations I'd ever experienced.

I was so enthusiastic about my new discovery that I urged everyone on set to try it. Naturally, there was a lot of interest, and people would gather around to listen. Later that night I'd get a knock on my bedroom door from a model wanting to experience it for herself. Tantra somehow helped me justify the random sex I was having. In my mind I was elevating my consciousness and helping my consenting sexual partners to elevate theirs. We were ascending the spiritual ranks together, and that made me feel like I was doing something positive.

My experiments with tantra were certainly interesting, and they definitely helped me continue on my spiritual path. What I discovered, though, was that tantra ideally should be shared with someone with whom you have an existing spiritual connection. Experimenting with some model I had just met on a shoot was fun, but it was limited. The spirituality I felt in my tantric adventures made me feel hopeful again, but I still lacked the one crucial element I was seeking: love.

12

Suicide Shifter

My career was at an all-time high. I was much in demand, working as often as I wanted and making more money than ever. When the Italian clothing company Corneliani asked me to fly to the Dolomites in Italy to shoot another ad campaign for them, I agreed immediately. I had been their main fashion model for ten years, thanks to their photographer, Fabrizio Gianni, and the work was always a pleasure. This time, to share that enjoyment, I took my father with me.

Dad was well traveled, of course, both

On location in Italy
for GQ . . .

as an international runner and in his navy career, so he wasn't quite
as excited about seeing the sights as my mom had been, but he loved
watching me work, and he was happy to spend time with his son.
I certainly loved having him around.

Fabrizio was a wonderful photographer to work with. I called
him "the Italian Bruce Weber." He always pronounced my name
"BROO-chay," and he told me I reminded him of his own father. He
was a sports fanatic, a scuba diver, a game hunter—in other words, a
real man's man. I once met another model on a Fabrizio shoot who
later became a good friend. Erick Jussen, known to everyone as "EJ,"
was such a natural storyteller that I thought of him as the models'
Pat Scullin; he reminded me of my Irish buddy who used to keep me

amused for hours on the lifeguard stand. EJ, Fabrizio, and I got along like a house on fire. We seemed to spend more time talking over long lunches or dinners than working, and my heart always soared when Fabrizio booked us for a shoot.

Doc X was living in Italy at that time, so Dad and I got to visit with him, too. Amazingly, X's newfound passion for photography, sparked by the camera I'd bought him years earlier, had taken him to the Philadelphia College of Art and then on to Milan. "Doc X is drawn to the fashion industry, B," he'd told me. "Doc X is going to become a fashion photographer." And that's exactly what he did. Within six months of arriving in Milan, he was working for *Max* magazine, Italian *Cosmopolitan,* and Italian *Bazaar.* He had his own apartment and was dating a gorgeous model. That winter I even persuaded X to

. . . and Corneliani.

come skiing with me in the Italian Alps, which was quite a feat, because he hated the cold and the snow as much as he loved the surf and the sand. X turned up wearing completely inappropriate clothing and clung to the ski lift the way a drowning cat might cling to a piece of driftwood in a river. "Doc X hates this!" he wailed. "Doc X needs to be lower down!" By the time we'd nursed him down the slopes, he had hypothermia and we had to hand-feed him hot soup in the restaurant, because his hands were shaking too much to hold the spoon. Sadly, his love affair with Italy was just as unsuccessful. The gorgeous model broke his heart, and a year later he was back in Avalon at the Doc X Mansion.

"Doc X hates the fashion world," he told me glumly. "It breaks people's hearts." So instead he started taking wonderful black-and-white photographs of the people and places he knew around Avalon, and he made some quirky documentaries. Best of all, he found his peace in surfing once again. For Doc X, Italy was an experiment that went horribly wrong.

As for me, I loved working with Italians because we spent more time eating than shooting. Chaotic as the Milan fashion shows were, on location there was a different atmosphere altogether. One of my next jobs was with the Italian photographer Aldo Fallai, for an English clothing chain called Next Directory. I spent a few weeks shooting the ad with Aldo in locations like Big Bear, Santa Monica, and Malibu, California. The best thing about Aldo was that he would shoot two rolls of film per shot and we would be done for the day, usually before noon. "Okay, now let's go to lunch," he would say. Somehow Aldo always got his shots with a few clicks of the camera, while other photographers struggled for hours, if not days, to get what they needed. I think his clients were always a little wary of his three-hour lunches until they saw the finished product.

The best thing about working in California was that I got to spend some time with Nick Constantino. He was still trying to make it as a Hollywood actor, but he was getting only a few commercials here and there. Although I felt for him, watching him struggle validated my decision not to give up everything and move to L.A. to chase a dream I'd never really had.

While I was in California shooting with Aldo, I received a call from my commercial agent in New York, who told me I'd been requested for a television commercial for Levi's. She wanted me to meet with the director, Roger Lyons, at the production offices in West Hollywood. I liked Roger right from the start. He asked me about my availability and my schedule, so I had a good feeling I would get the job. He sent me to see the casting agent, who was visibly shocked when I walked into the room. "I've been using a male model in a postcard as a guide for the type of model Levi's wants for this commercial," she told me, smiling. "The postcard was for Dim, the French underwear company." She picked up the postcard and showed it to me. "Recognize anyone?" *I* was the model on the postcard.

Once they realized I was that guy, I was booked. The deal called for me to be paid an initial fee of twenty-five thousand dollars for five days' shooting; then I would be paid additional royalties depending on how many different territories the ad was sold in. It was primarily intended for Europe, but the company had intentions of expanding it into Australia and possibly Japan if it was successful.

My co-star in the commercial would be the German supermodel Tatjana Patitz. I'd met Tatjana once before while she was doing a shoot for a friend of mine down in Jamaica. I also knew Tatjana's boyfriend, Rodney, from a Fabrizio Gianni job in Spain. A few days before I was due to start filming the Levi's commercial, I received a call from Rodney, whom I hadn't spoken to since the Spanish job.

I wasn't even sure how he got my number. He told me he'd also been up for the Levi's spot. Although we talked mostly about the casting, I had the feeling he was sizing me up, trying to get a read on my intentions toward Tatjana during the shoot. I understood Rodney's concern, but I had no intention of doing anything with Tatjana.

On the morning of the shoot, a car picked me up from Nick's apartment in West Hollywood and drove me out to the location, in the middle of the Mojave Desert. The production crew had already spent a week out there constructing an incredible set, creating an entire town in that wasteland. There was so much equipment and so many production trucks around, I felt as if I were arriving on the set of a big-budget movie.

Roger Lyons explained his vision for the commercial. For part of the shoot, I was going to be riding on an old 1947 Harley-Davidson "Shovelhead." The bike had a "suicide shifter," so called because you had to change gears by taking one hand off the handlebars to manipulate the gearshift stick. Roger wanted every detail to be authentic.

Roger told me, "You have that Marlon Brando energy, Bruce, and I need you to bring that energy to this commercial. You aren't shooting until the second day, so I want you to take the bike and get comfortable on it. I want it to be an extension of your character." So for the first day and a half, all I did was cruise around the desert on the Harley. Whenever I got bored, I'd practice my aikido sword work, with the wooden bokken I traveled with, on a nearby cactus, which always elicited a few stares from bemused crew members.

Like Doc X, I'd started to get interested in photography, and I always traveled with my own camera. I'd worked with so many talented photographers, like Weber and Ritts, who'd inspired me to see things in a new way, that now, when I looked through a lens, a different world emerged. I especially loved taking photos of landscapes, and sometimes I took behind-the-scenes shots of the other models working.

Tatjana was a lovely girl, and we hit it off right away. When she wasn't working, she'd jump onto the back of my Harley and we'd head off to the high desert so I could take pictures of Joshua trees, lizards, or barrel cacti. There was little conversation between us. She'd just get on the back of the bike, wrap her arms and legs around me, and hold on tight. At the end of her first day of shooting, Tatjana asked me if I wanted to have dinner with her. I knew that the crew was meeting at an old Mexican restaurant later, so I said, "Yeah, sure. I'll see you at the restaurant, right?"

"No, I mean just you and me," she said. "I want to get to know you better, Bruce."

Despite my recent call from Rodney, I figured what the hell. I was out in the middle of the desert with a beautiful girl who was asking me to dinner. It would have been rude to turn her down.

Tatjana showed up to dinner wearing a free-flowing white dress. Her curly blond hair was still wet from her shower. She looked absolutely gorgeous. As soon as we sat down at a table, she said, "Let's drink tequila."

When a supermodel wants to drink tequila with you, you don't ask questions—you drink tequila. And we weren't casually sipping margaritas; we were firing down shots of Jose Cuervo. I was trying to monitor myself so I didn't get too hammered, but it was no use. Everything was happening so quickly. Halfway through dinner I had already fallen under Tatjana's spell. I couldn't stop staring across the table into her piercing green eyes.

After our meal Tatjana invited me to her room. Despite all my good intentions, I accepted. Once inside, she locked the door and told me to sit on the bed. She then lit an army of small white votive

candles. When she had finished, she stood before me and undressed slowly, her naked body illuminated by the flickering light. We made love for hours.

From that moment on, she and I were immersed in an intense on-set romance. It felt as if we were mentally and physically locked in to each other. We spent every night of the shoot together, having deep conversations about our lives and dreams. She told me she was born in Hamburg, Germany, but had grown up in Sweden. She'd worked as a model in Paris from the age of seventeen and had recently moved to California to pursue acting.

Tatjana came across as deeply spiritual, but, like all spiritual seekers, she'd made her mistakes along the way. She told me a story about going to see a "healer" who promised to help her overcome her attachment to money. To do this, the old woman said Tatjana had to set fire to ten thousand dollars in cash and watch it burn to ashes. I didn't say anything to Tatjana at the time, but I'd heard of similar scams from other friends in the business. The healer would switch the ten thousand dollars with fake money and set the fake money alight while pocketing the real cash.

Our love affair made working together so easy. When the cameras rolled, the chemistry between us really worked. The story line for the commercial had me walking down some stairs in an old house in my underwear, hot, sticky, and drenched in sweat. Tatjana was sitting in the living room looking unbelievably sexy, with an old man and woman who were supposed to be her aging parents. They would all stare at me as I slowly made my way across the room, opened the old refrigerator, and pulled out my Levi's. I slipped them on, buttoned them up, and traded a seductive glance with Tatjana before heading through the door, jumping on my Harley, and disappearing off into the desert.

With Tatjana for Levi's "Mannish Boy" commercial in the Mojave Desert.

Roger did an incredible job, and when the commercial was cut, it looked amazing. Thanks to him and the casting agent, I was suddenly the new face of Levi's jeans. The producers were delighted. After we wrapped, Roger asked me, "How old did you say you were, Bruce?"

"I didn't say, but I'm thirty-six," I replied.

"Thirty-six? Shit, man, we thought you were in your twenties!" He laughed. "You're too old to be the Levi's guy, but don't worry, I won't tell anyone!"

It was the first time that anyone had said anything about the possibility that my age might be a professional liability. Although I looked much younger than I was and still photographed very well, when casting agents heard how old I was, there was a growing sense that I might be too old for some bookings. Although I'd only ever regarded modeling as a temporary means to an end, I now realized how much a part of my life it had become and how much I'd miss it if it was suddenly taken away.

After the wrap party, Tatjana came to see me. She said she felt confused. "I've fallen for you, Bruce, but I don't know what to do about Rodney," she said. "I thought I was in love with him."

At that point I crossed a boundary and did something I had never done to another male model before, and I've never done it since then, either: I ratted Rodney out. During the Spanish shoot, Rodney had told me about another model he'd had amazing sex with, so I told Tatjana. I felt guilty for stooping to such a level, but I was crazy about Tatjana and would have done anything to keep her.

Back in Los Angeles, Tatjana wasted no time in kicking Rodney out of her Malibu beach house. Afterward she came over to Nick's apartment, where we cooked up a crazy plan to run away together for a six-month vacation. I was going to fly to New York for my truck and then drive back out to L.A. to pick her up before heading down to Mexico. We figured we would live on the beach or find a yoga retreat. When we came back, we'd look for a house where we would live together forever. It was the perfect plan.

I flew to New York to prepare for the trip, and Tatjana flew off to do one last job before we could leave. It was a music video with a guy named Nick Kamen, a male model and musician who was a big pop sensation in England. She told me it wouldn't take longer than a week and that we'd keep in constant contact. I didn't hear a word from her for the entire week. I repeatedly tried the number at her hotel and left messages with the concierge. Something was obviously wrong. I finally tracked her down by phone when she returned to L.A.

"What's going on?" I asked. "I've been trying to reach you. Didn't you get my messages?"

She spoke so softly on the other end of the line that I had to strain to hear her. "I don't know about this trip anymore, Bruce."

Once again I couldn't believe what some woman was telling me. I'd canceled all my engagements and had spent the week planning my future with her, and now she was having second thoughts? I flew back out to Los Angeles the next day and drove to Nick's apartment. He didn't seem surprised to see me, and he started laughing when I told him about Tatjana. His sage comment: "Freaking Hulse, man. Running around with your head cut off."

I met Tatjana for coffee in West Hollywood. "I'm so confused," she told me, her eyes filling with tears. "I think I'm in love with Nick Kamen." I couldn't say I was surprised, but the blow still hurt. I was so eager to find "the one" that I kept choosing the *wrong* one.

The Levi's commercial hit Europe in the summer of 1988 and became an international sensation. I began fielding calls from my agents across the globe. The lucrative German catalog market wanted to book me for the next three months. Levi's flew me to England for a series of morning television interviews about the commercial and paid me twenty thousand dollars to fly to Dublin for the grand opening of their new store. I arrived in a limousine that was greeted by a mob of several hundred screaming teenage girls. I couldn't believe they all knew my name. "Bruce! Bruce! Over here, Bruce! We love you, Bruce!" I felt like a rock star. I even had two bodyguards. I have to confess that my sudden fame was unnerving. Those girls looked crazy! I sat at a table inside the store and signed autographs all day. I had never experienced fandom like that before, and for the first time I saw how creepy it was to be the focus of such intense adulation. Those hundreds of girls thought they knew me just because they'd seen my image on their TV screen.

Levi's had used the Muddy Waters song "Mannish Boy" in the commercial, and when the ad became a huge success, his record company put out a 45 record and used my image on the cover. The single ended up climbing to the top ten in the English music charts. I was given enough Levi's jeans, T-shirts, and jackets for a lifetime from that job, though I gave most of the clothing away. The commercial increased my profile within the industry considerably and brought me a good deal of work over the next few years. Everyone wanted "the Levi's guy." In all, I probably made more than a hundred and fifty thousand dollars for five days' work and a few extra promotional appearances. It was a whirlwind ride and the most money I ever made in a single year of working as a model. And my heart got bruised again along the way, too. What else was new?

Money meant freedom, and now that I was more flush with cash than I had ever been, I decided to get away from the frantic pace and fly down to Barbados for some much-needed rest and relaxation.

I took Tommy Preston with me, and New Zealander Richard Keogh, a hair and makeup artist I'd met on that New Mexico set with Lisa Marie, someone who shared my passion for surfing and martial arts.

We rented a little beach house and spent the days meditating, practicing yoga, and surfing. Our calming environment also gave us an opportunity to remove ourselves from the chaos of our normal lives and have deep conversations about love, death, and the future. We often spoke about finding the ultimate "shaman" woman, as we called her, a woman who is capable of living in both the physical and spiritual worlds. Such a creature understands and embodies life, death, sex, and love. You can take her rock-climbing or surfing because she has no fear. She can tell a dirty joke, but she's also intelligent and sophisticated. She has tremendous compassion and deep knowledge of spirituality. We knew that the shaman woman might have been an impossible ideal, a perfect woman who could not exist in the real world, but we all agreed that we'd never stop seeking her. However hard she might be to find, she was, I knew, the only girl I could ultimately settle down with.

One night the three of us were driving back from surfing on the northern part of the island when a black dog ran out in front of our car. There was nothing we could do to avoid hitting him. The dog was badly injured, but we watched in the light of our headlights as he picked himself up and limped off into the woods. We all jumped out and ran after him, but he was gone.

"We have to find that dog and save him," Tommy said.

Richard walked to the edge of the trees. "Yeah," he said, "we should follow him and see if he's really okay."

I looked around. This wasn't the best neighborhood to be in at night. The homes were run-down, and we'd seen some shady characters wandering around the street. From my previous trips to the island, I knew there were some dangerous areas in Barbados that you didn't want to find yourself in, especially after dark, and this place was definitely one of them. I was genuinely afraid of being knifed or robbed. My first impulse was to help save an injured animal, but I let my fear overrule my compassion. I convinced Tommy and Richard it was a bad idea to look for the dog. I said the dog could be rabid, or that he'd probably gone back to his owner. Reluctantly, they got back into the car.

The following morning we decided to surf at South Point. Early in the day, the breaks weren't great, but by noon they had picked up. I was paddling hard, trying to catch a wave, when I felt a sudden overwhelming pain in my foot. My first thought? *Shark!*

At that moment an image flashed through my mind of the black dog we'd hit the previous night. *We should have saved him,* I thought through the haze of pain. Then a massive red and purple jellyfish surfaced next to me. I paddled frantically away from the jellyfish, toward shore. If I hadn't been a strong swimmer, I might not have made it. The pain was excruciating as I pulled myself from the water, dropped my surfboard, and collapsed on the beach. I was going into shock, and I started convulsing. Tommy and Richard ran over to see what was wrong.

"I'm hurt bad!" I cried through chattering teeth. "Get help!"

Richard knelt down and grabbed my shoulders to stop me from writhing around in the sand. "Aw, mate, it's a jellyfish sting!" he said in his New Zealand twang. "We just have to piss on it." In a surreal sequence that I thought must be some sort of weird hallucination, Tommy and Richard whipped out their dicks and started peeing on my foot. Unfortunately, their urine only intensified the pain. My heart was by now pounding uncontrollably, and my convulsions grew even more severe.

"Get me to the hospital!" I was hyperventilating and genuinely thought I might die. They carried me to the car and were able to find a local clinic. I was not normally the type of person who relied on pharmaceuticals, but on this occasion I told the doctor, "Shoot me up with whatever you've got." He didn't disappoint. He injected me with adrenaline, painkillers, and cortisone. I spent the next ten hours rocking back and forth in agony. The only way I endured was to keep checking my watch and try to get through ten minutes at a time. It was by far the worst physical torment I have experienced in my entire life.

Through the waves of nauseating pain, the black dog kept finding his way into my thoughts. The night before, I had walked away from something I shouldn't have. In my drug-addled, pain-crazed state, I became convinced that there was some type of connection between the two events.

I had to stay in the hospital overnight, but I limped out the next morning. When we returned to the other side of the island, I told a few of the local surfers what had happened. "Oh, man, you got hit by the purple monster!" one said, shaking his head. "You can die from that." That explained why I'd felt so close to checking out.

After I recovered, I thought a lot about what had happened. There was an important lesson here for me to learn about karma, the cause-and-effect law that governs the universe. If I put negative energy out into the world, negative energy comes right back. Choosing to ignore the injured dog was selfish. Telling Tatjana about Rodney was selfish, too. From that point forward, I would try to be more mindful of the ethical implications of my behavior. Most of all I wanted to tune in and listen to what my instincts were telling me, instead of ignoring the obvious.

Whether I would follow through on these resolutions was another question.

13

The Good, the Bad, and the Beautiful

Not all my bookings were as successful or as lucrative as the Levi's commercial. Far from it. Many were poorly paid and tedious beyond belief, requiring me to work with some of the most temperamental people I've ever had the misfortune of meeting.

Not that I was complaining. As Donald Sterzin would say, I wasn't saving lives, I was only modeling clothes, for God's sake. What did I expect? I didn't have to possess any exceptional talent; the work mostly required me just to show up and do as I was told. Sure, I had to have a certain "look."

Then the designers had to determine whether my look was what they wanted for that year's clothing lines. The clothes changed from season to season, and so did the models. The only real continuity came from catalog work for companies such as Macy's, Eddie Bauer, Bloomingdale's, or J. Crew. Models with a classic, mainstream look could get five to ten years' work modeling catalogs, and many did.

I was fortunate enough to bear a subtle resemblance to a few popular actors. My seeming vaguely familiar not only helped people identify with me, it also helped advertisers because they got the "look" of Warren Beatty or Paul Newman without having to pay their enormous fees. I began to regard myself as similar to a used-car salesman. It was my job to sell my appearance to the consumer over and over again. I had to perfect different ways of making myself appear new and interesting with every click of the camera, which is a little more difficult for a man than for a woman. I couldn't add dramatic makeup or wear outrageous clothing or sophisticated hairstyles to enhance my modeling performance, as many of the women could. My hair was either short or long; that was about it. Sometimes I received a lot of direction from the photographer, and other times I had to rely solely on my instincts.

Over the years I have experienced just about every type of situation on set and on location for shoots, runway shows, and catalog work. There's one rule that usually prevails: The bigger the budget, the nicer the crew and executives are; the lower the budget, the more ruthless and unreasonable the clients and photographers are. Booked for a knock-down price themselves, they then try to squeeze everything they can out of you for as little money as possible, attempting to negotiate a lower day rate or pressuring you to agree to overtime without compensation.

Another golden rule on any set was this: Don't hit on the model

*"Marlboro Clothing"
in Monument Valley,
Utah.*

whom the photographer has his eye on. Most of the straight photographers made it clear that if you ever intended working with
them again, you had to give them first pick. If I couldn't figure out
which girl he was going after, the likelihood was that he was coming
after me. I quickly developed a finely tuned ability to discern which
model the photographer was zeroing in on within the first few hours
of a shoot. Many photographers told me that one of the reasons they
loved working with me was that I was one of the few male models
who never got in their way.

There was one photographer I worked with in Paris at the
height of my career who was a real mean son of a bitch. He was always shouting at his assistants and complaining about everything.
He didn't treat anyone with respect. The epitome of a wicked queen,
he screamed, ranted, and bitched all the time. Although I never let
him get under my skin, I thought the way he treated people was des-
picable. I never told him how I felt because he was quite famous and

offered me a lot of work over the years. My way of handling him was to show him constant kindness and unconditional love, a trick I'd picked up on the friendless construction sites of Philadelphia. Keep smiling, keep taking the constant insults with grace and tranquillity, and eventually they'll direct their venom at someone else. Thankfully, I had to tolerate guys like him for only a few days at a time, and

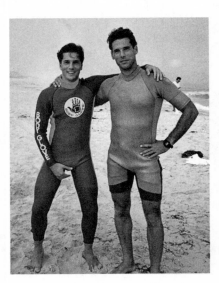

Taking a lunch-hour surf break with Jens-Peter (the face of Armani fragrance) on a Next Directory shoot in the Hamptons.

then I could walk away. I felt sorry for the people who worked with him every day.

Crew members could be just as tricky to deal with. The good stylists just dressed you in the clothes and then trusted you to do your job as a model. The others incessantly pinned and tugged at your clothing for no apparent reason, constantly micromanaging the fit. If the pants were too tight, they'd cut them up the back and tape them together. If the belts were too short, they'd slice and extend them with duct tape to give the appearance of a perfect fit. It didn't help that different clients expected different looks. The German catalogs wanted the clothing to be as tight as possible. Companies like J. Crew or the Gap were more interested in a relaxed, casual look. Photographers on those shoots actually insisted that wrinkles be visible, as if I'd just gotten up from a chair or had been wearing the clothes all day.

Less experienced hair and makeup people also prodded and

poked you between every click of the camera. Often this was their way of justifying their fees. Some makeup artists caked the stuff on so thick that I ended up looking like a vampire in an old horror movie. Eventually I came up with the lie that I was allergic to foundation, because I hated the way they made me look. After that, my skin was usually allowed to remain au naturel.

Although the prima donnas in a crew often tested me, I realized they were probably just trying to do their jobs. I tried to call on my Buddhist and aikido studies to help me deflect their negative energy without resorting to anger. For the most part, that worked, but there were a couple of times when it didn't. Once I was shooting an ad in Paris with an art director I couldn't stand, who was close to pushing me beyond my patience threshold. I was wearing a three-thousand-dollar suit, and we were set up in front of the Louvre. It had been an exceptionally long day, and everyone on set was worn out. We were all just trying to finish the job when a homeless drunk wandered up asking for spare change. The art director shooed him away brusquely, using a dismissive tone. If it had been me, I'd have given the guy a quick smile, handed him ten francs, and sent him on his way. Something about how the art director spoke to the bum really set the guy off. In the blink of an eye, the bum jumped on the art director and had him pinned up against the wall of the museum.

Everyone backed away, reluctant to intervene, and, to be honest, it wouldn't have displeased me terribly if the hobo had choked the art director to death in front of us all. But I couldn't just stand there and do nothing, so I approached slowly, using a soothing tone of voice, trying to assure the drunk that everything was fine. My father had taught me never to look a mad dog in the eye, so I kept my head down. All of a sudden, though, the drunk turned like a raging bull and focused all his anger on me. Noticing an empty wine bottle on the ground, he picked it up, cracked its neck on the sidewalk, and came straight for me, clearly intending me harm.

I probably could have dropped him on the spot with a couple of martial-arts blows, but I wasn't going to get into a fight with an angry drunk. Instead I ran toward him, screaming at him as if I were crazier than he was. While the rest of the crew watched in amazement, I yelled at him in an incoherent mix of French and English as he backed away, startled, and dropped the bottle, which shattered on the sidewalk. Out of the corner of my eye, I saw a policeman running toward us carrying a baton and a canister of tear gas. I backed off just as he began to spray it. More police arrived, and they dragged the bum away, muttering how much they hated the homeless.

On another shoot I had been flown to Italy to for a big ad campaign. The shoot took place in a photographer's studio, where the client had built an entire desert scene that looked amazing. The bad news, though, was that the photographer was extremely controlling and impossible to work with. He ordered me around like an underling. I've always tried to give photographers what they ask for, but there was no pleasing this guy. He kept telling me to "act more heroic" and to "give him better shape." I tried to interpret his directions, but there was nothing I could do to make him happy. "No! That's not it! That is *not* what I am looking for!" He'd walk over and demonstrate what he wanted, asking me to copy what he was doing. When I couldn't seem to do it, he'd say, "What is the matter with you?"

At his bidding I posed for countless photos in positions that made me look extremely effeminate. I wasn't afraid to go there. After my "gay" shoot with Nick, I knew I could play it soft and subtle as easily as I could play the strong athlete. No matter how hard I tried, though, he was still dissatisfied. I was more accustomed to working with photographers who not only loved my style but encouraged it.

I had never been demeaned or talked down to like this on a shoot. I didn't know how to handle his anger. I tried to stay positive and professional, hoping we'd connect somehow, but we never did that day.

The following morning I showed up on set determined to make the shoot a success. However, the photographer picked up right where we had left off, saying things like "No, no, no. That's terrible. Why can't you get it?" To make matters worse, I'd had a few drinks the previous night and hadn't meditated before coming to work, so I didn't have a clear head. It didn't take long for me to reach my tolerance threshold. I began to think that I really wasn't getting paid enough money to put up with this guy's shit for another day.

Finally, when I couldn't take one more minute of his disrespect, my rage just erupted out of me. I jumped up from my chair and yelled, "Listen!" to the photographer and his equally demanding assistants. "Hear this, all you assholes!" Pointing right at the photographer, I said, "Fuck you, you weasel!" In front of his entire crew, I berated him for his complete lack of professionalism and integrity. I told him I'd worked with some of the best photographers in the world, and it was clear to me he had no idea what he was doing. It was one of the few times in my career where I lost it—but boy, in that situation did it feel good. I told him that he didn't treat me with any respect and that I'd had enough; I was leaving. I walked out the door.

"Bruce, Bruce, come back!" I could hear the photographer calling piteously after me as I walked away. "What's the matter?"

By the time I got to my hotel, my phone was ringing off the hook. It was my agent, begging me to go back to the studio. He said the photographer was offering to double my fee if I returned to the set. I told my agent they could quadruple my money, but there was no way I was going back.

A few years later, I was on a job in Santa Barbara and introduced myself to the other male model, who smiled wryly and said he already knew who I was. "I was given my first big break in Italy the day you walked off that desert-scene set," he told me. "I'd actually been thinking about quitting the business when I got an emergency phone call to fill in for you, so thanks." My tantrum had changed the course of his career. He was so grateful for his big break that he didn't notice or care how crazy the photographer was. It was nice to know that someone else had been able to benefit from my own negative situation.

The most difficult jobs I had to endure were undoubtedly the German catalog shoots. Although the jobs paid me two to three thousand dollars a day, the work was mind-numbing. I was required to be nothing more than a breathing mannequin.

From the moment a shoot began, the rigors of the strict German regimen would begin. For one shoot I was five minutes late, and when I walked in, the red-faced client cornered me in a rage. "Where were you? This is not acceptable!" He was screaming and spitting as he spoke. Technically speaking, he was right, because my job was to be on time. There's no excuse for being late to a shoot; it's unprofessional and irresponsible. I always took every job seriously and was known for being a true professional. Having gotten off to a bad start, I was determined to make my best effort for the rest of the shoot. Ironically, I spent the next few hours in the van while the photographer figured out the lighting.

German catalog work usually entailed posing for shot after shot with only a few people on set speaking English or providing any helpful direction. Nobody communicated with me other than to tug at my clothes or change my position. I was essentially a robot obeying their commands. "Look left! Look right! Smile! Smile with no teeth!" It was boring, repetitive work. I wasn't even excited about the clothes,

On a German cigarette job in Arizona with Ellen von Unwerth.

because they were usually cheap and generic. I had no interest in seeing how the photographs came out or viewing the final catalog.

For another German catalog job, I flew to Miami and was driven out to a lake in the smallest van I'd ever seen. It turned out to be their only production vehicle and served a variety of purposes, including makeup area, dressing room, cafeteria, and refuge from the intense heat. The photographer had me standing out in the blazing Florida sun for half the day, and then he flew off the handle at me whenever I began to sweat. My only goal was to make the time pass as quickly as possible. I tried to pose so the clothes wouldn't wrinkle; otherwise the stylist would get mad at me and make me change outfits, so we'd have to start all over again. If there was another male model, then I would at least have a break while it was his turn. If I was working solo, there was no break at all. I'd spend my day moving back and forth between the wardrobe trailer and the set, going through as many as thirty changes a day. No matter how hard I worked to help them get the shots they needed, they were always moaning and groaning about some minor detail. It seemed you could never satisfy them.

On another German catalog shoot, I was flown to the factory in Frankfurt where they manufactured their clothes. At some point in the day, I was doing halves, which is when they photograph only your body, not your face. I was standing in the freezing-cold factory wearing just underwear from the waist down. At one point the German stylist walked up to me, shoved his hand down the front of my briefs, and angrily shouted "Not that side!" He yanked my dick over and said, "The other side!"

Even through such humiliations, I knew that I was lucky to be a working model. And for each horrible day of being treated like a piece of meat, there were far more days that were a blast, days that provided memories I would relive for the rest of my life. For me the enjoyment of modeling didn't come from the products or the clothes but from the people I met and the locations I worked in. For instance, I once did a Camel Clothing shoot on the Black River in Jamaica. Our entire crew followed a local guide through the jungle to a waterfall tumbling from a cliff forty or fifty feet above us. I thought back to my time at the abandoned quarry where we'd go after working all day on the trash truck with my buddies Charlie and Doc Dougherty. I told the photographer I could dive off the ledge if he wanted me to. He was really excited about getting the shot and asked our guide to lead me up to the highest point.

The guide was like Tommy Preston, shoeless and as surefooted as a mountain goat. The rocks were covered in moss and extremely slippery, so I was much more cautious and took my time. When we got to the top, the guide casually walked to the edge of the cliff and, without even a moment's hesitation, dived off. I watched him fall through the air and hit the water far below with a big splash. Once you were up on the ledge, it seemed much higher than it had looked from down below. The guide quickly bobbed to the surface and waved up at me. "Okay, mon, your turn!" he yelled.

I inched out to the edge of the cliff and steadied myself. From that elevation the view of the waterfall and the jungle was breathtaking. Adrenaline pulsed through my body, and I felt incredibly alive. The guide had made it, so I knew that the water was deep enough and that there were no jagged rocks lying in wait under the surface—or so I hoped. I crouched, took a deep breath, arced out from the ledge, and speared down into the water below. Hitting that water was the most amazing feeling, just as invigorating as leaping into the quarry had been when I was a kid. After the first jump, the guide and I found a few less dangerous ledges to dive from. The photographer took some fantastic shots, so he was delighted.

When the shoot wrapped, we stopped at a tiny shack on the side of the road where we all drank cold beer and listened to Bob Marley blasting out of the proprietor's sound system. It began to rain, and the Jamaican jungle looked amazing, a shimmering green cascade of bejeweled foliage. My skin still tingled from the water, and my head was light from the adrenaline and the beer; I felt totally immersed in nature and at peace. I noticed how good I felt, and I reminded myself of just how sweet life could be.

Moments like that one were reason enough to put up with all the bullshit and materialism and hedonism of this crazy industry I'd somehow ended up in. Sure, I liked making the money, but once I was okay financially, that wasn't what drove me. Of course I loved

Camel Clothing shoot on the Black River in Jamaica.

sleeping with all those beautiful women—who wouldn't? Setting me loose with a supermodel was like giving a box of matches to a pyromaniac. But it was those perfect oases of calm and serenity in faraway places I'd otherwise never get to see that really made it all worthwhile.

Another job that stood out in my mind was one where I was paid for literally doing nothing. This shoot was with photographer John Stember, for that Diet Coke shoot down in St. Barthélemy.

They flew ten of us to a gorgeous hotel on the east coast of the island, but the moment we landed, it started raining. A monsoon came in and hammered the island for the entire week we were there. We had no choice but to hang out at the bar, where we ran up the client's bill drinking cocktails. At night I was fortunate enough to hook up with an amazing Swedish model, and we'd lie in bed listening to the rain on the roof. At the end of the week, the weather still wasn't clearing, so we were all paid our full rates and flown home. Two weeks later I received a call asking me to go back and do it all over again. I could hardly believe my luck. In the end I made double the money, got to visit beautiful St. Bart's a second time, and made love to the Swedish model all over again. (This was the trip where the iguana caught me with my pants down!)

The photographer Stan Shaffer set me up with my favorite modeling job of my entire career. I'd done some good American catalog shoots with Stan, and I loved working with him; we'd always end up playing pool together, and he even bought me my own pool cue as a gift. Stan called one day and told me he was shooting a catalog for a new client, the Limited, a large clothing company based in Ohio. The Limited had recently purchased a small underwear company in San Francisco called Victoria's Secret. Their intention was to create a soap-opera ad concept to market their lingerie through catalogs. Stan told me I would be the only male model used in the campaign, which would consist primarily of bedroom scenes showing me with various lingerie models. I couldn't agree fast enough.

I practically sprinted over to Stan's studio, where he already had a bedroom set up to do the shoot. I sat off to the side for most of the first day, watching Stan photograph the most beautiful lingerie models I'd ever seen. There were gorgeous women everywhere, and since I was the only guy, the girls always made me the center of attention.

To amuse themselves they would tease me and try to get me hard by grinding their bodies against me during shooting. It was the start of a beautiful relationship between Victoria's Secret and me.

Over the next few years on Victoria's Secret shoots, I was fortunate enough to work with some of the world's top supermodels, including Lynette Walden, who became a successful actress; Jill Goodacre, who later married Harry Connick Jr.; and Frederique van der Wal, a sassy Dutch girl who also had an acting career. Occasionally Stan would insert me into a few shots here and there, but I was really nothing more than an accessory. The bras and underwear got more camera time than I did. I didn't care. I was never happier to be in the background than when I was doing a shoot for Victoria's Secret.

For an upcoming Victoria's Secret shoot in Barbados, I managed to convince the executives they should hire my buddy Big Pete as a bodyguard. Because I had been to the island before, I knew there were some dangerous spots, and Big Pete would keep everyone safe. Big Pete thought he'd died and gone to heaven when I gave him the news.

In Palm Beach, I did a Victoria's Secret shoot with a gorgeous young model who had been offered a full sports scholarship but had decided to pursue modeling instead. On the first day of shooting, I was in my usual position, sitting backstage watching the girls try on lingerie, when I noticed her looking over at me with a smirk on her face. After the other models had left and a few executives from Victoria's Secret went into the next room with Stan to discuss the wardrobe changes, she finally wandered over.

"You know how high-school girls keep pictures of guys on their lockers?" she said. "All the pictures in my locker were of you, Bruce. I can't believe I finally got to meet you in person."

Obviously I was flattered. This beautiful woman was telling me she'd had a crush on me since high school, and the idea really turned me on. There was an immediate sexual spark between us. Even though the client was in the next room, I pulled her into my arms and kissed her. Things rapidly got out of hand between us, and she ended up giving me an unforgettable blow job right there in the middle of the floor. Man, I loved my work!

The company ended up loving Stan's work on their catalog, and they left it largely up to him to pick the models. For the first three years, I was the only male model featured in the Victoria's Secret catalog. I later found out that for the first year at least I was paid more than the female models—a highly unusual discrepancy in the fashion industry, where the women usually make far more than the men. My agency had somehow managed to negotiate a great day rate for me. It didn't get much better than that for a male model. My buddies couldn't understand how I'd gotten so lucky. "Aren't they tired of you yet, Hulse?" Nick would ask. "I'm available. Tell them to call my agent." It was definitely an enviable gig.

About a year after one of the Victoria's Secret shoots, I bumped into a model I hadn't seen since we'd worked together on one of the catalogs. She was a really lovely girl, and we'd ended up in bed, enjoying each other enormously. This time, though, it was different. "There's something you should know, Bruce," she told me. "I got pregnant after the last time I saw you."

I was stunned. I didn't know how to react. Was it possible I had a child I didn't know about?

"Don't worry," she said, smiling sadly. "I got rid of it."

I was even more upset that she'd never told me. "If only I'd known, I could have done something, anything, to help out," I told her, taking her in my arms and holding her tight.

"It's okay," she said, pulling away. "It wasn't the right time for me to have a baby. I was busy modeling. I still am. Pregnancy just isn't part of the picture."

I kissed her good-bye and wished her well. Inside, I was hugely relieved. I didn't want to have a kid just because I'd had casual sex with someone. I don't think it's a good idea to have children out of wedlock, so if she had consulted with me, I would have agreed with her decision to have the abortion. Still, I felt responsible. If I had known, at least I would have been able to pay for the procedure and support her throughout what must have been a difficult process.

I wasn't happy about the idea of a human life being terminated, but I had never been given a choice in the matter. I began to wonder if any other women I'd slept with had faced the same predicament and hadn't told me. It was possible. For all I knew, I might have even had a child out there somewhere.

I always had unprotected sex. It seems ridiculous to say so now, but the truth is that most of the straight models did at that time. I never once thought about using protection. Sex for me was passionate, spontaneous. There wasn't time for condoms or questions about contraception. If the women were willing and as spontaneous as I was, I just assumed they were on the pill. Even after the AIDS epidemic began—an epidemic that hit the fashion industry particularly hard—I never thought about protecting myself. Like most straight people at that time, I thought it was a "gay" disease.

Even after I saw so many friends—photographers, models, hairstylists, and makeup artists—begin to die of the disease, I still thought I was untouchable. It was agonizing to watch the bodies of those I loved and cared for deteriorate, men like Donald Sterzin, whom Bruce Weber cared for at the end of his life. Or a wonderful model named Peter Keating who'd been one of the Paris "brotherhood," those models who were so helpful to me when I was first starting out there. Or a neighbor of mine who was a photographer–turned–landscape designer and who was one of the kindest people I'd ever met. I knew people who shied away from the lesions and the skeletal frames of the sick and dying; I always tried to be fully present.

Buddhists say that death is our greatest teacher, because it teaches us how precious life is. When I was still recovering from my depression after losing Nathalie and Sophie, I read an amazing book called *Who Dies? An Investigation of Conscious Living and Conscious Dying*, by Stephen Levine. In it Levine said that to prepare yourself for the immensity of death, you have to participate fully in life and ready yourself for whatever may come next. His words so moved me that I signed up for his seminar at Columbia University. The seminar involved dancing and walking in circles with thirty or so terminally ill people, all in various stages of their final days, to the strains of beautiful classical music. Then, in the very gym where I had once played basketball, with my father cheering loudly from the stands, we sat on the floor and gazed at each other, really examining one another's faces. For me it was a wonderful exercise in looking beyond the mottled skin or the lesions, the loss of hair or the yellowing eyes, until I could finally see the beautiful person beneath the shell.

Those remarkable classes brought out such mixed emotions in me. Here I was, six feet three inches tall, a hunk of virile male health in my prime, a fashion model, just back from a Victoria's Secret shoot in the Caribbean, where I had made love to a woman who was brimming with health and vitality. Yet the vulnerable young gay man, with his sunken eyes, or the cadaverous old woman opposite me, with her wispy white hair and transparent skin, suddenly seemed to be the most achingly beautiful people I had ever seen in my life. I couldn't stop the tears from streaming down my face.

14

Skin Deep

One of my favorite books is titled *After the Ecstasy, the Laundry,* by Jack Kornfield. The title alone appealed to me. After we experience the ecstasy of insight or enlightenment, the problems of everyday life still await us. Enlightenment isn't worth much if it can't help us live our normal lives and face our recurring challenges.

My greatest recurring challenge was undoubtedly my quest for love. I was always falling for the amazing women I met— Ginger, Nathalie, Andie, Paulina, Sophie, Tatjana—some of whom I thought I could spend the rest of my life with. But every time, either I would destroy what I had found by my own selfish actions or the woman would turn out not to be the "shaman woman" I had imagined her to be when I was infatuated. The older I got, the more I began to think that perhaps what I was seeking was unattainable. Still, the hopeless romantic in me couldn't give up the search.

Carey Lowell was a model I had known for some time because she was married to the photographer John Stember, the one who'd had me kissing my cousin Lisa Marie in that western shoot. Carey was a lovely girl, and we'd always gotten along really well. She was interested in meditation, and we talked a lot about our shared spiritual beliefs. I always thought John was a lucky man. Years later, after she'd split up with him, I bumped into Carey on the streets of New York. It was really good to see her again. She asked what I was doing, and when I told her I was on my way to an aikido class, she asked if she could come along and watch.

Carey was so taken with what she saw that she asked if she could join the class. She bought a uniform and came to a class the following week, and I helped show her some of the basic turns and movements, standing close, almost embracing her as I manipulated her arms and legs into the correct positions. The aikido dance we did together was highly erotic, and our energy (or "chi") levels were sparking crazily off each other. After the class she invited me back to her apartment, and before long we ended up in bed.

"I've always been attracted to you, Bruce," she told me afterward. "I really envy your free spirit."

I laughed sadly. "I'm not as free as you might think," I said. "I promise you, I have my own set of problems." We lay in bed talking all afternoon. It was a beautiful time for me, but by the time I left her apartment, we both knew we were destined to be friends, not lovers. Soon after our encounter, she got her role in the Bond movie *Licence to Kill* and married the actor Griffin Dunne, and we lost touch.

Now Carey is married to Richard Gere. The last time I saw her was on television, when the Dalai Lama received the Congressional Gold Medal from President Bush. The ceremony was held in the Rotunda of the Capitol, beneath the great dome, and the sight of the Dalai Lama surrounded by the portraits of our Founding Fathers almost moved me to tears. He spoke so eloquently that for a few minutes I was completely lost in his words. I was back in my ashram in Ithaca, listening to the words of Maharaj Ji; I was back with Guru Desai, my first guru; I was digging vegetables in the silence of the Mount Tremper monastery.

The television cameras panned around to show the specially invited audience—politicians, celebrities, and religious leaders sitting in rows to see this momentous occasion. Suddenly the faces of Carey Lowell and Richard Gere appeared on-screen, and I smiled. Carey looked radiant. I know that her husband is a practicing Buddhist and an active supporter of the Dalai Lama. I was happy that her spiritual journey had taken her to such a wonderful place, and I was glad that our paths had connected so soulfully along the way.

Seeing Richard Gere on television reminded me of the time I met his first wife, Cindy Crawford, while doing a Revlon shoot in a penthouse apartment off Central Park in 1988. She was the big sensation at the time, the new face of Revlon. When Cindy walked in, her beauty made my heart race. She was stunning without any makeup at all—a true natural beauty.

The photographer had me draped in a thick white terry-cloth

robe while Cindy sat on my lap wearing a short, low-cut dress. This was one of the sexiest photo shoots I had ever done, and he encouraged Cindy to show off her spectacular body. As the shoot progressed, I was getting more and more turned on. Unfortunately, the photographer was a nasty little man who ordered us around all day. Neither Cindy nor I could stand him. We chatted when we could between setups, but I never had the chance to get her alone to ask for her number. In fact, I think I may have been a bit intimidated by her. We wished each other well and went our separate ways.

A few months later, I was boarding a flight to Paris for a catalog job when I glanced up from the magazine I was reading and noticed Cindy walking straight toward me. "Hi, Bruce," she said with a huge smile. "You're on this flight, too? It's so good to see you." Once again I was amazed by her beauty and even more surprised that she had actually remembered my name. Cindy took her seat in business class as I made my way back to economy—another indication of the usual pay disparity between a top female supermodel and a successful male model. Luckily, the flight was almost empty, so I had an entire row of seats to myself to stretch out and sleep on throughout the overnight flight. I was just about to do exactly that when I saw Cindy walking down the aisle. I offered her the seat next to me, and we chatted for a while.

"I can't believe how tired I am," Cindy said after a time, stifling a yawn.

"Rest here awhile if you'd like," I told her.

She lay down across the empty seats I'd been planning to sleep on and gently nuzzled her head into my lap. *Boy,* I thought, *who knows where this could lead?* I gently stroked her hair, but eventually she dozed off, and I was trapped in my seat for the next six hours, unable to move, use the bathroom, or do anything else. I did at least

have the privilege of being able to say I've slept with Cindy Crawford, although really I should say she slept with me. Stuck in my upright position, I was too uncomfortable to sleep.

When we arrived in Paris, I asked Cindy if she wanted to get
together in the city. She explained that she was dating an actor who
was off working in India. I realized later that must have been Richard Gere. "Maybe we could just go to the museum or something,"
I offered. She nodded and said she thought that would be nice. I
told her I had to go to Milan for a fashion show, but I'd give her a
call as soon as I returned. She seemed agreeable. I was thrilled, because I really wanted to get to know her.

Milan was as crazy as ever, but in the mêlée of quick changes
and runway chaos, I spotted a beautiful model I had first seen six
months earlier. Her name was Marpessa, a Dutch model who was
the new "it" girl in Europe, the face of Dolce & Gabbana. Even
among the other gorgeous models, Marpessa was breathtaking. She
had a crackling energy and a sensuousness that made her hard to
forget. I tried to find her in the throng of people after the show, but
she had already left.

When I returned to Paris, I called my agent, Sophie, and asked
her if she had ever heard of Marpessa. "Oh, yes, I know her," Sophie
replied. "She's hot!"

"Listen, is there any way you can call her agency and leave my
name and number?" I figured it was a long shot, but it was worth a try.

"Oh, Bruce, you like Marpessa, huh?" Sophie teased. She was
intrigued by my request, because she loved to gossip and always had
the inside scoop on all the models, including me.

Later that night I received a call in my room. I was surprised to
hear Marpessa's voice on the other end of the line. My sudden nerves
caused me to mispronounce her name. "Hi, M-Marissa," I stuttered.

"Marpessa," she corrected. "How are you?"

"I'm good, I'm good. Uh . . . I just arrived back at my hotel in Paris, and I thought you might be in town and . . . you know, you might be at loose ends or something." I hoped I didn't sound desperate.

"I will be over in an hour to pick you up for dinner," she told me. She arrived in her Mercedes, and we drove around Paris, eventually ending up at a Danish restaurant, where we got to know each other properly. It turned out she was half Dutch and half Surinamese, which is what gave her that distinctive look. Her hair was long, curly, and wild, and her body was flawless.

After dinner she drove me back to her apartment. "Do you want to watch a movie?" she asked. We barely made it through the opening credits.

The following day, remembering my promise to Cindy, I phoned to see if she still wanted to meet me at a museum. I told her I'd bring a buddy along as a chaperone. My good friend EJ was in town, and I knew he'd be the perfect companion because of his natural storytelling abilities. "It's not a date. I promise to behave," I told her. Then I phoned Marpessa to see if she still wanted to meet me later that same night. I told her I had dinner plans but asked if she could come to my hotel around midnight. That way I could keep my promise to Cindy, knowing that Marpessa would be waiting for me at the end of the night.

After the museum Cindy, EJ, and I went to dinner at the famous L'Escargot restaurant. We sat outside, drinking wine and savoring the beautiful evening. I think was EJ was enjoying my date more than I was. He seemed to be infatuated with Cindy, asking her question after question. She was a sweet girl from the Midwest, and we listened to her stories about her childhood spent picking corn in Illi-

Marpessa in Avalon.

nois, but my mind kept drifting. I was attracted to a woman with a wilder streak.

Toward the end of dinner, I noticed a familiar black Mercedes pull up outside the restaurant. As the window lowered, I saw it was Marpessa behind the wheel. With her finger she motioned me over. Like a child caught with my hand in the cookie jar, I leaped up from the table. "What's going on?" she asked. "I thought you said you had something to do?"

"I did," I replied. "I'm having dinner with my buddy EJ. He brought along a friend of his."

Marpessa looked beyond me suspiciously, craning her neck to get a better look.

"Are we still on for tonight?" I asked brightly.

She paused for a moment. "Yes. I will see you later." She rolled up the window and drove away.

After dinner I walked Cindy back to her hotel room, wished her a polite good night, and returned to my hotel. As planned, Marpessa showed up at midnight, and we had another wonderful night together before I left for New York the following day.

Quite apart from the great sex, which was obviously important to me, I truly thought Marpessa was someone I could go the distance with. She was interested in living a meaningful life and told me she'd always had a dream to start a healing center. She spoke six languages, had traveled the globe, and was open to adventure. She seemed to possess many of the qualities I was looking for. Everything happened so fast between us that before I quite realized what was going on, she flew to New York for some bookings, said she needed somewhere to stay and moved into my apartment.

Big Pete had moved out earlier, so I was glad for the company. Neither of us had any idea how long she would be staying, but I was crazy about her, so I was happy to let things unfold. Pete had been having a hard time of his own after a breakup with a girl. Earlier in the year, I'd suggested he go to Kripalu, a spiritual retreat center in Massachusetts for some peace and reflection. The ashram was run by Guru Desai, the guru I'd met right after my bad acid trip. I hoped Pete's visit to the ashram would work out better than when I sent Doc X there; he and the yoga teacher ended up running off together—which wreaked havoc with the schedule of yoga classes! As it happened, Big Pete rediscovered his true calling at the ashram. To his and everybody else's surprise, it was gardening. He returned to his hometown of Princeton to become a landscape architect and organic gardener, along the way changing from Big Pete into the respectable professional Peter Soderman, which is who he still is today.

At first things were great between Marpessa and me. I took her rock climbing with Tommy Preston and surfing at Avalon with Doc X.

Marpessa was fearless at both. She loved to be active and seemed to be into nature as much I was. My buddies were polite and did all they could to make her welcome, but I never got the impression that they loved her the way they'd loved Nathalie or Elle. But they'd seen a few women come and go since then, and they were probably wary of opening their hearts to any new girlfriend of mine, in case it went wrong again.

Their instincts were right. As suddenly as our relationship had started, it began to fall apart. Somewhere along the way, the fun-loving girl who wanted to open a healing center gave way to a new and unfamiliar personality. Marpessa seemed angry with me all the time, and she never hesitated to let me know about it. I occasionally did curls with dumbbells on the living-room floor while watching television. For some reason this infuriated her. "You're so American!" she would say angrily. "I could never live with a man who lifts weights in the living room."

As time passed, I realized that Marpessa wasn't quite the earth-mother character I'd imagined her to be. She wasn't happy with my lifeguard persona, and we were just not a good match.

My friends and family were no longer subtle about their feelings for Marpessa. They told me in no uncertain terms how wrong they thought she was for me. They say love is blind, and in my love—or what I thought was love—for Marpessa, I certainly couldn't see what was obvious to everyone else. Despite our difficulties I had no intention of ending the relationship. In retrospect, I just don't think I could have faced being on my own again.

It wasn't long before the relationship's collapse became complete. Barely six months into our relationship, Marpessa told me, "I'm sorry, but I don't love you anymore, Bruce. I'm moving out." I thought we might be able to work through our differences, but

Marpessa had already made up her mind. She packed her sizable wardrobe and left.

Once again I sank into a deep depression. I couldn't eat or sleep. I looked like hell and felt horribly empty and alone. Why did this keep happening to me? How many more times did I have to endure this pain before I would find the peace I was so desperately seeking? Was it hopelessly naïve of me to think I could find love with the right woman one day? Each time my heart was broken, my confidence took another knock, and self-doubts and fears began to swamp me. My future had never seemed bleaker or more hopeless.

I escaped to the beach to find solace under the Avalon sun, in the one place where I felt I truly belonged. I hung out with my buddies and tried to find a path back to who I was. But I was no longer a lifeguard; the faces and the buildings and the atmosphere didn't feel the same, and the little shacks along the beach were all being developed into million-dollar mansions. If only I'd bought that house a few years earlier.

Doc X was spending a lot of time traveling back and forth between Avalon and his grandmother's house in Philadelphia, keeping an eye on her. She was getting old and frail, and he was worried about her. She'd raised him, and he always said that when she died, a part of him would die, too. While he was away, I turned over his vegetable garden for him, as I did every spring, and planted tomatoes, zucchini, and other vegetables so he could eat organically throughout the summer. The Glenn was a naval doctor now, traveling around the world. Shoe was a lifeguard down in Hollywood, Florida. A lot of my other friends were married and raising kids. My father had retired and was having trouble adjusting to life without the daily routine of going to an office. He seemed a little depressed. My sisters were tied up with kids and marriages and houses. I drove back to New York still feeling restless and unhappy.

I was booked for a photo shoot for *Cosmopolitan* with photographer Uli Rose at the brand-new and terribly chic Royalton Hotel on West Forty-fourth Street in New York. The job was familiar territory: There would be a girl in lingerie, and I'd be the guy in underwear. I had done so many shoots like it; this one would just be another day at the office. Politely introducing myself to the female model, I tried to hide the fact that I really preferred to be alone.

When I wasn't needed on set, I sat off to one side reading the newspaper, barely looking up. I wasn't even focusing on what I was reading. As the day wore on, though, something penetrated my solitary bubble: the contagious laugh of the model. Looking up, I saw that all the men on the crew seemed to love her. Half Mexican, half Irish, she had vibrant hazel eyes and a voluptuous, athletic body. Her name, I learned, was Katrina Olivas.

Once the shoot was over, I decided to walk home so I could get some exercise. I was trying to work through my depression by running around Central Park every day, and I also walked whenever I could. Katrina said that she lived downtown and offered to walk with me. En route she chatted away happily, telling me all about her life. She was from Dallas, and her mother and stepfather were holistic healers. She grew up riding horses, loved the outdoors, and seemed extremely down-to-earth. Even though I was deeply depressed, I could sense that she had a beautiful, radiant spirit, and, miraculously, my spirits began to lift, too. Yet I also found myself thinking, *Great. Here we go again.* Even though I was twelve years older than Katrina, I didn't feel the age difference, and she didn't seem to feel it, either. I wasn't ready for another relationship, but the more we walked and the more she talked, the more I felt that I wanted to get to know her better.

Katrina told me that her boyfriend, Jeff, was in Japan modeling. She told me she didn't know where their relationship was going, because she had serious doubts that he was the one. The fact that she used the phrase *the one* unnerved me, but I invited her to din-

ner, anyway. I could tell we both needed companionship, and I didn't want to brood alone in my apartment. Over dinner Katrina continued to speak eloquently and passionately about her beliefs. She explained that she'd grown up in a Christian denomination called Unity, which teaches that God is a universal presence that exists in all people. I was intrigued by the concept, because it seemed so generous and open. Unity, she said, promoted love and acceptance of everybody, since there was more than one path to God.

Her words were like a balm to my heart. I confessed to her that I'd been battling depression my entire life. I even admitted that I was sometimes suicidal. Katrina listened intently as I talked. It seemed she understood what I was telling her and wasn't passing judgment on me. It felt so good to be able to discuss my darkest issues with someone at last. We talked late into the night, and then we went back to my place and made love. As we lay in my bed afterward, I stroked her hair and kissed her forehead, and something told me to hold on to this amazingly special girl. This time the connection I felt wasn't frantic. It was quiet and easy.

Katrina and I started seeing each other almost daily after that. In addition to modeling, she was studying acting and living with a roommate in an apartment on Twenty-sixth Street. While her boyfriend was abroad, I essentially became Katrina's backdoor man. I was falling hard for her, though, so before long I told her I wanted her to be my proper girlfriend. She, however, had major reservations. One thing working against me was my reputation within the industry. She said she'd spoken with some models who had portrayed me as a major player—which, unfortunately, was true. Given what she'd heard, she was understandably reluctant to get more serious with me.

When Katrina's boyfriend finally returned from Japan and they were reunited, our relationship ended as suddenly as it had begun. I was devastated. I tried to maintain contact with her by sending postcards from wherever I was traveling. We occasionally bumped into each other when I was back in New York, but she had made it clear that she'd decided to stay with Jeff, and that was that.

I didn't give up so easily, though. I persuaded Bruce Weber to book Katrina as one of the models for a Versace commercial he was making, "Looking for Kicks," which was to feature the Belgian martial-arts expert Jean-Claude Van Damme. Known as "The Muscles from Brussels," Van Damme had risen to fame as a martial-arts actor in movies like *Bloodsport* and *Kickboxer*. Knowing my passion for martial arts, Weber rang and asked me to be the stunt coordinator, to play one of the stuntmen in the commercial, and to find three more stuntmen. My cousin Lisa Marie was going to be one of the women in the ad, along with a model named Helena Christensen. When I suggested he use Katrina, Weber asked me to send her to meet him, and the moment he saw her, he agreed.

The set was in a huge tenth-floor loft apartment on West Twenty-sixth Street, overlooking the Hudson River. I turned up with a friend, the New Zealander Richard Keogh, and "Fish," a huge guy from Trinidad whom I'd gotten to know at my aikido dojo. Fish was as tough as nails but had the biggest belly laugh of anyone I knew. I also brought along Daniel Bernhardt, a six-foot-four-inch Swiss model I'd met while shooting catalogs in Germany. As well as being a skilled practitioner of the martial arts and a great guy, Daniel was a major fan of Van Damme and longed to be an actor one day, so I thought it would be fun to have him on the set. "You be one of the stuntmen," I told him, "and you never know where it might lead."

Van Damme was only five feet nine inches tall, but he made up for his smallish size with attitude. He wasn't happy about working with us, but Bruce was insistent that I was the stunt coordinator and I would choose the stuntmen. We rehearsed the moves repeatedly in slow motion. As Van Damme came into the room, we lunged at him. This was followed by a punch-lunge maneuver and then a block-block, where one us went for him and he blocked us twice. He wanted us to really overreact to his kicks and moves, falling back with grimaces on our faces, making moaning noises. It was so staged. When I went for him, he was going to pick me up and throw me into a table. Richard was going to get flipped and slammed into the floor.

It was all choreographed perfectly in a sort of martial-arts dance, but when Weber said, "Action!" Van Damme took it all too seriously for our liking. He threw Richard to the floor and was supposed to pull his next punch, but instead he smacked Richard so hard in the head that you could hear the contact throughout the studio. I rushed over to where Richard was sitting on the floor, dazed, and I helped him to his feet. "Are you okay, buddy?" I asked.

Richard attempted a smile through his pain. "I'm okay, mate," he said, wincing. "I've had worse."

The rest of the day continued in much the same vein. To make matters worse, both Lisa Marie and Katrina came over to me to complain that Van Damme was really hustling them. That guy was a pain in the ass that day. The good thing was that I had a chance to spend some more time with Katrina. Daniel was the one who was most affected by the day, though. When Weber shouted, "That's a wrap! Thank you, everybody," the tall Swiss came up to me with a thoughtful expression on his face.

"You know, Daniel, Van Damme's okay, but I think you're stronger and bigger and better-looking than him," I said. "Maybe you should think more seriously about this acting idea."

I patted Daniel reassuringly on the shoulder. "You should move to L.A. and see if you can get a break. I'll put you in touch with my friend Nick, who's out there doing TV commercials. Do it, man. You've got nothing to lose." Happily, Daniel took the gamble, and he became a big martial-arts movie star. He took over for Van Damme in *Bloodsport 2, 3,* and *4,* and he had a part in *The Matrix Reloaded* and in a TV series called *Mortal Kombat: Conquest.*

Sadly, when the Weber/Van Damme shoot was over, I couldn't hang around with Katrina, as I had to rush to the airport to catch a flight to Paris for a Dior campaign. Helena Christensen flew with me, and although she was a sweet girl, I just wasn't interested. The whole way across the Atlantic, all I could think about was Katrina, about how comfortable it had been spending time with her, and how hot she had looked in her Versace dress. I liked who I was when I was around her. She was intelligent and funny and possessed all the qualities that any man would want in a beautiful woman. She would make a perfect life partner. Unfortunately, it looked as if somebody else had figured that out first. Which meant I was alone again.

Months before Marpessa and I broke up, we had planned a two-week Christmas and New Year's vacation to Costa Rica with Tommy Preston, Richard Keogh, my French agent Sophie, and her girlfriend. As the end of the year approached, I knew I no longer wanted to go, and I wondered what I could do instead. Katrina was spending the holidays with Jeff, and my hopes for her and me seemed futile. I thought maybe I'd just spend Christmas alone in New York or at home with my folks. My buddies insisted I still go on our vacation. "You can't just bow out now, B," Tommy pleaded. "We've paid for our plane tickets and everything. If you're not going, we're not going."

I eventually gave in to the pressure, not wanting to let Tommy and the others down. I had nothing else to do, and at least the surfing was supposed to be amazing in Costa Rica. To my surprise, Marpessa still wanted to come on the trip. She told me, "We'll just go as friends." I knew it wasn't a good idea, but I agreed.

We all flew down together, only to discover that there were no hotel rooms available. Our plan had always been not to really have a plan, but apparently everyone else staying in Costa Rica over the holidays had booked far in advance. We decided to rent a sailboat instead. We gave a couple of men at the local marina five hundred dollars and set out to sea, telling them that we wanted to gradually head down the coast, stopping at any interesting spots along the way. It was difficult to have Marpessa on that sailboat, a constant reminder that it was over between us. I tried not to let my feelings about what had happened with her and my unfulfilled longing for Katrina ruin my vacation, but it wasn't easy.

The surfing, however, was indeed amazing. As soon as one of us spotted some great breaks, Tommy, Richard, and I would grab our boards, throw them over the side of the boat, dive in, and paddle into the some of the most remarkable waves I have ever seen. There wasn't anyone else around for miles, not a single boat on the horizon. We lived like natives, catching fish off the back of the boat, gutting them, and cooking them for our supper. It felt wonderful to be in close contact with nature again.

One day we came across an incredible stretch of beach. It was the ideal spot to drop anchor and hang out for the day. The girls sunbathed nude while we surfed naked. It was like our own personal spot; we felt totally free. Until a man emerged from the forest carrying a pistol, that is.

"This is private property," he told us, scowling. "Put your clothes back on. You are being disrespectful."

I was extremely courteous and apologized for trespassing. I had no intention of arguing with a man carrying a gun while I was bare-ass naked. The girls weren't as agreeable. Sophie was a strong-willed Parisian who didn't like being told what to do. "What do you mean?" she cried indignantly. "We can do whatever we want." I pulled her aside and managed to calm her down. Fortunately, the man was more understanding than he had at first appeared, and once we put our bathing suits back on, he allowed us to remain there for as long as we wanted.

That night we made a campfire on the beach and cooked the tuna we'd caught during the day. As I stared into the flickering flames, I thought back to an experience I'd had a few years earlier, when I'd fire-walked at a seminar led by renowned life coach Tony Robbins. I told the others about it. When I was done, Marpessa taunted me, "Why don't you try it right now, if you think you can walk on fire?"

"Back then I did it with Tony Robbins's help," I replied.

My answer wasn't good enough. Marpessa was calling me out.

Jumping up, I took a log and raked the charcoal and ashes from the fire into a strip along the beach. When I finished, I looked up and saw Tommy and Richard staring at me like I was crazy. Maybe I was. We were at least a two-day sail from a doctor, so if I got badly burned, I'd be out of luck, but now my blood was up.

I stepped to the edge of the firewalk and hesitated. Lifting my head, I focused on a point off in the dark forest. I kept telling myself the one thing that I'd learned before: *Cool moss. Cool moss. Cool moss.* After a quick deep breath, I walked straight across the white-hot ashes.

Everyone went nuts when I reached the other side. To be honest, I was surprised I made it. My accomplishment gave my confidence a much-needed boost. Later, however, I realized what a stupid and pointless stunt it had been. What was I trying to prove? Nothing was going to change the way Marpessa felt about me. In fact, I think it just endorsed her opinions of what a loony American I was. After that vacation I never saw her again.

When I got back to New York, the hustle and bustle of the city streets stood in stark contrast to the tranquillity of the Costa Rican beaches. The noise and the pollution, the giant billboards and bright lights assaulted my senses. I'd grown up with a creek running through my backyard and fields I could play in. I needed to be more connected to nature. I was also paying an inordinate amount of money for an apartment I was barely living in, and it was time to scale back. I was making good money, but I was spending it too fast.

I told my buddy Tommy how I was feeling one day as we made our way up the sheer cliffs of the 'Gunks at New Paltz. Tommy seemed unusually distracted as I poured my heart out to him between climbs. Suddenly, halfway up the cliff face, when we were ten feet apart and at a point where neither of us could really move, he blurted out that he'd slept with Nathalie shortly after she and I had split up, when she was still on her own. "I've been meaning to tell you, B, but I just never found a good time."

Tommy knew that had I not been roped in and hanging off a cliff, my reaction might have been more emotional. There was no way I could punch the guy or throw a fit on the side of that rock. I used my emotions to power my way to the top, and by the time I reached the summit, I was no longer mad. In fact, I was relieved. I had screwed around on Nathalie so many times that it seemed only fair I was hurt in return. "I love you, T, and I forgive you," I told Tommy, hugging him. "You're my brother." Tommy meant too much to me to let a woman come between us, not even Nathalie.

I returned to my apartment alone, looked around, and realized that it was time to leave. If I remained in the city, I knew that my depression would claim me once more. I had to go someplace where I could keep searching for inner peace. I seriously considered leaving the industry altogether and going to live as a monk at the Mount Tremper monastery. My previous experiment with celibacy and a Buddhist life hadn't lasted long, but I was young and foolish then. Maybe this time I could go the distance. Or maybe I'd go live in Kripalu and become a teacher there, using my years of experience in meditation and connecting to the breath to help others. But the idea of being in the Northeast during the winter depressed me, and I felt instinctively—after all my modeling experiences in the Caribbean—that I needed to be somewhere warm.

15

Miami Heat

Miami had long been a preferred location for photographers, art directors, and models. The weather was glorious, the light was perfect, the Europeans loved the exchange rate, and everyone spoke English. More and more people in the fashion industry were moving down to Florida and setting up modeling agencies, production houses, and studios.

The more I pondered where I wanted to live, the more Miami made sense to me. I could finally invest some of my hard-earned money in a property overlooking the ocean, which would allow me to swim and surf every day. I could walk to work at the studios or to beach locations that fashion designers like Gianni Versace were using. Also, Florida would be the perfect place to develop my skills as a photographer, inspired by Bruce Weber and Doc X.

Weber had already rented a house for himself and his beloved golden retrievers in Key Biscayne and was spending the winters down there. It would be only a short flight to New York and New Jersey to see my family. Better still, the colleges in Miami had some good graduate schools, with courses in psychology and social work, so I could go to night school and finally get back on track with my original career plan.

In 1989 I found a great little condominium on Ocean Drive, right in the heart of South Beach, and bought it for next to nothing. My accountant didn't want me to buy in Miami. He thought Fort Lauderdale was a better bet. A conservative investor, he didn't think real estate was a good place to put money. Thankfully, I didn't listen to him. My new home was a small one-bedroom apartment on the ninth floor of a building that was built in the late 1960s. It had a little balcony with a view of the ocean. I could sit there, surrounded by the plants and vegetables I grew, and take in the sea air or photograph the pelicans flying majestically past. I could assess the surf each morning before I trucked on down to the beach to ride the breakers. It was an ideal existence, and my depression lifted almost immediately after I got there. I felt as good as I had during my lifeguard days, which had been the happiest years of my life.

Better still, my old friend Shoe was a short drive away, married with kids but still lifeguarding. He told me that another of our old buddies from Avalon, Tim McKee, was working right on the beach where I lived. The next morning I wandered up to one of the brightly

Todd "the God" Irvin and me at 465 Ocean Drive, Miami Beach.

painted lifeguard stands that are a unique feature of South Beach and surprised him. Man, it felt so good to sit with Tim and chew the fat about the old days: the races, the chicks, and old Scarhead. From then on I made sure I surfed and swam right in front of McKee's stand; he'd let me go way out and do whatever I liked, and then we'd meet up later for dinner and a few beers.

The largest modeling agencies operating out of Miami were Irene Marie and Michelle Pommier. They saw there was a movement to revitalize South Beach and were responsible for bringing a lot of business to the area. I signed up with Richard Pollmann and Nicole Brandt at Irene Marie and immediately began to get work. I had bookings from all over the world—English, French, Italian, and German catalogs, *GQ* editorials, Dutch magazines, Italian *Elle*, and Swedish editorials. I did some advertising for American Express, and I did campaigns for jeans from the United States, Holland, and Japan. I did editorial shoots with Weber and Fabrizio. I modeled Fruit of the Loom underwear. I was in European car commercials, and I did a Versace campaign with Nick Constantino, who had gotten tired of L.A. and was back into modeling. There was a lot of good-paying catalog work and a frenzy of shoots.

Most of the jobs were within walking distance of my apartment. I'd roll out of bed, run to the beach for a swim, go back home, take a quick shower, have breakfast in a café, walk to the location, do my job, and stroll home before meeting up with friends at night. South Beach was an incredibly easy place to live and work.

Before the fashion boom, Miami—especially South Beach—had been full of retired folks, and there were still many left. A lot of them grumbled about the dramatic changes taking place, but a few loved seeing all the young models flooding into town and fed off their vitality. There was one old lady named Ruth, who had a hunched back and who used to swim in the sea each morning at the same time I did. Every day I'd watch her hobble down to the beach and wade into the water. I'd hang around and make sure she was okay; then, when she was ready to come out, I'd swim over and help her get out of the surf, which was always the hardest part for her.

"Thanks, Bruce," she'd say with a smile. "When I was young like you, I was a really strong swimmer. I still swim every day!"

"Keep it up, Ruthie!" I'd say.

One of my neighbors in the building was an old rabbi who'd survived the Holocaust. This guy always had a huge smile on his face. Each morning, out by the pool, he'd go through this special exercise routine, which he said was based on kabbalah, an ancient form of Jewish mysticism. "I used to be a bodybuilder," he told me, grinning.

My parents came to visit me in South Beach, and they loved it. Dad especially liked the hot tub in my bathroom. I couldn't get him out of there. Mom liked to sit on my balcony with a book and watch all the people—the models, the Rollerbladers, the nude sunbathers, the retired folks, the drag queens, the foreign tourists, the gay couples, and the voyeurs, like her. Dad, who had once been an avid ice-hockey player, turned out to be a natural on Rollerblades, so when he and I weren't running up and down the beach together, we'd go skating along Ocean Drive, waving to all the people we knew, and many we didn't, and stopping at little cafés when we felt like it. I think Dad would have been happy to retire in South Beach.

Once I got settled, I called Nick Constantino and urged him to come to Miami. There was lots of work for models, and there was a major real-estate boom happening among the pretty pink houses and condominiums. Nick arrived soon after and saw the same opportunities I did. He became a regular in my crew. In South Beach we called him "the Dark Man," because he was the bad boy to whom women flocked. Nick rarely, if ever, chased girls. He just waited, and they came to him.

After my failures with Marpessa and Katrina, I had resolved not to commit to anyone else. I resigned myself to being the perpetual bachelor who never lacked female companionship but would never share his life with one special woman.

Nick would tease me about this. "The thing with you, Hulse, is that you enjoy the chase more than the actual catch," he said. "I watch you again and again go running around after these crazy girls. I won't even pick up the phone unless I know the girl is coming over. I don't want to take them out to dinner all the time and play the romantic." The truth was, Nick never had to.

South Beach was seasonal; the crowds began coming just before

Swedish editorial, Miami Beach.

Christmas and stayed through the end of April. Models arrived like a new crop every year from all over the world. It was like a United Nations of beautiful women. I could sit on my balcony and watch the parade of new talent walk by, portfolios in hand, in search of their next job. It was easy to meet girls if I wanted to, because I had the status of being an established male model on the scene. Whether I was sitting at a café or taking in some sun on the beach, there was no shortage of beautiful women happy to let me show them the sights. My only competition came from the French and Italian play-boys who flashed a lot of cash.

On days when I wasn't shooting, my routine was to start the day with a workout. Then I'd have breakfast, make a few calls, and take a long run or swim at the beach. After that I'd walk into town down

Ocean Drive to see who was around. I couldn't leave my apartment without seeing twenty or thirty people I knew.

I often saw Gianni Versace out in the local cafés, having his cappuccino and reading the paper. He always seemed so vivacious and happy. What did he know about life that I didn't? I'd worked in a few of his campaigns in Italy, and he was always kind to me. Every time he saw me on Ocean Drive, he'd say, "Bruce, you look fabulous. Look at you. I want to use you again." He was so accessible and friendly; I could sit and chat with him anytime. His nearby mansion hosted some of the hottest parties in town, though it wasn't always the best place to find a girl. The day I heard on the news that Gianni had been shot dead on the steps of his home by a young man who days later turned the gun on himself was one of the saddest days of my life.

In the halcyon time before Gianni's death, it was a wonderful experience being part of the burgeoning fashion environment in Miami. For a few short years, it was glorious. The innocence of the eighties was still prevalent. There was still a sense of fun, frivolity, and play that we knew couldn't last forever, but for a while it was fantasyland—or certainly my fantasy, at least.

In his novel *The Unbearable Lightness of Being*, Milan Kundera wrote that there were two kinds of womanizers: the romantic womanizer and the epic womanizer. The epic womanizer is a sex addict whose only aim is to screw women. The romantic womanizer uses sex as a way to continually search for that perfect woman, but he never finds her. I was the latter. I was the guy searching for perfection in a woman. What I found instead was casual sex.

For a while I thought I was living the perfect life in Miami. The guys were hustling the girls, and the girls were hustling the guys. There was a certain humor in it, but it was also sad in many ways.

A guy would talk about his "stable," the group of women in his address book. A girl had her stable as well. Occasionally people would go out and attempt to steal a "horse" from another stable. It was a game.

I had become so separated from my emotions that I began to equate having sex with a girl to going out to a new restaurant. Once you've enjoyed a delicious meal, you might find yourself returning to that same restaurant for another meal there, or you might acquire a taste for something else. I never deliberately deceived any of the women I was dating. From the outset I was entirely honest about my intentions, making it clear I wasn't looking for a relationship. As far as I was concerned, we were sharing a moment in time together and nothing more, each of us dancing the same tango. To my surprise, my candor was often attractive to a lot of women, many of whom seemed happy to have enjoyable, uncomplicated sex—nothing more, nothing less.

I had set myself up as a photographer in Miami, buying a Nikon camera and taking shots of alligators and sawgrass in the Everglades, and pelicans, sunsets, and colorful characters in and around South Beach. I'd ride out to the 'Glades on my motorbike on my days off, eat delicious fried frog legs from some funky roadside stall, and look for the perfect picture.

At home I did test shots for models. Weber always told me I was one of the few guys who had an eye for male beauty, and I'd sent him several models over the years, many of whom I'd photographed myself, like Doug Myers. Another was an Australian model and ex-cop named Russell James, whom I'd met through Tommy Preston in Hamburg. Weber went on to use Russell for Ralph Lauren, and Russell is now one of the best fashion photographers in the world; he's giving *me* work.

Knowing of my connections to Weber and others, a lot of

younger models started coming to me for advice and test shots. The women were especially keen on seeking me out. After all, wasn't I personally responsible for the career of Lisa Marie and Nathalie Gabrielli, among others? I wasn't playing the girls—not really. But I certainly enjoyed controlling that special seduction between lens and subject. What eventually happened to me in Miami, though, was that I learned that too much of a good thing isn't so great. I became increasingly uncomfortable with women who claimed to be fans of "the Levi's guy" or the "*GQ* cover guy" or the Victoria's Secret model. I'd receive letters or phone calls from fans propositioning me, which I found a big turnoff. The more women came on to me, and the more I watched the lizardy old playboys working the models along the Drive, the more I feared that I was going to turn into one of them unless I found my "shaman woman."

My salvation came in the unlikely form of a hulking boxer from Liverpool, England, named Gary Hope. I'd first heard of Gary when Big Pete had told me about him back when we were living in New York.

"Hey, Hulse, you gotta come down to Gleason's Gym and see this fighter," Big Pete had said. "He's crazy. He's banging the crap out of everybody." So I went to take a look at this character, and Pete was right—he was crazy. He was also impressive. He had this shock of bushy blond hair and was buzzing around the ring reciting the poetry of Octavio Paz and Pablo Neruda in his broad Scouse accent, knocking out anyone who came near him. "'Sleep, sleep cat of the night,'" he'd wheeze, between jabs, "'with episcopal ceremony—and your stone carved moustache.'" I loved it.

A couple of years later, I was at a Russian bathhouse in New York having a good sweat with Nick when I spotted a huge guy sweating in the opposite corner. It was Hope. I went over, said hello, and asked him how he was doing. He told me he'd fallen on hard times, so I asked him if he'd be interested in giving me some boxing training. "How does fifty bucks an hour sound?" I asked. His blood-shot eyes lit up.

Gary trained me at this sweaty little Puerto Rican gym on East Tenth Street, and we soon became friends. He joined Alcoholics Anonymous, cleaned himself up, and asked me to come along to a few of his meetings with him. Talk about lifting you out of your depression! Those people had heartbreaking stories to tell; they really helped me understand what suffering was. Gary himself was an amazing person who'd grown up working in his family's hair salon. He'd done some acting, and he loved poetry. Not only did he quote Neruda and Paz, he made up his own poems, and whenever he saw a girl he really liked, he'd say, "She's my Neruda."

When I moved to Miami, leaving New York and Gary behind, I could tell he was sad to see me go, so I phoned Bruce Weber and asked him if he needed a personal trainer down in Key Biscayne. "I know this great boxer," I told him. "You'll love him." So Gary Hope ended up living in Miami as Bruce Weber's personal trainer, encouraging us both as we swung sledgehammers around our heads to build upper-body muscle while he ate his way through Weber's refrigerator. After training, the two of them would sit at a coffee shop for hours, smoking cigarettes and talking about poetry, movies, actors, England, and life in general. I'd known that Weber would love him.

In Florida, Gary kept up his own boxing at the famed Fifth Street Gym, where Muhammad Ali had trained for his big fight with Sonny Liston. The spirit of "the Greatest" emanated from that dilapidated space, giving it an energy I'll never forget. The gym was on the third floor of a derelict building, with its ocean blue walls spat-

From left to right: Nick Constantino, Beau Jack, and Gary Hope at the Fifth Street Gym.

tered with years of blood and sweat. There was no air-conditioning, just the ocean breeze. Hollywood actor Mickey Rourke trained there, and whenever he arrived with his entourage, any music that was being played had to come off and Mickey's music had to go on. We never minded, though, because it always had a good beat.

One day while sparring with Gary at the gym, I came up with a crazy idea. "Why don't I see if I can get you some fights, and I'll manage you?" I said. "I could do it between modeling jobs and during the slack seasons." Gary stared at me through his padded helmet as I continued. "Then, when you've knocked everyone out of the ring, we'll build you up for a fight with Mike Tyson, and he can knock you out for a million bucks."

Gary spit out his mouthpiece, spraying me in saliva. "I'll knock Tyson flat, don't you worry."

And so, in my black jersey with GARY HOPE embroidered on my back, I took off with him for a tour of Wichita, Kansas; Omaha, Nebraska; and Paducah, Kentucky. I was his corner man and his coach. I bandaged his hands and patched his face; I sponged him down and took out his mouthpiece. I poured Gatorade down Gary's throat and bolstered his confidence each time these muscle-bound boxers fresh out of prison came for him with fists like melons. We stayed in cheap motels and drove for thousands of miles. It was real, and it was dirty, and it was tough as hell.

By the time we got back to Miami, I think we both knew that boxing was too hard a way to earn a living. Neither of us had the stomach for it. Gary was still hoping to be an actor, anyway, and having his face pummeled by maniacs wasn't the best way to get a screen test. I had one more request for him, though. I'd been sparring with him for a couple of years, and I figured it was time for the student to take on the master. Gary said I was crazy, but I insisted.

Word of my lunacy got out, and, to my horror, the Fifth Street Gym was packed with models, friends, and strangers for the six-round bout. *He's a smoker,* I told myself as I entered the ring without my usual face protection. *He's heavy. I just have to use my athleticism to dance around him, then surprise him when he's distracted.*

A veteran trainer laced me up, shaking his head all the while. Nick was my corner man, and even he looked scared. I came out fighting and hit Gary with a jab right away. I got another shot in and moved well, giving my confidence a nice boost. I came back with a left, then a right, and I clocked Gary with a solid uppercut. People began to cheer and call out my name. *Hey, this isn't so hard,* I thought.

Then Gary had me up against the ropes. I didn't realize quite how much I'd bounce back off them. Well, bounce I did, straight into his right hook, which slammed into my jaw like the sledgehammer he used to make me wield during workouts. I felt my legs buckle beneath me, and the next thing I knew, Gary's face was looming over me, etched with concern. "Man, am I glad to see you waking up," he said.

I never asked Gary to spar with me again. Soon afterward, as Gary Francis Hope, he got his first real acting role in *Fair Game,* a thriller set in South Beach starring my onetime sleeping companion Cindy Crawford. Gary is now back in New York, with a few other TV and film roles to his credit, and is working off-Broadway. He will always be one of my closest and dearest friends.

My experiences with Gary and the people at the gym made me appreciate by contrast how shallow the modeling industry could be. I was still earning good money, still having fun with women, but I was restless and feared I was heading into another depression. If I wasn't going to be a model for the rest of my life, and if boxing management wasn't for me, then what was I going to do? I was almost forty years old. I'd been in the business for ten years. How much longer could I keep this up?

Having decided that I really needed to get out of modeling, I went to Bruce Weber to talk it over with him. "I'm going to go back to school, or work in a hospice. I'm going to build myself a house, find a nice small-town girl, and settle down."

After a long pause, Weber laughed out loud. He and Donald Sterzin loved the drama of my crazy love life and always got a kick out of my exploits. He had every reason not to believe me. "You're going to go off and work in a hospice?" he said. "Don't be silly. There will always be time for that, Bruce. There's nobody out there in our business like you right now."

Soon afterward I was invited to a party on a yacht for Julio Iglesias, who had a house in South Beach. Various modeling agencies had sent beautiful women along as company for Julio and his friends. Gazing around me, I realized that these rough-looking guys were only about ten years older than I was. I was bored out of my mind, and I felt totally empty as I sat among all the fawning models. Leaving the party early, I rushed home and ran to the ocean with my surfboard. Sitting on my board, looking back at South Beach, I was grateful that day for the distance between it and me. Part of me wanted to float away from it forever and from the sleazy life I knew I could end up leading there if I wasn't careful.

Suddenly there was a splash beside me. A large, dark shape moved just beneath the water. My initial reaction was fear—it had to be a shark. Looking more closely, I saw that it was a manatee and her young calf swimming side by side in the crystal-clear water. I lay down on my board and started paddling, following them around for over an hour, listening to the mother softly calling to her calf in that ancient, lyrical music of the sea. I was filled with a peace and joy I will never forget.

I never wanted to leave the water that golden, sunlit evening, but when the manatee and her pup eventually swam off, I returned reluctantly to the shore. Back on the beach, a few yards from my door, I bumped into the one photographer I'd least liked working with. I had heard through the grapevine that he'd contracted AIDS, but nothing prepared me for the husk of a human being I saw walking toward me. Though he was only in his forties, he looked like a shriveled old man. All his strength and presence, his anger and bile, were gone. The disease had softened his soul. He looked up, and our eyes met, but I didn't know what to say. Still wet from the sea, I hugged him instead. Holding him tight, words came to me: "May God bless you."

He thanked me and shuffled on. I watched him go as the sun set across the water, standing there until I realized I was shivering from the cold. Seeing him was a reminder that it was time to stop squandering my time on this earth. I'd been Peter Pan, playing at love, skimming the surface, sleeping around for momentary pleasure, but avoiding the true commitment that led to maturity. I could so easily end up old and alone, with only paid models as my companions—or, worse, nobody at all. Time was slipping by, but my life could still change if I wanted it to.

Wake up, Bruce, said a little voice inside my head. *What are you waiting for?*

16

Lovers Meet

The Persian poet Rumi, who was born in present-day Afghanistan in the thirteenth century, wrote many beautiful verses about love, life, and the importance of truth that have inspired me. He has rightly become one of the best-loved poets of the world. One poem in particular spoke to me at that difficult time in my life in Miami, when I knew I had to finally face up to who I was and—more important—who I wanted to be. Rumi put it this way:

Let go of your worries
and be completely clear-hearted,
like the face of a mirror
that contains no images.
If you want a clear mirror,
behold yourself
and see the shameless truth,
which the mirror reflects.
If metal can be polished
to a mirror-like finish,
what polishing might the mirror
of the heart require?
Between the mirror and the heart
is this single difference:
the heart conceals secrets,
while the mirror does not.

I knew that it was time to look in the mirror of my life and face up to my own truth. When I did, I no longer liked what I saw in the reflection. I might have been considered by some to be the apotheosis of male beauty, but there was ugliness in my heart that was as obvious to me as the most disfiguring facial scar. To my shame, I had completely lost sight of the moral principles I'd been raised with and many of the spiritual principles I'd hoped to adopt.

All my Buddhist and Hindu practices, my meditations, my yoga, and my attempts to help others stepping out on their own spiritual journey had certainly somewhat counterbalanced the darker aspects of my life, but there was one thing missing. The key to unlocking the real me was the woman I knew was out there somewhere, who would be prepared to love me for who I was, good and bad, the old Bruce

Left, and below right: *Japanese advertising, Miami Beach.*
© FABRIZIO GIANNI

Italian Men's Vogue, *Mojave Desert.*
© KOTO BOLOFO

Above: *Gant campaign, Mexico.*
© MORTEN BJARNHOF

Spanish advertising.
© PEPE BOTELLA

Swedish editorial, Miami Beach.
© WWW.MATTIASEDWALL.COM

Italian Men's Vogue, *Scotland.*
© FABRIZIO GIANNI

Italian Men's Vogue, *Scotland.*
© FABRIZIO GIANNI

Morocco.
© MIKAEL JANSSON

Above: *Gant campaign, Mexico.*
© MORTEN BJARNHOF

Right: © CLAUS WICKRATH

Japanese advertising,
Miami Beach.
© FABRIZIO GIANNI

Nassau, Bahamas.
© FABRIZIO GIANNI

Morocco.
© MIKAEL JANSSON

Morocco.
© MIKAEL JANSSON

In tutte le città scozzesi, per Hogmanay, il capodanno, brindisi a base di Whisky. Ma il primo sorso dell'anno deve essere d'acqua, simbolo di purezza

British
UNA NUEVA PERSONALIDAD
Un ambiente clásico con un aire renovado tanto en diseños como en colorido

Spanish advertising.
© PEPE BOTELLA

Italian Men's Vogue, *Scotland.*
© FABRIZIO GIANNI

Italian Men's Vogue,
Mojave Desert.
© KOTO BOLOFO

Gant campaign, Mexico.
© MORTEN BJARNHOF

Morocco.
© MIKAEL JANSSON

A la puerta del hotel Cleevender, Bruce lleva un conjunto completo de la firma americana The 5miths.

*Japanese advertising,
Miami Beach.*
© FABRIZIO GIANNI

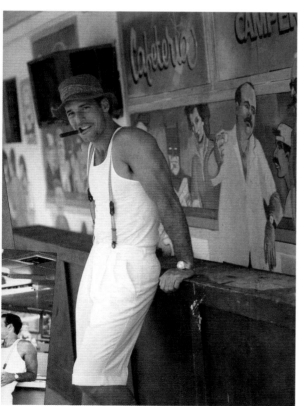

GQ, *New York City.*
© FABRIZIO GIANNI

Editorial with Yfke, 2008.
© STEVEN LIPPMAN

Hulse with all my past misdemeanors, and the new Bruce Hulse, the man I aspired to be: a loving husband and father, a friend for life, faithful, committed, and truthful.

I reached this epiphany early in 1992. The more I thought about it, the more I realized I needed to get away from South Beach. Much as I loved the swimming and surfing, hanging out with my buddies Nick, Gary, and the rest of the gang, talking to the old characters and living in a place where I could watch the pelicans and listen to the ocean, the temptations of Miami's hedonistic lifestyle had too strong a hold over me. My desire to be with beautiful women had always been my weakness. I needed to remove myself from an environment where my resolve was being constantly tested, at least until that resolve grew stronger.

My options were to stay near Miami for the work but move somewhere slightly less central to all the frenetic sexual activity, go back to Jersey and hang out with Doc X and my old buddies up on the eastern seaboard, or give up modeling altogether and return to psychology, carpentry, or even gardening—Big Pete seemed very happy designing landscapes at Princeton, after all.

I was walking down the street one day, considering my many choices, when I noticed a pretty girl sitting outside Caffé Milano on Ocean Drive. As I got closer, I suddenly recognized her. It was Katrina.

"Hello, Bruce," she said, flashing her vibrant smile. "Good to see you again. What are you doing in Miami?"

All my feelings for her engulfed me from the moment she said hello. She was truly a sight for sore eyes.

I sat down with Katrina and listened as she told me she was in Miami for work and planned to stay for a brief vacation. Despite the years that had gone by since we'd last met, we picked up right where

Caffè Milano, Miami Beach.

we'd left off. She was still with her boyfriend, Jeff, who was away on another job overseas, but I sensed some ambivalence about that relationship, and I hoped I was right. Being with Katrina felt like coming home, and I knew I couldn't risk losing her again. I wanted to make the most of this second chance I'd been given, because I was certain it wouldn't come around again.

Coffee turned into lunch and then dinner, and over the course of the next few days we became lovers once more. It felt so wonderful to have Katrina back in my arms. Her contagious laugh, which had first penetrated the black cloud that had descended on me after my breakup with Marpessa, made my heart soar every time. Because I liked who I was when I was with her, I didn't have to pretend to be anything I wasn't. She knew everything about me, the very worst of it, and yet she still seemed to care for me, unconditionally. Perhaps it was her upbringing in the Unity Christian community, with its emphasis on acceptance and love. Perhaps she was just such a warm-hearted person that she was prepared to overlook the flaws and foibles of the human heart to focus on what really lay within. The more time I spent with her, the more convinced I became that she was everything I had ever longed for in a partner.

For my fortieth birthday that March, Katrina threw a big bash for me in South Beach and invited all my friends. Nick was there, of course, and Gary, and all the good friends I'd made over the years. Tommy Preston, Big Pete, Doc X, and all my other buddies called or sent messages, and my parents telephoned, as they always did, first thing in the morning to say, "Happy Birthday, Bruce!" I felt surrounded by a bubble of love.

We drank and danced and partied and carried on until it was almost dawn. Everybody loved Katrina, and it was wonderful to see her in the midst of the people I loved, dancing and laughing and having as much fun as the rest of us. I was celebrating not only the fortieth anniversary of my birth but also the tenth anniversary of my entry into the crazy world of fashion. I was honoring my time in the industry and my years in South Beach; I was also letting go of the person I had once been and looking forward to the man I would yet become.

A few days later, Katrina admitted that soon after we'd first met, at the *Cosmo* lingerie shoot in the Royalton Hotel, she'd had a vivid dream where she saw herself in the ocean, holding a baby boy. "This may sound weird," she whispered, "but I knew that the little boy was your son and that we were destined to be together."

I still get goose bumps thinking about it. Her vision echoed my own deepest longings. It was as if my prayers were being answered. It had to be destiny. In all the years that had passed since we'd last met, in all the time I'd lost and wasted, some part of her had harbored the same feelings I had.

From that day on, we began spending every precious moment

together. We went for long drives in the Everglades and spent endless afternoons on the beach. I was never bored with Katrina. I trusted her completely. I could talk to her about anything. She was real. She was honest. She was of the earth. I knew she would make a wonderful mother to my children. Something about Katrina made me want to turn my life around. I was finally ready to make a lifetime commitment.

Katrina seemed to feel the same way, but first she had to break up with Jeff, which was going to be one of the most difficult things she'd ever had to do in her life. Jeff was a great guy, and he loved her. They'd been together for years, and she knew that splitting up with him would break his heart. I felt a huge burden of guilt on my shoulders for what she was about to do, but nonetheless, I knew—as did she—that their connection had attenuated long before I came back on the scene. As I drove her to the airport for her flight to New York, I knew she was taking a big step for us, and I hoped she knew I wouldn't let her down.

By the end of the summer of 1993, we were free to be together. Katrina agreed to move to Miami and share my apartment. She brought her two Doberman pinschers, who provided us with an instant family. Within weeks of her arrival, I knew that our being together was so right that I had to make it permanent. For the first time in my life, I had no desire to look outside my relationship. Katrina had fed my hungry ghost and helped me achieve that Buddhist state of peace I'd long striven for. She was the love I was born to adore. I wanted to spend the rest of my life with her. All my years of confusion and uncertainty fell away, and I was filled with the purest clarity when I thought of my future. I was focused and secure. Katrina Olivas would be my wife.

Browsing through the jewelry shops of Miami, I found a beautiful antique ring from the 1940s with two sapphires and a diamond in the center. My plan was to propose over dinner at our favorite restaurant, and then I couldn't wait to tell my family and all our friends. It was only when I arrived at the restaurant that my nerves started getting the better of me. It had never occurred to me until that moment that Katrina might turn me down. I'd been so busy thinking about taking the plunge and making this incredible commitment that I hadn't even considered her response. To combat my nerves, I started drinking shots of vodka. Pretty soon I realized I was not in the best shape to make my case, but somehow I managed to focus long enough to say what I'd come to say.

"Katrina, I know I've drunk too much, but that's only because I'm nervous, and that's because I've got something really important to ask you," I told her. "Will you marry me?"

Katrina paused and stared at my face. "Yes," she said. Then her eyes filled with tears.

I could hardly believe her answer. "Yes? You mean it? Really? You will?" I asked, jumping up and kissing her face, her nose, her eyes, my tears mingling with hers. It was the happiest moment of my life. After dinner we went back to our apartment and made love until sunrise, our bodies entwined in a rapturous, eternal embrace.

News of my engagement took a while to percolate through to all my friends and ex-girlfriends in Miami, so for a short time after Katrina accepted my proposal, I would still receive calls from models who were back in town and who wanted to see me.

One by one I had to tell them I was unavailable. I was always polite but honest, telling them I was getting married. Most thought I was kidding. When they realized I was serious, they tried hard to get me to stray. For the most part, my commitment to Katrina didn't seem to matter to them. Eventually I changed my number.

The transition from playboy to fiancé did take some getting used to, although the thought of betraying Katrina never once entered my head. I wasn't going to jeopardize losing the most sensational woman I'd ever met for a meaningless fling. Nonetheless, I was going cold turkey, which is never easy.

I was completely enamored of the concept of getting married, but at first I don't think I really understood what that entailed. I hadn't been in a long-term relationship since I'd gotten into modeling. Nathalie was the last girl I'd tried to be faithful to, and I'd been wildly unsuccessful there. When Katrina, who knew my history, saw me looking at other girls, it fed her own insecurities and created a lack of trust between us. I wasn't trying to upset her; it was just that old habits died hard. My glances at other women were a reflex for someone like me. I was working hard to change my ways, but it wasn't going to happen overnight. When Katrina suggested we see a therapist before getting married to work through our issues, I agreed.

Our new therapist was a great guy, but when I began to relate my stories of women and all the sex I'd had with different models over the years, he just laughed and shook his head at me, as if to say, "Some fantasyland you've been living in, Bruce!" I knew that a lot of my experiences were hard to believe, but they had happened. It took several weeks, and some confirmation from Katrina, before he came to accept that I really was telling the truth. His favorite question after that was "How did that make you feel?" which I never really knew how to answer in front of Katrina without hurting her.

Katrina, on the other hand, was much more comfortable talking about her feelings. I was way out of my element. I had to tread especially lightly when it came to my history. Over time I worked to prove myself to Katrina, who had been hurt in the past and needed to be sure of me. Those sessions forced me to acknowledge a lot of difficult things about myself, which were painful to admit but ultimately added momentum to the changes I was making in my life.

Katrina, too, reaped benefits from our therapy. After years of working as a model and achieving her independence, sometimes in the face of little or no respect, she had come into our relationship harboring fears of relinquishing her hard-won independence. Therapy allowed her to work through those issues, which eventually helped us connect with each other on an even deeper spiritual level. She could see my true identity beginning to emerge for the first time since I had been a young man. I liked who I was becoming and the distance I was creating from who I had been.

As part of our continuing quest for connection and enlightenment, we accepted an invitation from Tommy Preston to fly to New Mexico to meet his guru, Baba Ram Dass. A former Harvard professor, Ram Dass went to India on a spiritual quest and returned to the United States committed to the Hindu ethic of serving others

Sparring at the Manatee dojo with Katrina.

and seeking God. Tommy thought Ram Dass was wonderful, and he was eager for us to meet him.

Katrina and I both had amazing experiences that weekend (not including my bout of altitude sickness from hiking up the mountain). When Ram Dass met us, he smiled and told us we were meant to be together. Then, leaning closer, he warned, "But don't fall asleep!" It was one of the clearest and most sensible pieces of marriage advice we had ever been given, and we promised we wouldn't.

On a beautiful day, December 11, 1993, Katrina and I were married at the Raleigh Hotel in Miami. We printed a quote from a Matthew Arnold poem on our invitations:

> *Ah, love, let us be true*
> *To one another! for the world, which seems*
> *To lie before us like a land of dreams.*

Katrina's family flew in from Texas, and mine came down from New Jersey. My kid sister Carol told anyone who would listen how she'd taken the first shots of me in my mom's beret. "I started him off!" she bragged. Now a successful massage therapist, she had come to a good place in her life. April and Tom were there, too, still living in the house I'd help build. April was an art teacher and a talented potter, and Tom was an engineer. Their daughter Stephanie was one of our flower girls, along with Cedar, Carol's daughter. And Diane came, too, an environmental biologist, leaving her husband home to mind the kids. Lisa Marie came, with her fiancé Tim Burton, plus Uncle Corky, and of course some of Katrina's girlfriends, including Lynette Walden, with whom I'd worked on Victoria's Secret shoots.

My buddies Doc X, Tommy Preston, Todd the God, Nick Constantino, Big Pete, and Richard Keogh all made the trip, and they got to meet Gary and a few of my new buddies from Miami, as well as my agent Nicole. It was one of the only times I can ever remember us all being in the same place at the same time. Sadly, Bruce Weber couldn't make it. He was in California shooting a movie, but he sent us a sweet telegram wishing us every happiness.

I had asked my father to be my best man, because I couldn't choose among the rest of my friends. Dad was thrilled, although he was nervous about it. We asked a minister from Katrina's family's Unity church to officiate at the ceremony. I borrowed a beautiful Giorgio Armani tuxedo from Nick, and Katrina wore a beautiful, sexy, elegant white gown made by a designer in Brooklyn.

When the moment finally arrived and I turned and saw Katrina walking down the aisle toward me, I was completely overcome by emotion. Here, at last, was my bride. I knew how much courage it took for her to make this journey with me; I could see how petrified she was by the way she was trembling. In the vows we wrote to each other, I promised I would always be there for her from that moment on. As I read those words aloud, her shaking stopped.

I'm surprisingly old-fashioned. I grew up in a traditional family, and my parents had been married for almost fifty years. I knew that if and when I ever took marriage vows, I would hold them sacred. I was going to say them *one* time with *one* woman, which is why I had waited for Katrina. While a lot of guys view marriage as the end of the good old days, for me they were just beginning. As I heard myself saying the words *until death do us part*, I felt a deep part of me that had always been knotted tight suddenly relax and release. It was an incredible feeling.

At the reception dinner, our fifty guests drank fifty bottles of Veuve Clicquot champagne as a Dixieland jazz band danced and played their way between tables. It was such an exuberant celebration.

When we had a moment alone, Katrina teased me. "You were the backdoor man! Girls aren't supposed to marry the backdoor man." Thank God that she did.

Stan Shaffer, the photographer I'd done all those Victoria's Secret catalogs with, wandered into our reception with a big grin on his face. "I can't believe you're actually getting married!" he said. It turned out that he was staying at the same hotel. I was thrilled and surprised to see him. Had I known he was there, I surely would have invited him, although it was strange to have a reminder, on my wedding day, of the most wayward times in my former life.

The next morning Katrina and I flew to Egypt for a job I had booked long before the wedding, a fashion shoot with my favorite Italian, Fabrizio Gianni. We arrived in Sharm el-Sheikh, on the border with Israel, near the Red Sea. Katrina and I were so exhausted and drained after all the wedding preparations and the long flight that we both came down with a vicious virus. We ended up staying in our hotel room for three days, unable to get out of bed—and not in a good way. The shoot was for the Italian designer Corneliani, but, fortunately for us, the clothes we were supposed to be wearing were held up in customs and never arrived, so once we felt better, we spent the rest of the week snorkeling in the Red Sea.

Some months after Katrina and I returned home from Egypt, I took her on a proper honeymoon to Steamboat Springs, Colorado, for some romantic skiing. I remember lying in bed with her one snowy afternoon, watching some sappy movie on TV, both of us crying our eyes out—and laughing, too, because we were so happy to finally have found someone who was content to just lie in bed and weep over some silly film.

Although Katrina would have preferred that we move back to New York, I convinced her to stay in Miami. I think she thought that Manhattan would be a better environment for our relationship, but I needed to live near the beach and couldn't imagine going back to the city. There were so many dark memories there that I didn't want to revisit. Miami Beach might still have its temptations, but I was truly immune to them now, something Katrina was gradually coming to accept. We bought a house on South Shore Drive on Normandy Isle, with a pool, banana trees, parrots, and a dock. I set up what we called the "manatee dojo" out back to continue my mixed-martial-arts training, which was fun for me because my sparring partners and I could flip each other right off the dock.

Katrina signed with the Page Parks agency and was soon getting plenty of work in Miami. She'd been modeling since she was fourteen years old, so she had an established résumé as a lingerie and catalog model. She'd done a lot of work with Uli Rose and for *Donna* magazine. I was working, too, but I loved nothing better than coming home at night with a couple of lobsters and cooking us up some pasta, drinking some wine, and playing house. It felt so new and different to me.

The first two years of my marriage to Katrina were still challenging for us both. She was gradually learning to trust me, and I was learning to feel comfortable in my new lifestyle. Every now and then, Katrina's temper would flare if she spotted me giving even a single look in the direction of another woman. "Why did you marry me if you still want other girls?" she'd ask.

"I don't want anyone else!" I'd protest. "I'm still a man. It was only a glance. There's no disrespect involved." And there wasn't. I was just doing what came naturally. Katrina's insecurities came from inside her as much as did my philandering past. It would take time for both of us to work toward the place where we truly trusted each other, but we got there. We didn't let ourselves fall asleep.

17

Riding the Breakers

On the morning of my forty-second birthday, the telephone rang early, as usual. "I'll get it," I said, smiling at Katrina. "It's my dad."

But it wasn't my father. It was my mother, sobbing hysterically.

"Mom?" I said. "Mom, what is it?"

"He's gone!" she cried, her voice almost unrecognizable. "Your dad . . . he . . . he . . . had a heart attack. Early this morning—after his run. He's dead, Bruce!"

I don't remember much of the rest of our conversation. I spoke to one of my sisters and was comforted that they were all there with Mom. She told me Dad had gone for his usual morning "mall walk" with his buddies, but then he had collapsed just as he was leaving to come home and phone me.

I promised my sisters that Katrina and I would make arrangements to fly up as soon as we could. Putting the telephone back in its cradle, I felt a sudden, urgent need to escape from the apartment. I jumped into the car with Katrina and drove like a madman out to some desolate spot in the Everglades. I stopped the car in the middle of a cypress swamp. I wanted to get out of the car and start running, to imagine my dad running alongside me, stride for stride, encouraging me.

Come on, Bruce the Moose. Pick it up a little.

But when I opened the car door, my legs wouldn't work. Staggering to the side of the road, I fell to the ground. Katrina pulled me into her arms, and I lay there for what seemed like hours, listening to the sounds of the swamp, crying, talking, and thinking about my dad, with my wife rocking me like a baby.

I thought of all the wonderful things my father had taught me over the years. I thought of his beloved boat, *The Gibbut,* out at Cape May, and how painstakingly he'd restored it. I wanted to feel the soft wool of his navy sweater against my skin again, to hear his mellow voice giving an eminently rational explanation for the existence of UFOs. I thought of him grilling steaks for us when we were children, of how pale and quiet he'd been when Mom was in the hospital. I remembered him Rollerblading alongside me down Ocean Drive, as sprightly in his seventies as I was in my forties, waving and smiling to everyone we met.

I prayed for God to watch over my dad and envelop him in peace and love. I thought of the Buddhist teaching "Use death as your adviser." It was never more painfully clear to me how fragile life is or how important it is to make each and every action matter. Behind the smoke and mirrors, the superficial and the frivolous, all we really have in this world is love and each other.

The funeral was an incredible experience. So many people attended, including strangers who wanted to tell us how much Dad meant to them, too, friends we didn't even know he'd had. In addition to family and relatives, the church was filled with his mall buddies, and running friends, and people from his bridge club. I gave the eulogy and spoke mostly of my father's honesty and integrity, of how much he was going to be missed.

My mother was inconsolable. From the day she'd eloped with him as a young girl against the wishes of her strict Catholic family, my father had been the only man in her life. They had set up house together and loved each other unconditionally, through the good times and the bad, raising their children together in a loving and protective home. "We had a deal," she kept saying. "He was going to let me die first!" Now he was gone.

A few months after my father passed away, Katrina told me she was pregnant. The timing couldn't have been more bittersweet. I would so much have liked Dad to know that we were going to have a baby, but I hoped that maybe somewhere he did. Katrina and I embarked on the amazing journey of her pregnancy together. In an act of solidarity, I even gained ten pounds. We took birthing classes together, read books and articles aloud to each other, and prepared as best we could for the arrival of our baby. When Katrina's water broke, I was her coach, dutifully timing her contractions, holding her, and helping her breathe.

It was a long and intense labor, but our son Cade was finally born into this world on May 17, 1996. I was allowed to cut the umbilical cord connecting him to his mother, a moment I will never forget. I held his tiny hand as he stared up into my eyes and felt a connection I had never known.

That night I slept on a cot in the hospital room beside my wife and our newborn bundle of joy, who was curled up next to her in bed. As I drifted off to sleep, I thought about my dad and how proud he would have been to be a grandfather to my son. I said a little prayer and asked Dad to protect Cade throughout his life. I had a strong sense that my dad was present in the room that night, watching over us.

As thrilled as I was to be a father, after Cade was born, I found myself overcome with irrational fears and paranoia. I wasn't sure I was strong enough to handle the huge responsibility of fatherhood. I felt new extremes of vulnerability. This wasn't the depression with which I was so familiar, but more of a constant worry, day and night, that something would happen to my son and that I wouldn't be able to protect him. What I tried to remind myself of over and over again is that there is no way for any parent to completely protect a child.

At first I made the mistake of trying to control my fears, which was pointless. With Katrina's help I learned to accept that whether you like it or not, your kids are going to stumble and fall; they are going to get hurt. Depression may even enter into their lives one day. They will certainly be confronted with sadness and loss. But that is part of life. As a father I had to understand that there were so many things I'd have absolutely no control over. My job was just to be the best parent I could possibly be, to be truly present.

On Cade's first birthday, Bruce Weber called us up and asked us to bring Cade over to his house. "I'd like to take some photos," he said. This incredibly busy man, this genius behind the lens, devoted four hours of his time to taking the most gorgeous shots of Cade,

Katrina, and me in his garden, in his pool, on our own, and having lunch, as his birthday gift to our son. It was the most generous of gestures. (And by the way, only Bruce Weber could make a one-year-old look sexy!)

Weber also used Cade—and his doting parents—for a Jon Bon Jovi promotional movie over at his house, where we had to pretend to be friends of the singer and sit around a table talking animatedly to him over a meal as if we'd known him all his life. Bon Jovi was good company and, being a father himself, was great with Cade. It was our son's first professional booking. I said that if I had anything to do with it, it would be his last, although he has since shot an ad campaign for Ralph Lauren with Bruce Weber.

When Cade was two years old, Katrina and I decided to leave Florida for a picturesque beach community near Malibu, California. Despite our sadness at moving away from friends like Weber—who was employing me as his personal trainer by then—and all the other buddies we'd made in South Beach along the way, we both had a sense that fashion work in Florida was beginning to taper off. And Miami had changed, or at least our feelings for it weren't the same. Gianni Versace had been murdered, Ocean Drive had lost its charm, and it didn't feel like an ideal place to raise children. We still wanted to be near the ocean, and we agreed that California was the perfect destination. We both had friends who lived nearby, and we hoped that moving closer to Los Angeles would give us greater access to modeling and film work.

Seven years after Cade transformed my life, our daughter Halsey was born. Her arrival was a lot easier and quicker than Cade's, thanks in part to a doctor whose philosophy on natural childbirth mirrored our own. We've had some trying times with Halsey since her birth, because she suffers from severe eczema and allergies, which means she often has trouble sleeping at night, and we have to keep her from scratching her arms until they bleed. It's hard to see our little girl endure so much pain. We've tried every available remedy: specialty soaps, ointments, and steroid creams for the most severe flare-ups. We've also investigated Chinese herbs and medicines. It's been difficult, but we rely on each other for strength.

Despite the trials and tribulations of being a parent, my children have given me joy unlike any I've ever known. I feel reborn. Whenever I have to leave the house, I can hardly wait to get back home. I still want to stare at my children in wonder, to hold them, to hug and kiss them. I have a strong desire to be present for them as they grow up—and, of course, for Katrina. Having a family helped

me reprioritize my life, reminding me daily of what's really important. It has also helped me appreciate the impact some of my past
actions had on other people's lives. I now know that whatever path
my children choose, they, too, will make some mistakes along the
way. I can only be there to help them however I can.

As part of that process, Katrina and I taught our kids to pray at
an early age. We thought it important to instill a sense of spirituality
in them right from the start. I wanted to provide our children with as
much information as possible about the great spiritual traditions and
eventually let them find their own paths to spiritual fulfillment. I hope
they can find peace within themselves by absorbing what they need
from many religions. I don't want them to think that one path is nec-
essarily better than another. They are all helpful in their own ways.
Sometimes we attend the Lake Shrine, founded by Paramahansa
Yogananda, an Indian yogi and guru, which honors all religions and
teaches meditation and yoga. Other times we might go to a service
at our local Presbyterian church, as a respectful nod to my father.

It's interesting how children's prayers evolve as they grow up. At first, Cade's and Halsey's prayers would run along the lines of "God bless Mommy and Daddy." Now they are much more expansive: "God bless the world. God bless my friends. Thank you, God, for all of our abundance." When they face adversity in their lives— and I now accept that they will—I want them to have the tools to overcome and gain strength from their struggles, something that took me more than forty years to understand.

There is nothing I would rather do than spend time with my kids, whether it's working on circus routines with my daughter or coaching my son's Little League baseball team. Being with them has a tremendously calming effect on me. No matter what occurs during my day, anything is bearable when my daughter looks at me and says, "Daddy, I love you." It is at that moment that I can truly feel God smiling on me.

For my fiftieth birthday, Katrina threw a surprise birthday party for me at a local restaurant. Nick was there, having moved in just down the road with his wife, the German supermodel Patricia Hartmann, whom he met on a L'Oréal campaign. Todd the God, who had also gotten married, to a lovely Australian producer and writer named Leanne, was there with his daughter. They're local, too. Tommy Preston was in Vancouver, Canada, with his wife, Claudia, and their son, known to all as "Little X"; but he called and sent his good wishes, as did Big Pete from Princeton. Doc X was off surfing in Indonesia, so he sent me a postcard.

Hitting the milestone of fifty felt good. I was still working, still earning money as a model, but now when I went to a shoot, I showed off pictures of my kids instead of asking a girl, "What are you doing later?" Work for me was no longer about sex or hooking up. I met a hairdresser on a job a few years back who remembered me from Miami Beach. He couldn't get over the notion that I was married, with two kids. He kept telling me I used to be "the man" in those days, shaking his head in disbelief that I had comfortably settled into my suburban existence. As I listened to him go on and on about the old days, I laughed and told him that back then I was running around looking for something I never thought I'd find. And now I had.

As a middle-aged model, I am usually much older than the other models I work with, and I'm in a totally different phase of life from theirs. Occasionally some of them will ask me for stories about the old days. When I describe how crazy it was, I try to throw in a cautionary note; I try to tell them that a lot of lives are destroyed by drugs and that I don't think they're going to find happiness with all the girls they're running around with. Of course, they don't want to hear it, any more than I did when I was their age. But I feel that I have an obligation to at least put the truth out there. "You won't achieve fulfillment or peace in your life until you find your true partner," I say, trying to be as sincere as possible without sounding too preachy. They usually think about it for a moment and then ask something like "Hey, man, did you ever screw Cindy Crawford?" Sometimes the whole experience feels a little too close for comfort, like looking at an old photograph. I used to be just like them.

I have never stopped mentoring younger models, and I still send photos of those with the best potential to Bruce Weber and other photographers I know. But I also warn them of the fickleness of the industry and advise them to have a fallback plan.

My best advice to aspiring male models is to balance your career with something else, so you can make a smooth transition out of the business when the time comes. And it will. Few models have the staying power to keep working as long as I have, and my calls don't

On an Italian Vogue shoot at Universal Studios with Steven Meisel.

come in as often as they used to. If you have something else lined up, there will be less pressure on you to have to make your living as a model. Unfortunately, I never really planned for my future. I lived each day waiting for that phone call, always believing there'd be another assignment. I'm just lucky it all worked out.

Today the fashion industry has become far more competitive and demanding. In New York alone, there are probably thirty top agencies trying to push their clients. Movie stars, who had previously shied away from advertising for fear it might diminish their status in some way, have frequently taken the place of models. Whereas once models like me eagerly vied for the cover of *GQ*, now it's the latest hot celebrity on the cover. Companies no longer have to try to create a celebrity out of an unknown male model; now they can simply hire a celebrity with a built-in fan base, like Andy Garcia for Cadillac or Robert De Niro and Martin Scorsese for American Express. It isn't impossible for a male model to get a large designer contract, but it's much harder in our celebrity-obsessed world.

Starting around the time I turned forty-five, there was a noticeable decrease in the modeling work I was offered. Bernard Fouquet, a good buddy of mine, refers to us older models as "silverbacks." We're a new phenomenon in the industry, and some executives don't know exactly what to do with us. Thanks to natural attrition, there aren't many of us left. By my age most male models have lost their looks, or have moved on to become businessmen, or have fallen off the deep end. The good news is that there aren't bumper crops of new models coming along every year who are going to compete with us for jobs.

Despite my extensive experience, I still have to show up at castings and prove myself. There are no guarantees in this business. Amazingly, I still get that same surge of adrenaline when my agent calls. I don't think that will ever change. Twenty-five years ago, when I booked my first job with Paolo Roversi in Paris, I looked up to the sky and said, "Thank you, God." Today I say the exact same thing after every booking. I'm always grateful for the opportunity to work, because it allows me to provide for my family. Work is work. Work is good. Katrina feels the same way, although she really enjoys being with the children now, too. She's with Ford Models in L.A. and has done a lot of television commercials, as well as some acting in TV shows, like the action-adventure *Viper* and the sitcom *Just Shoot Me*. We have a pact that if she's working, I don't, and vice versa, so that one of us is always home for the kids. And we've got a backup plan: If some really extraordinary booking comes in that might cause a conflict, Grandma flies in from Texas to baby-sit.

Since moving to California, I've shot more than fifty television commercials. One of them involved playing a dad in a McDonald's commercial, where I had to bite into cold hamburgers more than a dozen times and spit the food into a bucket before the next take. I posed for the Callaway Golf catalog at the Trump National golf course in Palos Verdes.

I also did an amazing Abercrombie & Fitch shoot with Bruce Weber at San Onofre, California. In the shoot, Weber was paying homage to the psychedelic surfing movie *Rainbow Bridge*, which featured Jimi Hendrix's last American concert before he died. Weber had hired musicians and hippies with bongos for the shoot. He also brought in some of the greatest surfers of all time, like Nat Young and Shaun Tomson, former world surf champions. We all went down to the beach and paddled out into the water while Weber took his shots, and then he asked the champion surfers to go out and do their stuff. I came out and stood on the beach beside Weber, watching in awe. "Why don't you go and join them, Bruce?" he asked me.

I shook my head slowly. "Those guys are legends," I replied.

Lauren Hutton is one of the few female supermodels I've ever felt I had anything in common with, because of our versatility and longevity in the business. We've both survived modeling for decades. Over the years I've been called "the male Lauren Hutton," and I've never objected. We've both done almost everything in the industry, making us elders in the select group of models from my era who are still working. I always had the utmost respect for Lauren's long, successful career in a fickle and unforgiving industry.

I met Lauren for the first time in 2006 on a shoot for an ad campaign promoting an exclusive real-estate development in Utah. I found it strange that our paths hadn't crossed over the course of my twenty-five-year career. I was excited to meet her, even if we were to be playing the grandparents of a typical American family. It felt odd to be cast as Grandpa. In my mind I was still a young, virile lifeguard on Avalon Beach, and I had certainly never thought of Lauren Hutton as being Grandma. Still, work is work.

When I arrived on set and saw Lauren, I was immediately taken by her piercing blue eyes. She is still absolutely striking. There were only a few models on the three-day shoot, so I went up to her right away and introduced myself. "Hello, Lauren, how nice to meet you," I said, smiling and extending a hand.

She looked at me suspiciously.

"I'm Bruce, Bruce Hulse. I . . . uh, I play your husband in the shoot."

She hardly said a word. I soon realized that Lauren was a classic model diva. Despite her apparent lack of interest in me, I tried my best to do what I always do on location—make a connection that turns work into fun.

"Where are you living these days?" I asked.

She began to list the places where she kept homes, as if I were annoying her with my inquiry. I listened but quickly lost interest, because I could tell that there was no effort being made on her end. She didn't care. Perhaps the woman I had so admired for more than two decades was not the woman I'd imagined. Or perhaps she was so annoyed by being hired to play Grandma that she didn't really want to be there. I do know that I had to dig very deep to look loving when the cameras started shooting. She kept asking me my name, right up until the final day. We were polite enough, but I came away with the distinct impression that while I had grown accustomed to the idea that I might be the male Lauren Hutton, she had never once thought of herself as the female Bruce Hulse.

These days when I'm not in front of the camera, I'm behind it, as a professional photographer. There's a certain irony in the fact that I spend a lot of my spare time photographing weddings. After holding off on commitment for so long, now I'm inexplicably drawn to capturing these powerful emotional moments on film. Somehow my instincts have led me to become a documenter of happy beginnings.

I have also enjoyed my first major television work, as a host and judge on the Bravo series *Manhunt: The Search for America's Most Gorgeous Male Model,* which was a whole new ball game for me. Billed as "the fashion industry's first male supermodel," I had to get used to being recognized all over again, this time by adoring young gay fans as well as by women. The premise of the eight-part program was that a group of twenty hopeful young newcomers plucked from streets, bars, gyms, and colleges would compete for a hundred-thousand-dollar prize and a modeling contract with the IMG agency. Actress and singer Carmen Electra was the host, and swimsuit model Marisa Miller was my fellow judge. Having been scrutinized and evaluated constantly over the course of my career, it was refreshing to finally be the person doing the judging.

The cast and crew had an incredible time during the six-week shoot. I thoroughly enjoyed interacting with the young male models. Although I was supposed to assume the persona of a drill instructor, I felt much more at ease providing the guys with career advice and guidance after the TV cameras went off. Most of the *Manhunt* series was unscripted, so I had to improvise my dialogue, which wasn't an easy task for someone used to posing in silence. But the lack of scripting served the show well, giving it a spontaneous, freewheeling quality that distinguished it from many other reality shows.

Our first day of shooting took place at a skydiving facility just outside San Diego. I had a brief meeting with the director and producer to discuss their expectations for the day. The executive producer explained that I would walk down a dirt road to meet the contestants, who would be lined up next to each other, having been thrown half naked from a plane to the song "It's Raining Men."

On location in Utah for Talisker, 2006.

"We want you to introduce yourself, give a speech about male modeling, and then go down the line critiquing each model's appearance," one of the producers told me. This sounded like a tall order for the first day, but I knew that my experience and my instincts would take over. As I made my way down the line scrutinizing each of the contestants, I recalled everything my buddies and I used to say when we were teasing one another on photo shoots.

"Looks like you've got chicken legs there, buddy," I told one of the prospects. "You need to get on the squat rack and train." I carried on down the line, tearing each of the guys apart. "You call that a hairstyle? You look like you haven't had a haircut since 1984." All the guys knew that our job was to provide entertaining television, so they went with the act. No one took it personally.

One night we shot at a hotel in downtown Los Angeles. In this particular scene, I was supposed to walk into one of the rooms to wake up two male models for a midnight photo shoot on the roof with Marisa Miller. When the camera crew and I burst in through the door, the two contestants jumped out of a giant hot tub in the middle of the hotel room and sprinted into the bathroom naked. They slammed the door and wouldn't come out. I didn't know what to think. Then I noticed the two naked girls sitting in the hot tub staring at us.

Thinking the show's producers had orchestrated the entire scene, I began trash-talking the guys for leaving the girls out in the living room alone. "What kind of gentlemen are you?" I yelled at them though the bathroom door. "You have ten minutes to be up on the roof to shoot with Marisa!" After the director yelled, "Cut!" it turned out that the girls definitely weren't part of the production. In fact, the contestants had signed an agreement not to have anyone outside the show in their rooms, because of liability issues. Personally,

I would have been more surprised if the models *didn't* have girls up in their rooms. After a few phone calls to the lawyers, everything was straightened out, and we continued shooting.

Jon Jonsson, the model who eventually won the competition, has since been working regularly. Our paths have crossed on a few occasions, and I recently shot a Mervyns catalog with him in Malibu. It is so rewarding for me to see him, because I feel I played an integral part in advancing his career. Bruce Weber used Jonsson and me, plus the four runners-up from *Manhunt,* for an Abercrombie & Fitch shoot in Santa Barbara, which was another fun spin-off from the series. Another was *The Shot,* a series on VH1, produced by my friend Russell James, the former model who is now a photographer. In the series Marisa Miller and I had to pose as models on a sailboat off Long Beach, California, while ten aspiring fashion photographers clicked away, hoping to be picked as the next new up-and-coming fashion photographer. Half of them knew what they were doing and got it right. The other half got so seasick they couldn't hold their cameras straight.

Manhunt and *The Shot* were wonderful experiences, because I was able to showcase a new side of myself, which is closer to my true personality. The long days in front of the camera taught me a tremendous amount and helped build my confidence to pursue similar projects. I was finally able to tap in to that talent for acting Bruce Weber always claimed I had, and to explore my potential as an entertainer.

I continued dabbling in sports management, managing a Russian fighter named Alex Rafalsky, with the help of a martial-arts trainer named Rico Chiapparelli, whom I'd met when I taught him jujitsu in New York. I sent Rico to meet Bruce Weber, and of course Weber loved him, using him for Abercrombie & Fitch and Calvin

Klein and having Rico serve as a producer for a whole spread Weber did about the University of Iowa wrestling team. He also used Alex in a Versace campaign, where he looked incredible, this huge Russian in those sleek suits. Rico went on to do a lot of modeling after that, but now he's pretty much concentrating on sports. Rico and I recruited a mixed-martial-arts fighter by the name of Randy Couture, now known as "The Natural," the only five-time champion in Ultimate Fighting Championship history. Rico uses me to negotiate contracts for him, and I negotiated Randy's with the UFC.

Perhaps most fulfilling of all, I started writing again. I wrote a screenplay, *Cooler by a Mile*, which is basically about my teenage years at Avalon. I created a story line about a three kids who go out to the New Jersey shore to take the lifeguard test and how they spend the rest of that summer in that most sacred of places to me. It's a coming-of-age story about three lost boys finding themselves at Avalon. It follows their swim races, their adventures with falling in love for the first time, smoking pot, and discovering sex in the sand dunes under the stars. Bruce Weber loved it, and I hoped it was just the first screenplay of many, in what is for me an exciting new creative outlet.

Doc X was another one of my old buddies who had moved to California, into the house of his new girlfriend, a few blocks from where we lived. He was still doing his photography and making documentaries, and he had also set up a charity in memory of a kid from Avalon who'd died of cancer. I would go back to Jersey with X once a year to be a judge for the races and the surfing contests he arranged to raise money for the charity. X also became a popular personal trainer in L.A., maintaining his strict vegetarian, non-smoking, nondrinking habits of a lifetime.

His personal life, however, was a mess. He had a great new girlfriend, Karen Voight, the exercise guru, who had asked him to move in with her, and he swore that this was the one. "Doc X really likes this gal," he told me with a wry smile. "Doc X sees how happy B is and thinks he might even get married and have kids one day. Who knows? This could be the Doc X way." We really liked Karen, too, and we couldn't have been more pleased. The trouble was, as soon as he moved in, X started fooling around on Karen in his usual cavalier fashion. When we found out, he made the same old excuses: "It's just the Doc X way."

Needless to say, Karen eventually kicked him out, and X was on his own again. To keep himself busy, he flew to Hawaii with Tommy Preston to film some shots for X's surfing documentary, *The Water-hole,* about two young surfers from Avalon who went to Oahu in search of the perfect wave. He and Tommy had become close in recent years. Even though Tommy was in real estate now, having married his Canadian wife, Claudia, and moved to British Columbia, he and Doc X shared the same sort of laissez-faire philosophy about life. I loved that they found so much pleasure in surfing and hanging out together.

Tommy called me unexpectedly one day in January 2003 from Hawaii. He had some bad news. "It's X," he told me, his voice breaking. "He's not well, B. He's been having some trouble doing normal things, so I took him to the hospital. He's got brain cancer, man. It's inoperable."

I felt as if someone had just punched me in the solar plexus. For a few minutes, I couldn't catch my breath. Doc X? Dying? At forty-six? That vital, life-loving free spirit whom I'd first met when he was a rebellious fifteen-year-old on Avalon Beach? The guy who lived such a healthy life that he wouldn't eat candy? We all thought he'd live to be a hundred. My mind just couldn't take it in.

Me and Doc X.

X flew straight back to New York, where he saw several specialists who all told him the same thing. His particular type of brain cancer, one neurosurgeon said, tended to be found in surfers who took in excessive amounts of polluted seawater. He underwent chemotherapy, which made him feel so sick he could barely stand it. When it became obvious that he wouldn't survive the illness, he stopped the treatments and moved back to Los Angeles to spend the time he had left surrounded by his many friends, including Tommy and me. We cared for him around the clock, making sure he was bathed, giving him his medication, and fixing his favorite vegetarian meals. We kept a CD of Tibetan monks chanting in the background, and we had his favorite incense burning continuously. We wanted to create as peaceful an atmosphere as possible for his final days.

Doc X had always loved going to the movies. It was his favorite thing to do. Without fail, every time we sat down in a theater, he would turn to me with a smile and say, "You know, B, I love the movies!" Now, when he was feeling up to it, I brought in some DVDs and set up a mini-theater in his house, with all his buddies around. He had never watched the sci-fi TV series *Taken,* so I bought the twenty-hour box set, and Doc X, Tommy, and I sat down with a few other buddies and watched that whole darn series from beginning to end in the last weeks of his life. He enjoyed every scary moment of it. It made me happy to see Doc X smile, because I knew he was in such pain. I watched him suffer through all his treatments, hurting and sick, but he lived as he always had—without fear.

On a few occasions, I took Doc X down to the beach to watch the waves roll in. I would sit for hours holding his hand while we talked about life. The closer he got to death, the more Doc X opened up to me. He confessed that his biggest regret was never learning how to love and never truly loving a woman the way he wanted to. He admitted that he had hurt every woman he'd dated. I reminded him there were plenty of women who'd hurt him, too, but it didn't seem to make a difference. The more he spoke that day, the more his remorse became clear. He'd obviously been bottling it all up for years. His emotions must have touched a chord in my own heart, because one of the hardest things I've ever had to do was to listen to X speak of his empty years of looking for and never finding love.

"You loved *me,*" I told him, and X nodded, close to tears. "Perhaps you failed in some areas of your life," I said, "but you weren't really dealt a fair hand." Never having had a father figure as a role model made it difficult for X to trust women. "I forgive you, X," I told him finally, sensing that this was what he needed to hear. "I forgive you for all of the pain you believe you've caused." I told him that God asks us to admit our sins only in order to receive His forgiveness. "If you can forgive yourself, you'll finally be free from this burden."

Not long after that, one of Doc X's old girlfriends showed up at his place to see him. She told him that she'd made a terrible mistake in breaking up with X and that she had married the wrong man. She made it clear she wanted to sleep with him "one last time." It was a nice moment in a period of overwhelming despair. Poor X was too ill to oblige, but it warmed my heart to see his big smile.

Our conversations became a daily practice to help him be at peace. Soon we began talking about the positive things he'd done in his life, shifting our emphasis from his past mistakes. The more I reassured Doc X about God's love, the more I reaffirmed my own beliefs. In the end, even though he could no longer speak or eat, I believe that Doc X began to forgive himself. You could see the love and acceptance in his big, luminous blue eyes.

Doc X's funeral was held in an old cemetery in Philadelphia where I used to spend joyous summer afternoons skateboarding as a young boy. What an odd feeling to have such cheerful memories at a time of such deep loss. All our lifeguarding buddies attended the ceremony. It was good to see so many familiar faces turn out to pay their respects to an incredible soul. Even though I was with him right until the end, I still couldn't believe that Doc X was gone. I found some relief in the fact that he'd died with so much courage and integrity. He set the bar high for all of us to follow.

His family asked me to deliver the eulogy. It was an honor to talk about Doc X's zest for life. He had lived, as he would have said, "the Doc X way." He was a great friend, a true light in this some- times dark and dreary world. He had touched so many souls by al- ways being there for us all and lending support in any way possible. He would talk for hours with people, curious to know about their lives, and he was a good listener as well as a wonderful storyteller. He was passionate about his politics and about the environment. He was even in *Guinness World Records*, for doing the most sit-ups in two minutes.

I told the assembled mourners, "I was at Studio 54 with Doc X in the seventies, and chasing models around Milan in the eighties, and surfing and working with him in California in the nineties, but the most important part of the Doc X way was Avalon. Avalon was his spiritual home, and X was its unofficial mayor." I told them that he had probably already set up his own Avalon in heaven and was kneeboarding through the stars.

X's beach house in Avalon was always a place anyone could go for good conversations, friendship, delicious vegetarian meals, and a retreat from the world. Sadly, almost immediately after his death, Doc X's estate sold his house to a developer, who tore it down and constructed a massive beach house that X would have hated. It was truly the passing of an era.

18

A Happy Beginning

It is a perfect Malibu day. The sun glitters on the water, and the sky is an impossible azure. Katrina lies beside me, gently dozing in the sun, her perfect body tanned and gorgeous. I lean over and kiss her on the lips. "I love you, babe," I tell her, and she hooks her long arms around my neck and kisses me back.

"I love you, too, Bruce," she tells me. And that's all it takes to keep me going.

Our wonderful children, Halsey and Cade, sit a few feet away from us, scraping out a trench in the soft white sand and filling it with seawater, giggling and pushing each other playfully, happy and free. This is the childhood I'd always wanted them to have: beach, fresh air, parents who adore each other, and friends and family around them to protect and nurture them as they make their way in this life.

Todd is there, with his daughter Ainsley, and Nick with his two children, Lucca and Anna. All of us are relaxing on this idyllic California day, sunbathing, reading, playing with our kids, chatting, and laughing together. To anybody walking past, we must look like something from the pages of a lifestyle magazine: four models and their five happy children, picnicking on the beach.

My skin tingles from too much sun, so I jump up and grab my surfboard. I run out toward the waves, the sand hot beneath my feet. I can feel my breath moving, my heart pounding, my muscles taut, everything within me ready as I hit the water. The shock of it takes my breath away, but I keep going, keep pushing on through the surf, paddling now, deeper and deeper.

In my mind I'm a kid again, swimming out as fast as I can around that distant buoy at Avalon, desperate to be one of the first twenty back to shore. I'm surfing with Doc X, paddling out beyond the breakers as we holler to each other above the roar of the ocean. I'm a lifeguard, slicing through the water to rescue some poor little surf grommet who's crashed into the end of the pier and come up with a bloody nose. The feel of the salt against my skin, the sensation of the water cooling me down is so familiar, so comforting, I could be in the womb of my childhood again. Safe. Protected. Loved.

Turning, I pull myself up onto my board and look back at the beach. Behind it, purple mountains lie misty on the horizon. In the distance I can just make out our happy little group, all the people I love most. Cade and Halsey are off to one side, digging for glory.

From left to right: Todd Irvin, me, and Nick Constantino with our kids, Malibu, California.

Katrina is sitting up now, her hand shielding her eyes, watching me from afar. Todd and Nick are also keeping an eye on their surf buddy way out on the high rollers.

I close my eyes and recite a version of a Buddhist prayer that I often repeat to myself in moments of stillness: "May my family and friends, and all those I love, be free from suffering. May there be peace and love in this world. May we all reach a state of enlightenment."

I open my eyes again. As my lower legs dangle off the board into the water, I think of all the times I've sat like this, looking back: at Avalon Beach, on a hundred different shoots all over the world—in Mexico, Hawaii, the Caribbean, Miami. I was trying to put some distance between myself and the people and the places I knew, to give it all some sort of perspective.

In the past, that sense of space and perspective had always been welcome. I had often longed to just paddle away, or I wished I could catch a breaker that would help me escape from the world that imprisoned and bewitched me. No longer, though. Now, as I look back on the place I'd just come from, I feel an overwhelming sense of joy and peace. I have a beautiful, loving wife. I have two incredible children who will one day make their own mark on this world. I have friends who have stuck by me through thick and thin and who live nearby so we can all grow old together. My long, difficult spiritual journey is not yet over, but it has reached a good place for now. I have found myself in the hearts and minds of these people, these wonderful, life-giving souls whose spirits lift my own.

Behind me I can feel the ocean swelling. A wave is gathering, and I can tell it's going to be a good one. Leaning forward, preparing myself, I paddle with my hands and wait, wait for the moment. Then, just as the wave comes up behind me, a swirling force of nature, as fierce and strong as the love in my heart, I pull myself upright on my surfboard and begin to ride it in.

My feet flat on the wet fiberglass, my toes curled over for traction, my arms outstretched, I am that little boy again at Cape May, riding the white water all the way in to the sand, flying, free, and at one with the waves. I am Bruce Hulse, I am Doc X, I am Big Pete, The Glenn, Shoe, Stoover, Rob, Pat Scullin, and Chris Gilday. I am all the lifeguards at Avalon. I am anyone who has ever caught a wave, who knows that feeling of exhilaration.

The water rises and rises beneath me, holding me aloft, high above the land and the ocean, bringing me home. Katrina, Nick, and Todd see me coming in, and they stand, as one, to watch in open appreciation. Cade and Halsey stop what they are doing and run toward me, calling out to me. "Daddy! Daddy!" they cry, running into the surf, as Todd and Nick begin whistling and Katrina stands beside them, laughing and clapping and shouting her encouragement.

Tears stream down my face, mingling with the spray and sun and the surf. I am laughing and crying at the same time, happier and more contented than I've ever been. I am safe. I am protected. I am loved.

I am finally the man I had always hoped I could be.

Acknowledgments

There are so many people who have helped me along my path, some of whom have already been mentioned in this book, some of whom I mention here, and some of whom I may unintentionally omit. Forgive me if you fall into that last category, but know that you have my thanks and appreciation for the contribution you made to the remarkable journey that has been my life.

My thanks to Alan Nevins at The Firm, who championed this project, and to Shaye Areheart at Harmony Books, who published it; to Laura Morton and especially Wendy Holden; to my sisters April, Carol, and Diane; to Tom and Eric Lang; to Calvin Klein; to Gary Hope and Mark McKenna; to Mario Testino, Fabrizio Gianni, Uli Rose, Claus Wickrath, Ellen von Unwerth, and Paolo Roversi; to Pete Soderman, Stu Hoover, Chris Gilday, Ali Franco, Richard Pollmann, and Rob Graham; Ram Dass, Klaus Puhlmann, Nan Bush, Bernard Fouquet, Lisa Marie, Rico Chiapperelli, David Hebble, GiGi Hughes Leitch, Jim Moore, Henry Smith, Renee Rhyner, Stuart Krasnow, Nicole Brandt, Laura Barra, Corky Smith, Jim Shoemaker, Billy Glenn, Carlo Bosco, Patricia Cadiou-Diehl, Carl Spaeth, Sophie Fraise, Erick Jussen, Dr. Denise Philips, Dr. Jacobus Schmidt, Sarah Robarts, Guru Amrit Desai, Richard Keogh, Bob Horowitz, and Joe Iacopino. And my gratitude goes out to all the women I have loved, who helped me in my quest to find the woman I am destined to be with until the end of my days.

Photography Credits

Grateful acknowledgment is made to the following copyright holders for permission to use their photographs.

Carlo Bosco: pages 28, 228

Nick Constantino: page 307

Fabrizio Gianni: pages iii, v, vii, 147, 196, 197, 210

David Hebble: pages 273, 283

Frank Horvat: page 90

Bruce Hulse: pages 12, 170, 185, 202, 240, 259

Bruce Hulse Archive: pages ii, iv, viii, 3, 4, 8, 15, 25, 32, 35, 43, 94, 109, 112, 124, 174, 186, 203, 213, 214, 219, 222, 235, 251, 268, 288, 293, 298

Cade Hulse: page 285

Carol Hulse: page 7

Katrina Rae Hulse: pages 302, 305

William F. Hulse: pages 14, 19

Rico Puhlmann: pages 101, 117

Herb Ritts Foundation: pages 135, 142, 165, 194

Uli Rose: pages 157, 264

Paolo Roversi: page 59

Ellen von Unwerth: pages 70, 160

Bruce Weber: pages xix, xxii, 46, 66, 82, 104, 120, 248

www.MattiasEdwall.com: page 254

Terry Xughes: pages i, vi, xv, 79, 278

Index

Page references in *italic* refer to photographs.

H

hairdressers, 127–28, 214–15
Halsband, Michael, 181, 182
Halston, 119
Hansen, Patti, 143–44
Hanson, Pamela, 2, 6
Hartmann, Patricia, 286
Haverford High School Fords,
    18–20, *19*
Haverford State Hospital, 11–12,
    16, 17
Hendrix, Jimi, 290
Hinduism, 41, 273–74
Hintnaus, Tom, 95
homoeroticism, 164–66
Hoover, Stuart "Stoover," 26, 106,
    111–12, 158, 188
Hope, Gary, 257–61, *259*, 267, 269,
    275
Horvat, Frank, 87, 92
"hot shots," 134–36
Hughes, Terry "Doc X," 24, 33–34,
    85–86, 91, 106, 131, 133, 140,
    150–52, *170*, 171, 236, 238, 267,
    269, 274–75, 286, 296–301, *298*
  death and funeral of, 297–301
  GQ lifeguard piece and, 108–10, 111
  home of (Doc X Mansion), 33,
    109, 109–10, 130, *170*, 301
  Hulse given romantic advice by,
    150–51, 167–68
  Hulse's spiritual journey and, 39
  at Kripalu spiritual retreat, 236
  living in Italy, 197–98
  personal life of, 296–97, 299–300

  as photographer, 109, 151, 183–84,
    197, 200, 250, 296
  as secret millionaire, 34
Hulse, April (sister), 4, 10, 68, 170,
    274
Hulse, Bill (father), 3–5, *4*, *12*, 18,
    20, 27, 30, 49, 63, 85, 98, 177,
    183, 215, 282, 285
  boating and, 5, 44
  death of, 279–81
  Italy trip of, 195–96, 197
  Miami visit of, 253
  retirement of, 238–39
  as runner, 3, 22, 68
  son's depressions and, 16–17,
    35–36
  son's modeling career and, 72, 85,
    87–88, 118
  son's wedding and, 275
  wife's alcoholism and mental
    problems and, 9–10, 11–12
Hulse, Bruce:
  acting career considered by,
    137–40, 199
  as artists' model, 29–32, 134
  as basketball player, 14, 16, 18–20,
    19, 32–33, 34, 41–44, *43*, 90, 130
  boxing as interest of, 257–61,
    295–96
  childhood and teenage years of,
    3–5, 9–22, 296
  college years of, 22–37, 41, 134, 138,
    155–56; *see also* Cornell
    University
  as construction worker, 37–38,
    44–45, 56, 214

Hulse, Bruce *(continued)*:

depressions of, 15–22, 34–36, 45, 131, 171–72, 177–78, 182, 183, 184, 190, 238, 240, 247, 261

as father, 281–86, *283, 285, 302, 307*

fiftieth birthday of, 286

finances of, 115, 130–31, 206, 246

first cover of, 116–19, *117*

first girlfriend of, 13, 15, 20–21, 22, 26–27

first modeling job of, *59,* 64–65, 68, 69, 71–72

first photo shoot of, 5, *7,* 53

first runway work of, 68, 69, 71–72, 73–74

fortieth birthday of, 269

in graduate school, 44–45, 51, 52, 250

honeymoon of, 276

Katrina's relationship with, 239–41, 267–77; *see also* Olivas, Katrina

as lifeguard, 22–26, *25,* 33–34, *35,* 39–40, 56, 69, 85, 105, 106–11, 125, 129

LSD-induced breakdown of, 15–22

Marpessa's relationship with, 233–38, 244, 245–46, 253

martial arts training of, 36, 62, 178–81, 230, 241, *273,* 277

meditation practice of, 3–4, 21, 39, 47–48, 60, 62, 107, 131, 184

modeling career begun by, 52–65

Nathalie's relationship with, *see* Gabrielli, Nathalie

as photographer, 200–201, 250, 256, 292

psychology as interest of, 20, 44–45

as runner, 21–22, 68, 177–78

sexual encounters of, 63, 72–73, 74, 92–93, 95, 100–101, 103, 106, 144–51, 153–59, 161–63, 166–73, 182–83, 190–93, 201–5, 223–26, 229–31, 240–41, 255–57, 271–72, 277, 287

slowdown in modeling career of, 287–89

Sophie's relationship with, 153–59, 161–63, 166–73; *see also* Billard, Sophie

spiritual journey of, 3–4, 21, 36–40, 45, 47–48, 49, 60, 155–56, 177–81, 191–93, 207, 209, 231, 245–46, 247, 266–67, 273–74, 285, 306

as surfer, 4, 5, 40, 244–45, 304–7

in television commercials, 199–204, *203,* 205–6, 241–43, 290

in television series, 292–95

test shots of, 53

thirtieth birthday of, 87–88

wedding of, 274–76

yoga as interest of, 3–4, 21, 22, 39

Hulse, Cade (son), 281–86, *283,* 303–4, 306, *307*

birth of, 281–82

first birthday of, 282–83

Hulse, Carol (sister), 4, 5, *7,* 10, *33,* 53

Hulse, Diane (sister), 4, 10, 274

Hulse, Halsey (daughter), 284–86,
    285, 302, 303–4, 306, *307*
Hulse, Mrs. (mother), *12,* 18, 20, 22,
    26, 27, 30, 44, 49, 56, 68, 167, 183
    alcoholism and depression of,
        9–12, 27, 80
    husband's death and, 279–80, 281
    Italy trip of, 176–77, 196
    Miami visit of, 253
    son's depressions and, 16–17,
        35–36
    son's modeling career and, 72, 118
"hungry ghosts," 175
Hutton, Lauren, 290–92

I

Iglesias, Julio, 262
Iman, 94, 96–97
IMG agency, 292
Interview, 118
Ireland, Hulse's promotional
    appearances in, 206
Irene Marie, 251
Irvin, Todd "the God," 55, 60, 74,
    117–18, 188–90, *251,* 274–75, 286,
    304, 305, *305,* 306
    romantic overlaps of Hulse and,
        189–90
Italian *Bazaar,* 197
Italian *Cosmpolitan,* 197
Italian *Elle,* 251
Italian *Vogue, 288*
Italy, 176–77, 195–98
    Corneliani shoot in, 195–97, *197*
    Doc X's sojourn in, 197–98

GQ shoot in, *196*
Hulse's conflict with
    photographer in, 216–18
Milan runway shows in, 125,
    126–30, 198, 233
Ives, Michael, 55

J

Jack, Beau, *259*
Jackson Hole, Wyoming, *GQ* shoot
    in, 123–25
Jagger, Bianca, 119
Jamaica, Camel Clothing shoot in,
    220–21, *222*
James, Russell, xviii–xix, 256, 295
J. Crew, 212, 214
Jeff (Katrina Olivas's boyfriend),
    240, 241, 244, 268, 270
Jens-Peter, *214*
Jocelyn (First Agency's talent
    scout), 55, 56–57, 58, 60–61, 62,
    81, 163, 188
Jonsson, Jon, 295
Jussen, Erick "EJ," 196–97, 234–35

K

Kamen, Nick, 205
Karan, Donna, 126
Keating, Peter, 226–27
Keogh, Richard, 207–9, 242–43,
    244, 245, 246, 274–75
Klein, Calvin, 87, 114, 126, 295–96
    Hulse's first meeting with, 81,
        83–85, 86

rock climbing of, 184–87, *186*, 246–47

surfing documentary made by, 297

Pullman, Rico, 118

R

Rafalsky, Alex, 295–96

Rahula, Walpola, 36

Rainbow Bridge, 290

Ram Dass, Baba, 273–74

Rask, Annette, 89–90, *90,* 92–93, 163

Rector, Kelly, 94

Revlon, 231–32

Richards, Keith, 143

Ritts, Herb, *124,* 133–37, 164–65, 176–77, 200

    Barbados shoot for *Mademoiselle* and, 133–36, *135*

Robbins, Tony, 245–46

rock climbing, 184–87, *186,* 246–47

Rodney (Tatjana Patitz's boyfriend), 199–200, 201, 204, 209

Ronin, Jim "Rono," 110

Rose, Uli, 239, 277

Rossellini, Isabella, 77

Rourke, Mickey, 259

Roversi, Paolo, *59,* 64–65, 71, 97, 289

Rumi, xvii, 265–66

runway work, 64, 125–30, 233

    Hulse's first booking for, 68–69, 71–74

Ruth (Hulse's girlfriend in Philadelphia), 48, 49, 50

S

St. Barthélemy, Diet Coke shoot in, 191, 222–23

Santorini, Greece, Calvin Klein shoot on, 90–91, 93–103

Scorsese, Martin, 289

Scott, Sir Walter, 63–64

Scullin, Pat, 85, 106, 196–97

Severance, Joan, 71, 94, 96–97

Shaffer, Stan, 223, 224, 225, 276

"shaman" woman ideal, 207

Shields, Brooke, 84

Shoemaker, Jim "The Shoe," 14–15, 23, *25,* 85, 106, 238, 250

shorinji kempo, 36

Shot, The, 295

Soderman, Peter "Big Pete," 24–26, 106, 107–8, 110, 130, 139, 176, 177, 188, 257, 269, 274–75, 286

    as bodyguard, 224

    Hulse's New York City apartments shared by, 111–12, 113, 236

    at Kripalu spiritual retreat, 236

    as landscape architect, 236, 267

Soto, Talisa, 123

South Jersey Lifeguard Championships, 33

Spain, shoots in, 199, 204

Sports Illustrated, 32, 98, 183

Stella Artois, 144, 148

Stember, John, 114, 132, 153, 154–55, 222–23, 230

About the Author

BRUCE HULSE, recently named one of the top ten male models of all time, is a Cornell graduate with a degree in Buddhist studies. He also attended West Chester University, where he focused on graduate-level clinical psychology. Most recently, Bruce appeared as a judge on the Bravo reality show *Manhunt: The Search for America's Most Gorgeous Male Model*. Today, Bruce is an accomplished surfer, a professional photographer, a fitness consultant, and continues to be one of the longest-working models in the industry. He lives in Southern California with his wife and two children.